270+ Recipes for
Incredible Low-Carb Meals

THE
ULTIMATE
KETO
COOKBOOK

BRITTANY ANGELL
Creator of BrittanyAngell.com

PAGE STREET
PUBLISHING CO.

PAGE STREET
PUBLISHING CO.

Copyright © 2020 Brittany Angell

First published in 2020 by
Page Street Publishing Co.
27 Congress Street, Suite 105
Salem, MA 01970
www.pagestreetpublishing.com

Distributed by Macmillan, sales in Canada by The Canadian Manda Group.

24   23   22   21   20   1   2   3   4   5

ISBN-13: 978-1-62414-963-4
ISBN-10: 1-62414-963-4

Library of Congress Control Number: 2019943007

Cover and book design by Rosie Stewart for Page Street Publishing Co.
Photography by Brittany Angell; photos on pages 32, 117, 118, 123, 139, 184, 243 by
Becky Winkler
Author photo by Tre'

Printed and bound in the United States

I would like to dedicate this book to Kenna Dickman.
Thank you, Kenna, for all your hard work, for keeping me
sane and for all your contributions to this book!
I couldn't have done it without you.

Contents

Sides, Salads and Soups 181

Bread and Pasta 225

Homemade Liqueurs and Cocktails   431

Keto Basics   480

Introduction:
My Story

In my early twenties, freshly graduated from college with a degree in fine arts, I ventured out into the world looking for a career, completely unsure how to apply what I had studied to a real-life adventure. I thought I hit the jackpot when I was hired to work at a stained glass studio. I grew up in a 1920s-era house and adored our leaded windows and always admired stained glass windows in old buildings and churches. I was excited to jump into this new venture and to learn all that I could. Each day, being young and clueless I worked in a factory-type space that had a broken ventilation system. We wore regular clothing (no protective suits), and I was quite literally touching and breathing in lead five days a week for a year straight.

I left that job after about a year and within six months my health began to completely spiral out of control. First, I suffered from major digestive distress, then my gallbladder became inflamed and caused a lot of ongoing pain. Then I found out that I was prediabetic, and had severe adrenal fatigue, and I began developing a huge assortment of food allergies and sensitivities. Finally, after three years of seeing many different doctors, I was diagnosed with Hashimoto's disease. Getting a diagnosis came to me as a huge relief, which may sound strange, but it was an answer I *needed*. I am the type of person who will do whatever it takes to find answers and having a diagnosis meant I could take it on and do everything in my power to heal.

It took another six years for me to also discover that I had serious lead poisoning not only within my bones and muscles, but within almost every single red blood cell in my body. I did a lot of different treatments, made my eating a priority, discovered and went on several immune modulators and little by little turned my health around. These days, now ten years into the journey I'm able to look back, amazed by how far I have come. I'm a true believer in the fact that we can heal and turn things around, and food is often an important part of that equation.

While getting sick was not a path I would have ever chosen for myself, I firmly believe that everything happens for a reason. This experience lit a flame in my heart for supporting people suffering with allergies, needing to follow a special diet to heal. I myself relied heavily on a keto-type diet long before it was ever a popular option or known about much at all. I have experienced the healing power of keto and believe in its abilities to help people far beyond weight loss! I have been pouring my heart into thousands of special diet and allergen-free recipes for the last eight years and I'm so excited to share them with you here!

Brittany Angell

Breakfast

Breakfast can be the most difficult-to-figure-out meal when on a keto diet. At some point eggs and bacon begin to feel really overdone. This chapter opens up an entirely new world of delicious and fun possibilities, making breakfast the best meal of the day.

When it comes to sugar-free and low-carb drink options, most syrups sold in stores are made of ingredients that I don't feel great about buying. This chapter is filled with coffee-house favorites that taste just as good, but without the guilt.

← See recipe on page 43.

Homemade Yogurt in Nine Flavors

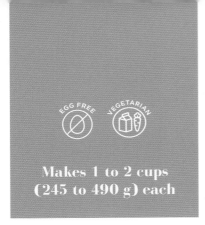

EGG FREE   VEGETARIAN

Makes 1 to 2 cups (245 to 490 g) each

If you are ever tempted by all the delicious flavored yogurts at the grocery store, this collection of sugar-free yogurt mix-ins will be a fun option for you. All are sweetened with stevia and made with low-glycemic fruits or vegetables. Feel free to use any type of unsweetened yogurt as your base, such as those made from cow's milk, goat milk, almonds, cashews or coconut. Most of those options are widely available in stores.

Cranberry Orange Yogurt

¾ cup (75 g) frozen cranberries

¼ to ½ cup (60 to 120 ml) water (enough to cover the cranberries)

1 tbsp (6 g) orange zest

½ tsp stevia extract or monk fruit extract

1 cup (245 g) unsweetened yogurt (dairy or nondairy)

⅛ tsp Himalayan salt, to taste

Add the cranberries to a small saucepan and add enough water to cover the berries. Bring to a boil, then reduce to a simmer until most of the water has evaporated, 10 to 15 minutes. Remove the pan from the heat. Add the orange zest and stevia or monk fruit extract. Stir to combine. Add the cranberry mixture to the yogurt and salt to taste.

Key Lime Pie Yogurt

2 tbsp (30 ml) lime juice

¼ tsp lime zest

½ to 1 tsp stevia extract or monk fruit extract, to taste

½ cup (123 g) unsweetened yogurt (dairy or nondairy)

⅛ tsp Himalayan salt, to taste

¼ cup (20 g) unsweetened toasted coconut flakes

In a small bowl, combine the lime juice, lime zest and stevia or monk fruit extract. Add the lime mixture to the yogurt and salt to taste. Garnish with the unsweetened toasted coconut flakes.

Blueberry Lavender Yogurt

1 cup (230 g) frozen blueberries

¼ to ½ cup (60 to 120 ml) water (enough to cover the blueberries)

1 tsp lemon juice

¼ tsp lavender extract

1 tsp stevia extract or monk fruit extract

1 cup (245 g) unsweetened yogurt (dairy or nondairy)

⅛ tsp Himalayan salt, to taste

Add the blueberries to a small saucepan and add enough water to cover the berries. Bring to a boil, then reduce to a simmer until most of the water has evaporated, 10 to 15 minutes. Remove the pan from the heat. Add the lemon juice, lavender extract and stevia or monk fruit extract. Stir to combine. Add the blueberry mixture to the yogurt, stir to combine and add salt to taste.

Lemon Poppy Seed Yogurt

2 tbsp (30 ml) lemon juice

¼ tsp lemon zest

1 to 1¼ tsp (5 to 6 ml) stevia extract or monk fruit extract, to taste

1 cup (245 g) unsweetened yogurt (dairy or nondairy)

1 to 2 tsp (3 to 6 g) poppy seeds

⅛ tsp Himalayan salt, to taste

In a small mixing bowl, combine the lemon juice, lemon zest and stevia or monk fruit extract (start with 1 teaspoon and add more to taste). Add the yogurt and poppy seeds, stir to combine and add salt to taste.

Blackberry Lime Yogurt

½ cup (75 g) frozen blackberries

¼ to ½ cup (60 to 120 ml) water (enough to cover the blackberries)

1 tbsp (15 ml) lime juice

¼ tsp lime zest

¾ tsp stevia extract or monk fruit extract

1 cup (245 g) unsweetened yogurt (dairy or nondairy)

⅛ tsp Himalayan salt, to taste

Add the blackberries to a small saucepan and add enough water to cover the berries. Bring to a boil, then reduce to a simmer until most of the water has evaporated, 10 to 15 minutes. Remove the pan from the heat. Add the lime juice, lime zest and stevia or monk fruit extract. Stir to combine. Add the blackberry mixture to the yogurt, stir to combine and add salt to taste.

(continued)

Pumpkin Spice Yogurt

⅔ cup (160 g) canned pumpkin

2 tsp (5 g) ground cinnamon

½ tsp ground ginger

½ tsp stevia extract or monk fruit extract

½ tsp vanilla extract

½ cup (123 g) unsweetened yogurt (dairy or nondairy)

⅛ tsp Himalayan salt, to taste

In a small mixing bowl, combine the pumpkin, cinnamon, ginger, stevia or monk fruit extract and vanilla extract. Stir well, then add the yogurt. Stir to combine and add salt to taste.

Espresso Yogurt

¼ cup (60 ml) strong dark roast espresso

¼ tsp cocoa powder

1 tsp vanilla extract

¾ to 1 tsp monk fruit extract

1 cup (245 g) unsweetened yogurt (dairy or nondairy)

⅛ tsp Himalayan salt, to taste

In a small mixing bowl, combine the espresso, cocoa powder, vanilla extract and monk fruit extract. Stir well, then add the yogurt. Stir to combine and add salt to taste.

Recipe Note:

I have found that monk fruit extract works better with cocoa or chocolate than stevia extract.

Savory Beet and Thyme Yogurt

½ medium red or yellow beet, finely chopped

½ tbsp (8 ml) avocado oil

¾ tsp dried thyme

¼ tsp lemon juice

¼ tsp Himalayan salt

¼ tsp ground black pepper

1 cup (245 g) unsweetened yogurt (dairy or nondairy)

Preheat the oven to 450°F (230°C).

In a small mixing bowl, stir the finely chopped beet, avocado oil, thyme, lemon juice, salt and pepper to combine.

Tear off a square of aluminum foil and place the beet-and-thyme mixture in the center. Wrap the foil around the mixture. Roast in the oven for 15 minutes, or until the beet is fork tender. Allow the beet to cool, then place it in a blender with the yogurt or use an immersion blender in a small bowl. Blend on high until combined. Serve immediately.

Chocolate Hazelnut Yogurt

2 tbsp (10 g) cocoa powder

⅓ cup (80 ml) sugar-free maple syrup or sugar-free honey

2 tsp (10 ml) hazelnut extract

1 tsp vanilla extract

¼ to ½ tsp monk fruit extract

¼ tsp Himalayan salt

1 cup (245 g) unsweetened yogurt (dairy or nondairy)

In a medium mixing bowl, stir the cocoa powder, maple syrup, hazelnut extract, vanilla extract, monk fruit extract and salt to combine. Add the yogurt and stir to combine. Serve immediately.

Recipe Note:

I have found that monk fruit extract works better with cocoa or chocolate than stevia extract.

Substitution Notes for ALL Yogurt Recipes:

- To make these *nut free*, use regular yogurt or coconut milk yogurt.

- To make these *dairy free*, use store-bought dairy-free unsweetened yogurt or Homemade Cashew Yogurt (page 492).

- To make these *Paleo*, swap out the sugar-free maple syrup or honey for real and omit monk fruit extract and/or stevia.

EGG FREE · DAIRY FREE · VEGETARIAN

Makes 1¼ cups (365 g) per recipe

Chia Seed Pudding in Four Flavors

You can't ask for a quicker or easier snack than chia pudding. Make a batch at night before bed and you will have a delicious treat waiting for you for breakfast the next morning. Or you can throw it together and eat it 10 minutes later after it thickens a little. For these recipes, I have found that canned coconut milk tastes the best. Unsweetened nondairy milk or heavy cream will also work, but the texture is the best when using full-fat canned coconut milk.

Almond Joy Pudding

1¼ cups (300 ml) canned unsweetened full-fat coconut milk

¼ cup (43 g) chia seeds

½ tsp stevia extract or monk fruit extract

½ tsp vanilla extract

¼ tsp almond extract

⅛ tsp Himalayan salt

3 tbsp (15 g) unsweetened shredded coconut

3 tbsp (32 g) keto-friendly chocolate chips, plus more for garnish

Whole almonds, for garnish

Combine the ingredients, except the almonds, in a medium bowl. Stir until well combined. Cover and refrigerate for at least an hour before serving. Garnish with the chocolate chips and almonds. Keep covered in the refrigerator for up to 3 days.

Substitution Note:

To make this **Paleo**, use honey or maple syrup in place of the stevia or monk fruit extract. The amount required will be different; sweeten to taste.

Chocolate Mousse Pudding

NUT FREE

1 cup (240 ml) canned unsweetened full-fat coconut milk

¼ cup (43 g) chia seeds

3 to 4 tbsp (45 to 60 ml) sugar-free maple syrup

2 tsp (10 ml) vanilla extract

¼ tsp Himalayan salt

3 tbsp (15 g) unsweetened cocoa powder, to taste

Fresh raspberries, for garnish (optional)

Combine the ingredients, except the raspberries (if using), in a medium bowl. Stir until well combined. Cover and refrigerate for at least an hour before serving. Garnish with the raspberries (if using), when serving. Keep covered in the refrigerator for up to 3 days.

Substitution Note:

To make this **Paleo**, use honey or maple syrup in place of the stevia or monk fruit extract. The amount required will be different; sweeten to taste.

Coconut Cream Pie Pudding

1¼ cups (300 ml) canned unsweetened full-fat coconut milk

¼ cup (43 g) chia seeds

2 tbsp (10 g) unsweetened shredded coconut

2 tbsp (30 ml) sugar-free honey or ½ tsp stevia extract or monk fruit extract

½ tsp vanilla extract

⅛ tsp Himalayan salt

Dairy-Free Whipped Topping (page 484), for garnish (optional)

Combine the ingredients, except the whipped topping (if using), in a medium bowl. Stir until well combined. Cover and refrigerate for at least an hour before serving. Garnish as desired. Keep covered in the refrigerator for up to 3 days.

Substitution Note:

To make this *Paleo*, use honey or maple syrup in place of the stevia or monk fruit extract. The amount required will be different; sweeten to taste.

Lemon Pitaya Poppy Seed Pudding

1¼ cups (300 ml) canned unsweetened full-fat coconut milk

¼ cup (43 g) chia seeds

½ tsp stevia extract or monk fruit extract

1 tbsp (9 g) poppy seeds

¼ tsp vanilla extract

⅛ tsp Himalayan salt

2 tbsp (30 ml) lemon juice

1 tbsp (5 g) pink pitaya supercolor powder

Zest of 1 lemon

Lemon slices, for garnish (optional)

Combine the ingredients, except the lemon slices (if using), in a medium-size bowl. Stir until well combined. Cover and refrigerate for at least an hour before serving. Garnish as desired. Keep covered in the refrigerator for up to 3 days.

Substitution Note:

To make this *Paleo*, use honey or maple syrup in place of the stevia or monk fruit extract. The amount required will be different; sweeten to taste.

Pumpkin Spice Rum Granola

Anyone who knows me knows I am a huge fan of all things pumpkin spice. Combined with the rum and sugar-free maple syrup, the flavor of this granola is delicious and comforting. I have found with the keto diet that I sometimes really miss eating crunchy foods, and this recipe totally resolves that craving for me. Unlike regular granola filled with carbs and sugar, this is guilt free, and it has lots of protein and is super filling.

Dry Mixture

1 cup (145 g) whole raw unsalted almonds

1 cup (100 g) raw unsalted walnuts

1 cup (110 g) raw unsalted pecans

1 cup (64 g) raw unsalted pumpkin seeds, divided

½ cup (70 g) raw unsalted sunflower seeds

1 cup (75 g) unsweetened coconut flakes

½ cup (75 g) flax meal

Wet Mixture

½ cup (120 ml) sugar-free maple syrup or sugar-free honey

½ cup (100 g) keto brown sugar

2 tbsp (30 ml) rum extract

4 tbsp (56 g) salted butter or coconut oil

1 tbsp (8 g) pumpkin pie spice

2 tsp (5 g) ground cinnamon

½ tsp Himalayan salt

Optional Toppings

Keto-friendly chocolate chips or cacao nibs

Unsweetened coconut flakes

Hemp seeds

Berries

Preheat the oven to 300°F (150°C). Line an oversized baking sheet (or two standard-sized pans) with parchment paper.

For the dry mixture, place the whole almonds into a food processor and pulse until halfway broken down. (Be aware this happens quickly.) Add the walnuts, pecans, ½ cup (32 g) of the pumpkin seeds and the sunflower seeds. Process until coarsely chopped and you have a nice variety in sizes and textures of nuts and seeds. Pour the mixture into a bowl and stir in the coconut flakes, flax meal and remaining ½ cup (32 g) of the pumpkin seeds. Set aside.

For the wet mixture, in a small saucepan, whisk together the maple syrup, brown sugar, rum extract, butter, pumpkin pie spice, cinnamon and salt. Bring to a simmer and remove from the heat. Pour the wet mixture over the dry mixture and stir so that the dry mixture is well coated. Pour the combined mixture onto the prepared baking sheet(s) and spread out the granola, leaving it in clumps. Bake for 20 minutes, then remove from the oven and gently stir (it may start sticking to the baking sheet; be sure to loosen and flip it). Return it to the oven and bake for another 18 minutes. Remove from the oven to cool fully. When the granola is completely cool, stir in any optional toppings. Store the granola in the refrigerator (to keep it crisp) for up to 1 week.

Substitution Notes:

- To make this *nut free*, use only a mixture of seeds (sunflower and pumpkin).

- To make this *dairy free*, use the coconut oil instead of butter. Butter-flavored coconut oil would be ideal. Also use dairy-free chocolate chips or cacao nibs.

- To make this *Paleo*, use real maple syrup and coconut palm sugar in place of brown sugar.

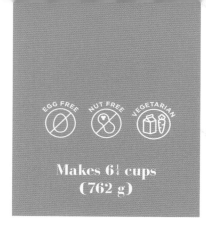

**Makes 6¼ cups
(762 g)**

Dry Mixture

2 cups (280 g) raw unsalted sunflower seeds, divided

2¼ cups (144 g) raw unsalted pumpkin seeds, divided

1 cup (75 g) unsweetened coconut flakes

2 to 3 tbsp (14 to 21 g) spirulina powder

½ cup (75 g) flax meal

½ cup (80 g) hemp seeds

Wet Mixture

½ cup (120 ml) sugar-free maple syrup or sugar-free honey

½ cup (100 g) keto granulated sugar

4 tbsp (56 g) salted butter or coconut oil

2 tbsp (30 ml) lemon juice

1¼ tsp (3 g) ginger powder

½ tsp Himalayan salt

¼ cup (43 g) chia seeds

Optional Toppings

Unsweetened coconut flakes

Hemp seeds or pumpkin seeds

Berries

Keto-friendly chocolate chips or cacao nibs

Seedy Spirulina Superfood Granola

I used to love a spirulina bar that was made with seeds, spirulina and banana. This recipe is my take on that bar, made keto. Spirulina has tons of health benefits, including being high in protein and vitamins, improving gut health, lowering cholesterol, reducing blood pressure and helping your body detox.

Unfortunately all brands are not created equal, and some have a very strong, unpleasant smell and flavor. I use and love the brand Terrasoul Superfoods Spirulina Powder as it has little to no odor or flavor. It makes this granola intensely green and adds a big boost of nutrition but cannot be tasted in the finished recipe.

Preheat the oven to 300°F (150°C). Line an oversized baking sheet (or two standard-sized pans) with parchment paper.

For the dry mixture, place 1¾ cups (245 g) of the sunflower seeds and 2 cups (128 g) of the pumpkin seeds in a food processor and pulse until coarsely chopped and you have a nice variety in sizes and textures of seeds. Be aware that this happens quickly. Pour the mixture into a bowl and stir in the coconut flakes, spirulina powder, flax meal, hemp seeds, remaining ¼ cup (16 g) of pumpkin seeds and remaining ¼ cup (35 g) of whole sunflower seeds. Set aside.

For the wet mixture, in a small saucepan, whisk together the sugar-free maple syrup, granulated sugar, butter (or coconut oil), lemon juice, ginger powder and salt. Bring to a simmer and remove from the heat. Pour the wet mixture over the seed mixture and stir so that the dry mixture is well coated. Stir in the chia seeds. Pour onto the prepared baking sheet(s) and spread out the granola, leaving it in clumps. Bake for 20 minutes, then remove from the oven and gently stir. Return it to the oven and bake for another 18 minutes, then remove from the oven to cool fully. When the granola is completely cool, stir in any optional toppings. Store the granola in the refrigerator (to keep it crisp) for up to 1 week.

Substitution Notes:

To make this *dairy free*, use the coconut oil instead of the butter. If using chocolate chips, opt for dairy free or cacao nibs.

To make this *Paleo*, use real maple syrup instead of sugar-free maple syrup. You can add an extra ¼ cup (25 g) of coconut palm sugar if you like your granola sweet. Omit keto granulated sugar.

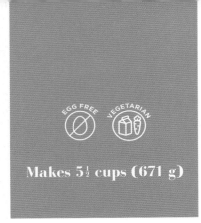

Makes 5½ cups (671 g)

Mocha Chip Granola

Chocolate and coffee are a match made in heaven and they work perfectly together in this mocha-flavored granola. You may find it odd to put ground coffee in the recipe, but I assure you that once it's baked you will only get a hint of coffee in the flavor and won't notice any gritty coffee-bean texture. The coffee is entirely optional, so feel free to leave it out if you wish.

When making the recipe you need about 4 cups (572 g) raw unsalted nuts/seeds, but which ones you use is entirely up to you. I tend to leave out cashews because they are the highest in carbohydrates. You can follow the mixture I used, or come up with your own combination. The results will be consistently good.

Dry Mixture

2 cups (290 g) raw unsalted whole almonds

1 cup (100 g) raw unsalted walnuts

½ cup (32 g) raw unsalted pumpkin seeds

½ cup (70 g) raw unsalted sunflower seeds

1 cup (75 g) unsweetened coconut flakes

½ cup (75 g) flax meal

Wet Mixture

4 tbsp (56 g) salted butter or coconut oil

¾ tsp Himalayan salt

3 tbsp (15 g) cocoa powder

½ cup (120 ml) sugar-free maple syrup or sugar-free honey

½ cup (100 g) keto brown sugar (or keto granulated sugar)

1 tbsp (15 ml) vanilla extract

1½ tbsp (5 g) finely ground coffee beans (dark roast is best)

Optional Toppings

Keto-friendly chocolate chips or cacao nibs

Unsweetened coconut flakes

Hemp seeds

Preheat the oven to 300°F (150°C). Line an oversized baking sheet (or two standard-sized pans) with parchment paper.

For the dry mixture, place the whole almonds in a food processor and pulse until halfway broken down (be aware this happens quickly). Add the walnuts, pumpkin seeds and sunflower seeds. Process until coarsely chopped and you have a nice variety in sizes and textures of the nuts and seeds. Pour into a bowl and stir in the coconut flakes and flax meal. Set aside.

For the wet mixture, in a small saucepan, whisk together the butter (or coconut oil), salt, cocoa powder, sugar-free maple syrup, brown sugar, vanilla and coffee. Bring the mixture to a simmer, then remove from the heat. Pour the wet mixture over the nut/seed mixture and stir so that the dry mixture is well covered. Pour the granola onto the prepared baking sheet(s) and spread out the granola, leaving it in clumps. Bake for 20 minutes, then remove from the oven and gently stir (it may start sticking to the baking sheet; be sure to loosen and flip it). Return it to the oven and bake for another 18 minutes. Remove from the oven to cool fully. When the granola is completely cool, stir in any optional toppings. Store the granola in the refrigerator (to keep it crisp) for up to 1 week.

Substitution Notes:

- To make this **dairy free**, use the coconut oil instead of butter. Butter-flavored coconut oil would be ideal. Also use dairy-free chocolate chips or cacao nibs.

- To make this **Paleo**, use real maple syrup instead of sugar-free maple syrup. You can add an extra ¼ cup (25 g) of coconut palm sugar if you like your granola sweet. Omit the keto sugar.

**Makes 1 to 2 servings
per recipe**

Smoothie Bowls in Three Flavors

Smoothies or smoothie bowls are not typically considered keto. With a little creativity I worked my way around that. Smoothies are typically comprised of mostly frozen fruit, which you can have with keto but in smaller amounts. Bananas are often a filler/thickener ingredient and they have too much sugar and carbohydrates to maintain ketosis. I opted instead to freeze cubes of yogurt in one tray, and in another I froze full-fat coconut milk from a can. You'll need to make these the night before, but they are great to have in the freezer to throw into all kinds of smoothies or even soup. You may find it odd that I have salt included in these recipes but I promise it is needed. It really helps round out the flavor from stevia. If you aren't a fan of stevia you can sweeten with a sugar-free syrup instead.

Frozen Coconut Milk

1 (15-oz [444-ml]) can full-fat unsweetened coconut milk, room temperature

To make the frozen coconut milk, shake the can of coconut milk and pour into an ice-cube tray; freeze overnight.

Frozen Yogurt

1 cup (245 g) unsweetened plain yogurt (dairy or non-dairy)

To make the frozen yogurt, fill the holes of an ice-cube tray with the yogurt; you will need three cubes per recipe so fill at least three holes, or more if you have extra yogurt. Freeze the yogurt overnight.

(continued)

Photo on left, Acai Blueberry Lavender Smoothie Bowl (page 30)

Acai Blueberry Lavender Smoothie Bowl

1 (3.5-oz [100-g]) packet frozen unsweetened puréed acai, mostly thawed under hot running water

5 cubes Frozen Coconut Milk (page 29)

3 cubes Frozen Yogurt (page 29)

½ cup (120 ml) cold water

½ cup (115 g) frozen blueberries

¼ tsp Himalayan salt

1 tsp vanilla extract

¼ tsp lavender extract

1 tsp stevia extract or monk fruit extract (or more, to taste)

Add all of the ingredients to a blender except the stevia and blend on high until smooth. Start with adding 1 teaspoon of stevia or monk fruit extract and then add more, ¼ teaspoon at a time, to taste.

Pour the smoothie into bowls and add your toppings of choice (see the Recipe Notes on page 33). Store any leftovers in an airtight container in the refrigerator. It should keep for 3 to 4 days.

*See image on page 28.

Raspberry Pink Pitaya Smoothie Bowl

5 cubes Frozen Coconut Milk (page 29)

3 cubes Frozen Yogurt (page 29)

½ cup (120 ml) cold water

2 tsp (4 g) pink pitaya powder (or more for extra vibrant color)

½ cup (70 g) frozen raspberries

¼ tsp Himalayan salt

1 tsp vanilla extract

1 tsp stevia extract or monk fruit extract (or more, to taste)

Add all of the ingredients to a blender except the stevia and blend on high until smooth. Start with adding 1 teaspoon of stevia or monk fruit extract and then add more, ¼ teaspoon at a time, to taste.

Pour the smoothie into bowls and add your toppings of choice (see the Recipe Notes on page 33). Store any leftovers in an airtight container in the refrigerator. It should keep for 3 to 4 days.

(continued)

Butterfly Pea Flower Smoothie Bowl

5 cubes Frozen Coconut Milk (see page 29)

3 cubes Frozen Yogurt (see page 29)

1 to 2 tsp (1 g) blue butterfly pea supercolor powder

½ cup (120 ml) cold water

½ cup (75 g) frozen strawberries

¼ tsp Himalayan salt

1 tsp vanilla extract

1 tsp stevia extract or monk fruit extract (or more or less, to taste)

Add all of the ingredients to a blender except the stevia and blend on high until smooth. Start with adding 1 teaspoon of stevia or monk fruit extract and then add more, ¼ teaspoon at a time, to taste.

Pour the smoothie into bowls and add your toppings of choice (see the Recipe Notes below). Store any leftovers in an airtight container in the refrigerator. It should keep for 3 to 4 days.

Recipe Notes for ALL Smoothies:

- You can add any of the following topping ideas to these recipes: pumpkin seeds, poppy seeds, sunflower seeds, black sesame seeds, hazelnuts, chia seeds, hemp seeds, strawberries, blueberries, raspberries, blackberries or unsweetened coconut flakes.

- A powerful blender will work best. You may need to stop the blender a few times to press everything down with a spatula. It takes a little extra time to blend, but the results are worth it.

- If your smoothie bowl melts too much while it's in the blender or while you are putting the toppings on, you can stick the bowl right in the freezer for 15 to 20 minutes and it will quickly firm back up. If you leave it in the freezer for 1 to 2 hours, it will end up more like a frozen yogurt bowl, which is also delicious.

Substitution Notes for ALL Smoothies:

- To make this *dairy free*, use dairy-free yogurt.

- To make this *Paleo*, use regular honey or maple syrup in place of the stevia or monk fruit extract. The amount required will be different—sweeten to taste.

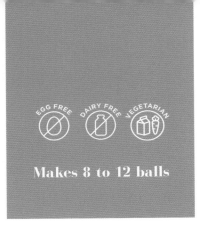

EGG FREE · DAIRY FREE · VEGETARIAN

Makes 8 to 12 balls

Homemade Protein Balls (Fat Bombs) in Five Flavors

Protein balls are an easy no-bake snack. Keep them stocked in your refrigerator for a quick breakfast to keep your diet on track. Here we have five flavors that are sure to satisfy your every mood. There are a variety of sugar-free maple syrups available in stores and online, and they are not all created equal. I have come to love two sugar-free brands: Lakanto Maple Flavored Syrup and Sweet Leaf Stevia Syrup (Maple Flavored). I find that the Sweet Leaf brand is sweeter cup for cup, which works best when also using tahini in a recipe because it can be bitter. Both brands can be found online. For the superfruit powders, I used Suncore Foods brand. You can swap out the black goji powder or pink pitaya for any other color/flavor that they sell.

These recipes can be customized. This is the base recipe that I used to create all of the flavors. Feel free to experiment and make your own or use it to make substitutions to the recipes provided. All protein balls taste best chilled!

Protein Ball Base

1 cup (75 g) shredded unsweetened coconut

¾ cup (112 g) flax meal or finely processed nuts or seeds

½ cup (128 g) any unsweetened nut or seed butter (almond, tahini, peanut, etc.) or ¾ cup (75 g) raw coconut butter

⅓ cup (80 ml) sugar-free maple syrup (may need an extra 2 tbsp [30 ml] if using coconut butter to make sticky), or sugar-free honey

1 tbsp (10 g) chia seeds

2 tsp (10 ml) vanilla extract

⅛ tsp Himalayan salt

To make the protein ball base, in a large bowl, combine the unsweetened coconut, flax meal, nut or seed butter, maple syrup, chia seeds, vanilla extract and salt and mix until well incorporated. Form the mixture into eight to twelve equal-sized balls, or proceed to the directions for any of the flavors on the following pages.

Recipe Note:

Every brand of nut/seed butter is different. Therefore they may all perform a little differently in these recipes. If you find your protein balls are a bit dry and are not holding together, add a little bit more nut/seed butter. A little bit more maple syrup or honey can help too.

Coconut Lime Macadamia Protein Balls

½ cup (66 g) chopped macadamia nuts

1 recipe Protein Ball Base (page 36), using coconut butter and the extra maple syrup

¼ cup (20 g) shredded unsweetened coconut

Zest of 1 large lime

Mix the macadamia nuts into the Protein Ball Base until well incorporated. Form the mixture into eight to twelve equal-sized balls.

In a small bowl, combine the coconut and the lime zest. Roll the balls in the mixture to coat. They can be eaten immediately or placed in a sealed container in the refrigerator for up to 1 week.

Substitution Notes:

- To make this *nut free*, omit the macadamia nuts and swap in a seed of choice. Use nut-free options in the base recipe.

- To make this *Paleo*, use regular maple syrup instead of the sugar-free maple syrup.

Carrot Cake Protein Balls

¾ cup (40 g) shredded carrots

1 tsp ground cinnamon

½ tsp ground ginger

¼ tsp ground nutmeg

1 recipe Protein Ball Base (page 36), using almond butter

Mix the carrots, cinnamon, ginger and nutmeg into the Protein Ball Base until well incorporated. Place the mixture in the freezer for 10 minutes or the refrigerator for 30 minutes. This will help the mixture solidify. Form the mixture into twelve equal-sized balls. They can be eaten immediately or placed in a sealed container in the refrigerator for up to 1 week.

Substitution Notes:

- To make this *Paleo*, use regular maple syrup or honey instead of the sugar-free maple syrup.

- To make this *nut free*, use seed butter in the base recipe and a flax or seed option.

(continued)

Chocolate Chai Protein Balls

2 tsp (5 g) ground cinnamon

½ tsp ground cardamom

½ tsp ground ginger

¼ tsp ground nutmeg

¼ cup + 2 tbsp (45 g) cacao nibs

1 recipe Protein Ball Base (page 36), using coconut butter and the extra maple syrup

1 tbsp (5 g) cocoa powder (optional)

Mix the cinnamon, cardamom, ginger, nutmeg and cacao nibs into the Protein Ball Base until well incorporated. Form the mixture into twelve equal-sized balls.

Optional: Put the cocoa powder in a small bowl. Roll the balls in the cocoa powder to coat. They can be eaten immediately or placed in a sealed container in the refrigerator for up to 1 week.

Substitution Notes:

- To make this *nut free*, use nut-free option in the base recipe.

- To make this *Paleo*, use regular maple syrup or honey instead of the sugar-free maple syrup.

Black Goji Berry Protein Balls

¾ cup (100 g) salted and toasted macadamia nuts

1 cup (75 g) shredded unsweetened coconut

½ cup (120 ml) tahini

⅓ cup (80 ml) sugar-free maple syrup or sugar-free honey

1 tbsp (10 g) white chia seeds

1 tsp vanilla extract

2 tbsp (15 g) sapphire wolfberry superfruit powder

⅛ tsp Himalayan salt

In a food processor, pulse the macadamia nuts until finely ground. Put the ground macadamia nuts in a bowl and add the coconut, tahini, maple syrup, chia seeds, vanilla, superfruit powder and salt and mix well until everything is incorporated. Form the mixture into twelve equal-sized balls. They can be eaten immediately or placed in a sealed container in the refrigerator for up to 1 week.

Substitution Notes:

- To make this *nut free*, swap the macadamia nuts for ¾ cup (112 g) of flax meal or another seed of choice.

- To make this *Paleo*, use regular maple syrup or honey instead of the sugar-free maple syrup.

Pink Dragon Fruit Protein Balls

¾ cup (100 g) salted and toasted macadamia nuts

1 cup (75 g) shredded unsweetened coconut

½ cup (120 ml) tahini

⅓ cup (80 ml) sugar-free maple syrup or sugar-free honey

1 tbsp (10 g) white chia seeds

1 tsp vanilla extract

2 tbsp (15 g) pitaya superfruit powder

⅛ tsp Himalayan salt

In a food processor, pulse the macadamia nuts until finely ground. Put the ground macadamia nuts in a bowl and add the coconut, tahini, maple syrup, chia seeds, vanilla, superfruit powder and salt and mix well until everything is incorporated. Form the mixture into twelve equal-sized balls. They can be eaten immediately or placed in a sealed container in the refrigerator for up to 1 week.

Substitution Notes:

- To make this *nut free*, swap the macadamia nuts for ¾ cup (112 g) of flax meal or another seed of choice.

- To make this *Paleo*, use regular maple syrup or honey instead of the sugar-free maple syrup.

EGG FREE DAIRY FREE

Makes 8 to 10 large sausages

Homemade Breakfast Sausage Three Ways

Breakfast sausage is an easy, make-ahead dish. When bacon is called for, I removed the salt from the recipe because bacon is typically plenty salty. Here are three of my favorite ways to create a sure-to-please breakfast dish.

Maple Pecan Bacon Pork Sausage

8 slices bacon, chopped

1 lb (454 g) ground pork

1 cup (110 g) chopped pecans (optional)

¼ cup (60 ml) sugar-free maple syrup

½ tsp stevia extract or monk fruit extract

1 tsp ground black pepper

½ tsp ground cloves

½ tsp cayenne pepper

In a large skillet over medium heat, add the chopped bacon and cook until crisp, about 6 minutes. Remove the bacon from the pan and place on a paper towel to drain, leaving the bacon fat in the skillet over low heat while you make the sausage.

In a large mixing bowl, combine the ground pork, chopped pecans, maple syrup, stevia or monk fruit extract, black pepper, ground cloves, cayenne pepper and the cooked bacon until well incorporated. Form eight to ten equal-sized balls of the sausage mixture and flatten to about ¼ inch (6 mm) thick.

Increase the heat under the skillet with the bacon fat to medium and place each sausage patty in the pan. Allow the patties to cook for about 4 minutes, then flip and cook for another 3 minutes, or until cooked through. Store in a container in the refrigerator for up to 3 days.

Substitution Notes:

- To make this *nut free*, omit the pecans.

- To make this *Paleo*, use real honey or maple syrup in place of sugar-free and omit the stevia or monk fruit extract.

Sage and Cranberry Turkey Sausage

1 lb (454 g) ground turkey

1 cup (100 g) fresh cranberries, finely chopped or pulsed in a food processor

3 tbsp (45 ml) sugar-free maple syrup or sugar-free honey

¼ tsp stevia extract or monk fruit extract

1 sage leaf, chopped, or 2 tsp (1 g) ground sage

¼ tsp Himalayan salt (or more to taste)

½ tsp ground black pepper

½ tsp garlic powder

½ tsp dried thyme

¼ tsp ground cloves

3 tbsp (45 g) coconut oil or ghee

In a large mixing bowl, combine the ground turkey, cranberries, maple syrup, stevia extract, fresh or ground sage, salt, black pepper, garlic powder, thyme and cloves until well incorporated.

Place the coconut oil or ghee in a large skillet and place over medium heat. Form eight equal-sized balls of the sausage mixture and flatten to about ¼ inch (6 mm) thick. Place each sausage patty in the pan and allow them to cook for about 4 minutes, then flip and cook for another 3 minutes, or until cooked through. Store in a container in the refrigerator for up to 3 days.

*See photo on page 10.

Substitution Notes:

- To make this *Paleo*, use real honey or maple syrup in place of sugar free. Omit the stevia or monk fruit extract.

- To make *dairy free*, use coconut oil.

Maple Apple Cinnamon Turkey Sausage

1 lb (454 g) ground turkey

1 small apple, finely chopped

3 tbsp (45 ml) sugar-free maple syrup

¼ tsp stevia extract or monk fruit extract

2 tsp (5 g) ground cinnamon

¼ tsp Himalayan salt (or more to taste)

1 tsp ground black pepper

¼ tsp ground clove

¼ tsp cayenne pepper

3 tbsp (45 g) coconut oil or ghee

In a large mixing bowl, combine the ground turkey, apple, maple syrup, stevia extract, cinnamon, salt, black pepper, clove and cayenne pepper, until well incorporated.

Place the coconut oil or ghee in a large skillet and place over medium heat. Form eight equal-sized balls of the sausage mixture and flatten to about ¼ inch (6 mm) thick. Place each sausage patty in the pan and allow them to cook for about 4 minutes, then flip and cook for an additional 3 minutes, or until cooked through. Store in a container in the refrigerator for up to 3 days.

Substitution Notes:

- To make this *Paleo*, use real honey or maple syrup in place of sugar free. Omit the stevia or monk fruit extract.

- To make *dairy free*, use coconut oil.

VEGETARIAN

Makes 7 muffins

Lemon Poppy Seed Muffins with Toasted Sliced Almonds

As if lemon poppy seed wasn't delicious enough on its own, the toasted almonds on the top of this muffin add a great texture and flavor. Out of all the muffins in this book this has to be one of my favorites.

3 large eggs

2 tbsp (30 ml) melted butter or mild oil of choice

½ cup (100 g) keto granulated sugar

4 tbsp (60 ml) heavy cream or unsweetened full-fat coconut milk (from a can) or other milk of choice

Zest of 1 lemon

1 tbsp + 1 tsp (20 ml) lemon or lime juice

¼ tsp Himalayan salt

¾ tsp double-acting baking powder

1 cup (116 g) blanched almond flour

¼ cup (20 g) oat fiber

2 tsp (6 g) poppy seeds

½ cup (54 g) raw/unsalted sliced almonds

Preheat the oven to 350°F (175°C). Line a muffin tin with seven paper liners.

Add the eggs, melted butter, sugar and cream to a blender. Blitz on high for 45 seconds. Add the lemon zest, lemon juice, salt, baking powder, almond flour and oat fiber. Blend on high again for 30 seconds. Stir in the poppy seeds.

Fill the muffin liners three-fourths full and top the muffin batter with the almonds. Place on the center rack of the oven. Bake for 25 to 30 minutes, until a toothpick comes out clean, the muffins are firm to the touch and the edges are perfectly golden brown. Allow the muffins to cool fully.

Store at room temperature in a sealed bag or container for up to 1 week or freeze for up to 1 month. These muffins taste great the day they are made but continue to taste better in the days following.

Recipe Notes:

• These flours have a tendency to stick to the muffin liners a bit. If you would like to avoid that, a greased silicone muffin tray can be used instead.

• For the best results, use gram measurements and recommended brands on page 491.

Substitution Notes:

• To make this **dairy free**, use the oil and full-fat coconut cream options.

• To make this **Paleo**, omit the oat fiber. Swap out the sugar for coconut palm sugar or granulated maple sugar. Use the full-fat coconut milk option.

Carrot and Zucchini Muffins with Toasted Hemp Seeds

I love this combo of carrot and zucchini as it gives these muffins the perfect texture and moisture level. Rather than topping the muffins with crumb topping, I opted to try something different and sprinkle them with hemp seeds. Adding that extra bit of texture and flavor really made this recipe stand out.

3 large eggs

2 tbsp (30 ml) melted butter or mild oil of choice

½ cup (100 g) keto granulated sugar

4 tbsp (60 ml) heavy cream or unsweetened full-fat coconut milk (from a can) or other milk of choice

2 tsp (10 ml) vanilla extract

1 tsp lemon or lime juice or apple cider vinegar

2 tsp (5 g) ground cinnamon

¼ tsp Himalayan salt

¾ tsp double-acting baking powder

1 cup (116 g) blanched almond flour

¼ cup (20 g) oat fiber

½ cup (25 g) grated carrot, squeezed of extra moisture

½ cup (90 g) grated zucchini, squeezed of extra moisture

¼ cup (40 g) hemp seeds (optional)

Preheat the oven to 350°F (175°C). Line a muffin tin with eight paper liners.

Add the eggs, melted butter, sugar and cream to a blender. Blitz on high for 45 seconds. Add the vanilla, lemon juice, cinnamon, salt, baking powder, almond flour and oat fiber. Blend on high for 30 seconds. Stir in the carrot and zucchini.

Fill the muffin liners three-fourths full. Sprinkle the tops with the hemp seeds (if using). Place on the center rack of the oven. Bake for 35 to 38 minutes, until a toothpick comes out clean, the muffins are firm to the touch and the edges are perfectly golden brown. Allow the muffins to cool fully.

Store at room temperature in a sealed bag or container for up to 1 week or freeze for up to 1 month. These muffins taste great the day they are made but continue to taste better in the days following.

Recipe Notes:

- These flours have a tendency to stick to the muffin liners a bit. If you would like to avoid that, a greased silicone muffin tray can be used instead.

- For the best results, use gram measurements and recommended brands on page 491.

Substitution Notes:

- To make this *dairy free*, use the oil and full-fat coconut cream options.

- To make this *Paleo*, omit the oat fiber. Swap out the sugar for coconut palm sugar or granulated maple sugar. Use the full-fat coconut option.

Makes 8 muffins

Blueberry Lemon Crumb Muffins

This recipe will not disappoint. The texture of the muffins is perfect and doesn't have that overly eggy texture that I have found in most low-carb muffins. The crumb topping is also delicious and adds an extra bit of lemon flavor from some zest mixed in.

Muffins

3 large eggs

2 tbsp (30 ml) melted butter or mild oil of choice

½ cup (100 g) keto granulated sugar

4 tbsp (60 ml) heavy cream or unsweetened full-fat coconut milk (from a can) or other milk of choice

Zest of 1 lemon

1 tbsp + 1 tsp (20 ml) lemon juice

¼ tsp Himalayan salt

¾ tsp double-acting baking powder

1 cup (116 g) blanched almond flour

¼ cup (20 g) oat fiber

1 cup (230 g) frozen blueberries

Crumb Topping

¾ cup (87 g) blanched almond flour

2 tbsp (25 g) keto granulated sugar

¼ tsp Himalayan salt

Zest of ½ lemon

2 tbsp (30 ml) melted butter or mild-tasting oil

Preheat the oven to 350°F (175°C). Line a muffin tin with eight paper liners.

To make the muffins, add the eggs, melted butter, sugar, cream and lemon zest to a blender. Blitz on high for 45 seconds. Add the lemon juice, salt, baking powder, almond flour and oat fiber. Blend on high for 30 seconds. Gently stir in the blueberries.

To make the crumb topping, in a bowl, combine the almond flour, sugar, salt and zest. Mix just until crumbs form. Stir in the melted butter gently until clumps form. Set aside.

Fill the muffin liners three-fourths full with the batter and then top with the crumb topping. Place on the center rack of the oven. Bake for 35 to 38 minutes. Tent the muffins with aluminum foil after the first 20 minutes of baking to prevent the crumb topping from burning. Bake until a toothpick comes out clean, the muffins are firm to the touch and the edges are perfectly golden brown. Allow the muffins to cool fully. Store at room temperature in a sealed bag or container for up to 1 week or freeze for up to 1 month. These muffins taste great the day they are made but continue to taste better in the days following.

Recipe Notes:

- These flours have a tendency to stick to the muffin liners a bit. If you would like to avoid that, a greased silicone muffin tray can be used instead.

- For the best results, use gram measurements and recommended brands on page 491.

Substitution Notes:

- To make this *dairy free*, use the oil and full-fat coconut options.

- To make this *Paleo*, omit the oat fiber. Swap out the sugar for coconut palm sugar or granulated maple sugar. Use the full-fat coconut milk option.

VEGETARIAN

Makes 8 muffins

Blackberry Lime Muffins

Out of all the muffin flavors this one may be my favorite. If you haven't tasted blackberry and lime together now is the time to test it out: The flavors are a match made in heaven. Blueberry-lemon is considered by many to be the be-all, end-all flavor combo but I would argue this one is even better!

3 large eggs

2 tbsp (30 ml) melted butter or mild oil of choice

½ cup (100 g) keto granulated sugar

4 tbsp (60 ml) heavy cream or unsweetened full-fat coconut milk (from a can) or other milk of choice

Zest of 1 lime

1 tbsp + 1 tsp (20 ml) lime juice

¼ tsp Himalayan salt

¾ tsp double-acting baking powder

1 cup (116 g) blanched almond flour

¼ cup (20 g) oat fiber

1 cup (150 g) frozen blackberries, cut in half

Preheat the oven to 350°F (175°C). Line a muffin tin with eight paper liners.

Add the eggs, melted butter, sugar, cream and lime zest to a blender. Blitz on high for 45 seconds. Add the lime juice, salt, baking powder, almond flour and oat fiber. Blend on high for 30 seconds. Gently stir in the blackberries.

Fill the muffin liners three-fourths full. Place on the middle rack of the oven.

Bake for 33 to 35 minutes, until a toothpick comes out clean, the muffins are firm to the touch and the edges are perfectly golden brown. Allow the muffins to cool fully.

Store at room temperature in a sealed bag or container for up to 1 week or freeze for up to 1 month. These muffins taste great the day they are made but continue to taste better in the days following.

Recipe Notes:

- These flours have a tendency to stick to the muffin liners a bit. If you would like to avoid that, a greased silicone muffin tray can be used instead.

- For the best results, use gram measurements and recommended brands on page 491.

Substitution Notes:

- To make this *dairy free*, use the oil and full-fat coconut milk options.

- To make this *Paleo*, omit the oat fiber. Swap out the sugar for coconut palm sugar or granulated maple sugar. Use the full-fat coconut milk option.

VEGETARIAN

Makes 8 muffins

Pumpkin Chocolate Chip Muffins

With fall comes pumpkin everything so I've got you covered with this recipe. You will enjoy the season's best flavor without an ounce of guilt. For the chocolate chips, my favorite brand is Guittard. Their extra dark chocolate chips are decently low in carbs, and because they don't have any sugar alcohol they taste like regular chocolate.

3 large eggs

2 tbsp (30 ml) melted butter or mild oil of choice

½ cup (100 g) keto granulated sugar

4 tbsp (60 ml) heavy cream or unsweetened full-fat coconut milk (from a can) or other milk of choice

½ cup (116 g) pumpkin purée

2 tsp (10 ml) vanilla extract

1 tsp apple cider vinegar

¼ tsp Himalayan salt

¾ tsp double-acting baking powder

1 cup (116 g) blanched almond flour

¼ cup (20 g) oat fiber

2 tsp (6 g) pumpkin pie spice

½ cup (84 g) keto-friendly chocolate chips

Preheat the oven to 350°F (175°C). Line a muffin tin with eight paper liners.

Add the eggs, melted butter, sugar and cream to a blender. Blitz on high for 45 seconds. Add the pumpkin purée, vanilla extract, apple cider vinegar, salt, baking powder, almond flour, oat fiber and pumpkin pie spice. Blend on high for 30 seconds. Stir in the chocolate chips.

Fill the muffin liners three-fourths full. Place on the middle rack of the oven. Bake for 35 to 38 minutes, tenting the muffins with aluminum foil the last 10 to 12 minutes. Bake until a toothpick comes out clean, the muffins are firm to the touch and the edges are perfectly golden brown. Allow the muffins to cool fully.

Store at room temperature in a sealed bag or container for up to 1 week or freeze for up to 1 month. These muffins taste great the day they are made but continue to taste better in the days following.

Recipe Notes:

- These flours have a tendency to stick to the muffin liners a bit. If you would like to avoid that, a greased silicone muffin tray can be used instead.

- For the best results, use gram measurements and recommended brands on page 491.

Substitution Notes:

- To make this *dairy free*, use full-fat coconut milk and swap the chocolate chips for ¼ cup (30 g) cacao nibs or dairy-free chocolate chips.

- To make this *Paleo*, omit the oat fiber. Swap out the sugar for coconut palm sugar or granulated maple sugar. Use the full-fat coconut milk option.

52 THE ULTIMATE KETO COOKBOOK

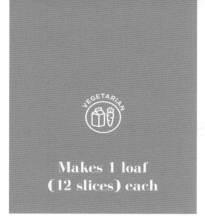

**Makes 1 loaf
(12 slices) each**

Quick Bread in Two Flavors

These quick breads come together quickly and easily. For the best results for these recipes, use a kitchen scale to weigh all the ingredients using the gram measurements provided—even for the liquids.

Red Velvet Quick Bread

4 tbsp (60 ml) mild oil or melted butter

⅓ cup (75 g) water

¾ cup (159 g) keto granulated sugar

4 large eggs

2¼ cups (261 g) blanched almond flour

2 tsp (9 g) double-acting baking powder

¼ tsp Himalayan salt

1 tsp vinegar or lemon juice

1 cup (168 g) keto-friendly chocolate chips

1 tbsp (5 g) dark cocoa powder

4 tsp (24 ml) red food coloring

Topping

Cream Cheese Frosting (page 234)

1 cup (100 g) sliced berries

Shaved dark chocolate

Preheat the oven to 350°F (175°C). Line a 9 x 5-inch (23 x 13–cm) loaf pan with parchment paper.

Combine all the ingredients in a large bowl and whisk until smooth. Pour into the prepared pan. Bake for 40 to 50 minutes, until a toothpick comes out clean and the bread feels set when you shake the pan.

Top with the Cream Cheese Frosting, fresh sliced berries and shaved dark chocolate. Serve hot, or store in a sealed bag or container for up to 1 week.

Substitution Notes:

- To make these *dairy free*, use oil instead of butter and use dairy-free chocolate chips.

- To make these *Paleo*, swap out the sugar for coconut palm sugar or granulated maple sugar. Use dairy-free chocolate chips.

(continued)

Pesto and Mozzarella Quick Bread

Quick Bread

4 tbsp (63 g) pesto

⅓ cup (75 g) water

4 large eggs

2¼ cups (261 g) blanched almond flour

2 tsp (9 g) double-acting baking powder

¼ tsp Himalayan salt

1 tsp vinegar or lemon juice

1 tbsp (10 g) garlic powder

1 tbsp (2 g) dried basil

2 cups (225 g) shredded mozzarella

Optional Toppings

1 cup (160 g) baby tomatoes, sliced in half

1 tbsp (15 ml) avocado oil

Pinch of salt and pepper

3 tbsp (45 g) pesto

A few leaves of basil or spinach, cut into ribbons

Preheat the oven to 350°F (175°C). Line a 9 x 5-inch (23 x 13–cm) loaf pan with parchment paper.

Combine all the quick bread ingredients in a large bowl and whisk until smooth. Pour into the prepared pan. Bake for 40 to 50 minutes, until a toothpick comes out clean and the bread feels set when you shake the pan.

To make roasted tomatoes, preheat the oven to 450°F (232°C). Place the tomatoes on a small rimmed baking sheet. Toss with oil, salt and pepper. Roast 20 to 25 minutes, or until tomatoes are blistered and begin to burst.

Brush the bread with the pesto and top with the roasted tomatoes and basil or spinach. Serve hot, or store in a sealed bag or container for up to 1 week.

Substitution Note:

To make this *Paleo*, omit the cheese and use a dairy-free pesto.

Makes 4 to 6 servings

1 small head cauliflower, roughly chopped

2 cups + 2 tbsp (204 g) blanched almond flour

3 cups (720 ml) chicken broth

4 tbsp (56 g) butter, unsweetened nondairy milk or butter-flavored coconut oil

2 tsp (12 g) Himalayan salt

1½ tsp (3 g) black pepper

1 tsp garlic powder (optional)

Optional Toppings

Cooked shrimp

Sharp cheddar cheese

A pinch of cayenne

Cooked bacon

Keto Grits

Creamy grits for breakfast—yum. The cauliflower rice is a great keto substitute in this recipe. Now you can enjoy grits without the worry of all the starch. You can enjoy these mock grits as is, or mix in cheddar cheese, a pinch of cayenne and shrimp to take it up a notch.

Place the cauliflower in a blender or food processor and pulse until it is a rice-like consistency. Measure 3 cups (350 g) of the riced cauliflower, saving any remaining "rice" for another use.

In a medium saucepan, bring the "riced" cauliflower, almond flour, chicken broth, butter, salt, black pepper and garlic powder (if using) to a gentle boil over medium heat and whisk often, until thick, 15 to 20 minutes.

Serve with shrimp, cheddar cheese, cayenne and bacon, if desired.

Substitution Note:

To make this *dairy free* and *Paleo*, use butter-flavored coconut oil and omit the cheese topping.

Makes 8 scones

Blackberry Almond Caramel Scones

These scones might be even more delicious than they look. Fresh blackberries are a must! They taste incredible with the homemade caramel sauce and slivered almonds. Thanks to the lupin and oat fiber these scones are fluffy but still flaky.

2 large eggs

1 tsp lemon juice or apple cider vinegar

⅓ cup (80 ml) unsweetened nondairy milk

2 tsp (10 ml) almond or vanilla extract

1½ cups (150 g) lupin flour

½ cup (40 g) oat fiber, plus more for dusting

⅓ cup (65 g) keto granulated sugar

½ cup (115 g) salted butter or shortening

½ tsp Himalayan salt

1 tsp double-acting baking powder

½ cup (75 g) fresh blackberries, halved, plus more for garnish

⅓ to ½ cup (36 to 54 g) raw, unsalted sliced almonds

Keto Caramel (page 359), for drizzling (optional)

Preheat the oven to 425°F (220°C). Line a baking sheet with parchment paper.

In a small bowl, combine the eggs, lemon juice, milk and almond extract and set aside.

In a large bowl or food processor, combine the lupin flour, oat fiber, sugar, butter, salt and baking powder; mix until the butter forms pea-size pieces. If using a food processor, move the dry ingredients to a large bowl. Combine the wet ingredients with the dry ingredients and mix until the dough starts to come together. Add the blackberries and combine.

Place a piece of parchment paper on the counter. Dust the parchment paper with a little of the oat fiber and transfer the dough to the parchment. Gently shape the dough into a round that has even thickness across the top (about 1 inch [3 cm] thick). Be careful not to overmix the dough, or the berries will break. Once the round is formed, top the dough with the almonds and lightly press the almonds into the dough. Cut the circle into eight separate wedge-shaped pieces. Transfer the dough pieces to the prepared baking sheet.

Bake, covered with foil, for 10 minutes on the center rack in the oven. Remove the foil and bake for an additional 2 minutes, or until the almonds are perfectly toasted.

Drizzle the scones with caramel sauce (if using) and additional fresh blackberries, if desired, and serve. Store in a covered container in the refrigerator for 1 week.

Substitution Note:

* To make this *dairy free*, use dairy-free butter or palm shortening and dairy-free milk.

**Makes 9 to
10 biscuits**

Savory Caprese
Biscuits

*If you enjoy a caprese salad, then be sure to put this scone
recipe at the top of your "to make" list. These fluffy, flaky,
savory biscuits are perfect in every way with their tomatoes
and fresh basil! If you really want to channel the caprese vibe,
you can drizzle a little balsamic vinegar over the biscuits
when serving.*

2 large eggs

1 tsp lemon juice or apple cider
vinegar

⅓ cup (80 ml) unsweetened
nondairy milk

1½ cups (150 g) lupin flour

½ cup (40 g) oat fiber, plus
more for dusting

½ cup (115 g) salted butter

½ tsp Himalayan salt

1 tsp double-acting baking
powder

1 cup (132 g) mozzarella balls
cut in fourths, or shredded
mozzarella

½ cup (80 g) baby tomatoes,
halved

¼ cup (6 g) fresh basil, plus
more for garnish (optional)

½ cup (56 g) grated mozzarella
cheese

Balsamic vinegar, for drizzling
(optional)

Preheat the oven to 425°F (220°C). Line a baking sheet with
parchment paper.

In a small bowl, combine the eggs, lemon juice and milk, then
set aside. In a large bowl or food processor, combine the lupin
flour, oat fiber, butter, salt and baking powder; mix until the
butter forms pea-size pieces. If using a food processor, move
the dry ingredients to a large bowl. Combine the wet ingredients
with the dry ingredients, then add the mozzarella chunks. Mix
just until the dough starts to come together, being careful not to
overmix. Add the tomatoes and basil and combine.

Place a piece of parchment paper on the counter. Dust the
parchment paper with a little of the oat fiber and transfer the
dough to the counter. Top the dough with another piece of
parchment. Using your hands, press down and out so that the
dough becomes an even rectangle about 1½ inches (4 cm) thick.
Using a 2-inch (5-cm) biscuit cutter, cut out the biscuits from
the dough. Place each biscuit on the prepared baking sheet.
Bake for 6 minutes.

Remove the baking sheet from the oven and sprinkle the biscuits
with the grated mozzarella cheese. Return the baking sheet to
the oven and bake for an additional 6 to 7 minutes. Drizzle with
balsamic vinegar and sprinkle with more chopped fresh basil if
you'd like. Store in a covered container in the refrigerator for up
to 1 week.

Recipe Note:

- For the best results, use gram measurements and
  recommended brands on page 491.

Substitution Note:

To make this *dairy free*, use dairy-free butter or shortening and
dairy-free milk. Omit cheese or use nondairy cheese of choice.

Super Green Breakfast Bowl with Sesame-Crusted Soft-Boiled Eggs

Fresh and healthy, this big green breakfast bowl is absolutely delicious. The sesame-crusted eggs take the flavor and texture over the top.

Lemon Vinaigrette Dressing

½ cup (120 ml) avocado oil

2 tbsp (30 ml) lemon juice

1 tsp Himalayan salt

¼ tsp black pepper

1 tsp yellow mustard (or Dijon)

Sesame-Crusted Eggs

4 large eggs

2 tbsp (18 g) toasted sesame seeds

1 tsp cumin powder

⅛ tsp Himalayan salt

Salad

6 cups (120 g) arugula or baby kale (or a mix)

1 avocado, peeled, pitted and thinly sliced

8 oz (227 g) asparagus, steamed until bright green

Pistachios, removed from shells

To make the salad dressing, whisk the oil, lemon juice, salt, pepper and mustard together in a bowl. Set aside.

To make the eggs, bring a pot of water (deep enough for the eggs to fully submerge) to a rapid boil. Add the eggs and set a timer for 6 minutes. For slightly less runny eggs, boil the eggs for 7 minutes. Then, quickly remove the eggs with a slotted spoon and gently place them in a bowl with cold water running over them to cool them.

On a small plate, mix together the toasted sesame seeds, cumin and salt. Carefully peel the eggs. Roll them in the sesame mixture and set aside.

For the salad, place two to three handfuls of greens in each bowl. Top with the avocado, asparagus, sesame-crusted eggs and a small handful of pistachios, then drizzle with the salad dressing. Serve immediately.

Recipe Note:

Pistachios are higher in carbs than most nuts. If you're trying to keep your carbs super low, omit them or just watch your portions.

Substitution Notes:

- To make this *egg free*, omit the eggs.

- To make this *nut free*, omit the pistachios.

Makes 12 servings

Roasted Garlic and Sausage Baked Custard Sheet Pan

Think of this recipe as a major upgrade to a frittata or quiche. What many people don't realize is that the egg-to-milk ratio used to make a perfect custard can take a recipe from what is expected to exceptional. This custard is heaven on earth.

To Roast

2 cups (320 g) grape tomatoes, halved

20 cloves garlic, lightly chopped

2 bell peppers (any color), chopped

1 red onion, sliced

¼ cup (60 ml) avocado oil

½ tsp Himalayan salt

½ tsp black pepper

½ tsp fresh or dried thyme

6 Italian sausage links

Custard

4 cups (945 ml) heavy cream or unsweetened full-fat coconut milk (from a can)

8 large eggs

1 tsp Himalayan sea salt

¼ tsp black pepper

⅛ tsp cayenne

For Topping

6 oz (170 g) mozzarella balls

1 to 2 cups (20 to 40 g) arugula

Preheat the oven to 450°F (230°C). Cover a large baking sheet with parchment. Place the tomatoes, garlic, peppers and onion on the baking sheet. Drizzle the oil on them and add the salt, pepper and thyme. Stir to coat the vegetables. Place the sausage links on the tray last, then roast for 30 to 35 minutes. Stir the veggies and sausage once halfway through roasting. Set aside to cool while making the custard. After you remove the tray, turn the oven down to 350°F (175°C).

To make the custard, warm the heavy cream in a saucepan until it just barely starts to simmer, then remove from the heat immediately. Pour the cream into a blender and add the eggs, salt, pepper and cayenne. Blend on low and then move gradually up to high. Blend on full power for 1 minute. Turn off and set aside.

Line a 9 x 13–inch (23 x 33–cm) baking pan (not sheet) with parchment paper. Chop the sausage links into ½-inch (1.2-cm) pieces. Place two-thirds of the roasted veggies and meat on the bottom of the pan and spread it out evenly. Pour the custard over. Par bake for 27 to 30 minutes until almost set. Remove from the oven and add to the top the remaining roasted veggies and sausage. You can press it down into the top ever so gently. Place the mozzarella balls on top, evenly dispersing them. Sprinkle with arugula and bake 20 to 25 minutes more until custard is fully set.

Remove from oven to cool. It can be topped with some additional arugula if desired. Serve warm, or cover and place in the fridge until ready to serve. It can be reheated in the oven at 300°F (150°C) until warmed through or placed in the microwave. It slices best after it has been refrigerated. Store in an airtight container in the refrigerator for 7 to 10 days.

Substitution Notes:

- To make this *dairy free* and *Paleo*, use the coconut cream instead of the heavy cream. Omit the mozzarella cheese.

- To make this *vegetarian*, omit the sausage.

Crepes Two Ways

Makes 10 crepes per recipe

My family is friends with the Flying Wallendas and one day we were invited back by Tino and Olinka to join them for breakfast. Olinka made crepes for us and I became completely obsessed with learning how to make them myself. I made this basic vanilla crepe recipe with just the tiniest hint of sweetness so that they could work in sweet or savory applications—you can eat them filled with yogurt or with leftover chorizo taco filling. If you wish to go the yogurt route I highly recommend adding a few teaspoons of superfruit powder to the yogurt; the powders add gorgeous color and some nutrition. Pink pitaya, black goji berry and blue butterfly pea powders are my favorite as they produce the most vibrant color without adding many carbs.

The Vanilla Crepes are so versatile and delicious. If you aren't sure if you are a crepe person, start here first. These crepes can be paired with just about any topping you could want.

Vanilla Crepes

6 large eggs

4 oz (114 g) cream cheese (dairy or nondairy)

3 tbsp (45 ml) water or unsweetened nondairy milk

1 tsp vanilla extract

2 tbsp (30 ml) sugar-free maple syrup

¼ tsp Himalayan salt

¼ cup (29 g) blanched almond flour

1 tbsp (16 g) psyllium husk powder

Add all the ingredients to a blender. Process on high for about 1 minute. The batter will thicken after a minute, so it is important to process for a full minute or your crepe batter will be too thin.

Preheat a crepe pan over medium–low heat and use a paper towel to wipe a thin layer of oil onto the pan. Make sure that your pan is nonstick or really well-seasoned cast iron. If you use too much oil on the pan the crepes will not spread correctly.

Pour ⅓ cup (80 ml) of batter into the center of the pan and either use a special crepe tool to spread batter thinly and evenly *or* pick up the pan and quickly tilt and rotate the batter around the pan so that it ends up thin and in a circle. You only have about 20 seconds to get the batter spread out before it begins to cook.

Allow the crepe to cook for about 1 minute. (This time will vary depending on how hot your pan gets.) You will know the crepe is ready to flip when the edges are lightly golden and the crepe lifts easily from the pan. Using a thin fish spatula works best for flipping. Cook for about 1 minute on the other side. Repeat to make nine more crepes.

(continued)

Chocolate Hazelnut Crepes

6 large eggs

4 oz (114 g) cream cheese (dairy or nondairy)

3 to 5 tbsp (45 to 75 ml) water

2 tsp (10 ml) hazelnut extract

3 tbsp (45 ml) sugar-free maple syrup

½ tsp Himalayan salt

¼ cup (29 g) blanched almond flour

1 tbsp (16 g) psyllium husk powder

3 tbsp (15 g) cocoa powder

⅓ cup (70 g) keto granulated sugar

Homemade Nutella

1 cup (135 g) raw unsalted hazelnuts

½ tsp vanilla extract

1½ tbsp (22 ml) avocado oil or other mild-flavored oil

2 cups (360 g) keto-friendly chocolate chips

1 tbsp (9 g) keto powdered sugar (Swerve brand recommended)

Pinch of Himalayan salt

Fresh berries, for topping

Substitution Notes for BOTH Crepes:

- To make this *dairy free*, use dairy-free cream cheese and dairy-free milk.

- To make *Paleo*, use real maple syrup and coconut palm sugar. Use the dairy-free substitutions.

Add all the ingredients to a blender. Process on high for about 1 minute. The batter will thicken after a minute, so it is important to process for a full minute or your crepe batter will be too thin.

Preheat a crepe pan over medium–low heat and use a paper towel to wipe a thin layer of oil onto the pan. Make sure that your pan is nonstick or really well-seasoned cast iron. If you use too much oil on the pan the crepes will not spread correctly.

Pour ⅓ cup (80 ml) of batter into the center of the pan and either use a special crepe tool to spread batter thinly and evenly *or* pick up the pan and quickly tilt and rotate the batter around the pan so that it ends up thin and in a circle. You only have about 20 seconds to get the batter spread out before it begins to cook.

Allow the crepe to cook for about 1 minute. (This time will vary depending on how hot your pan gets.) You will know the crepe is ready to flip when the edges are lightly golden and the crepe lifts easily from the pan. Using a thin fish spatula works best for flipping. Cook for about 1 minute on the other side. Repeat to make nine more crepes.

To make the nutella, preheat the oven to 350°F (176°C). Line a rimmed baking sheet with parchment paper. Put the hazelnuts on the sheet and toast in the oven for 12 to 13 minutes. Remove the hazelnuts from the oven and let cool, then rub the hazelnuts between your hands or a kitchen towel to remove as much of the skin as possible. Place the hazelnuts in a food processor with the vanilla and avocado oil and process until it becomes a smooth nut butter.

Place the chocolate chips in a microwave-safe bowl and heat up for 30 to 60 seconds until melted when stirred. Add the melted chocolate into the food processor with the powdered sugar and a pinch of salt. Process until smooth and creamy.

Serve the crepes with the Homemade Nutella and fresh berries.

Recipe Notes:

Start with the smaller amount of water listed in the recipe. If your crepes are a bit too thick, add a little bit more water, 1 teaspoon at a time, until the batter smoothly runs off your spoon. Do not overprocess your batter. If the batter gets warm, it will start to thicken quickly. If your crepes are sticking, this means your pan is no longer nonstick. If it's cast iron it may need to be better seasoned. If your crepes are burning or cooking too quickly, turn the heat down.

Perfect Fluffy Blueberry Pancakes

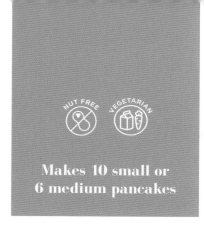

Makes 10 small or 6 medium pancakes

¾ cup (76 g) lupin flour

¼ cup (20 g) oat fiber

⅓ cup (42 g) keto powdered sugar or keto granulated sugar

1 tsp double-acting baking powder

¼ tsp Himalayan salt

2½ tsp (12 ml) vanilla extract

3 large eggs

¼ cup (60 ml) mild-flavored oil, melted coconut oil or melted butter, plus more for the pan

½ cup (120 ml) water or unsweetened nondairy milk

1 cup (230 g) berries (blueberries, blackberries or raspberries) or ½ cup (84 g) keto-friendly chocolate chips (optional)

Sugar-free maple syrup and butter, to serve

I have worked on so many test runs of pancakes over the years that I could make them in my sleep. Nailing the perfect keto pancake has brought its challenges and I have made many that were good. It wasn't until I found lupin flour that I hit the jackpot with a pancake that tastes completely the same as regular high-carb pancakes. I hate the concept of settling for less, no matter which diet you are on, so I'm really truly thrilled with this recipe. There are a few different brands of lupin flour online, but I recommend using the Lupina brand. The grind of the flour is perfect and it doesn't have a bitter aftertaste.

Combine the lupin flour, oat fiber, sugar, baking powder, salt, vanilla, eggs, oil and water or milk in a medium or large bowl and whisk the batter until smooth. Add the berries (or chips, if using) and fold them in.

Heat a nonstick or well-seasoned cast-iron skillet to medium heat and add a little oil or butter. Pour about ¼ cup (60 ml) of batter per pancake into the pan, and when bubbles form and then start to pop, flip the pancakes and cook until lightly browned. If they brown too quickly, turn down the heat a little.

Serve with sugar-free maple syrup and butter.

Recipe Note:

For the best results, use gram measurements and recommended brands on page 491.

Substitution Note:

To make this *dairy free*, use mild-flavored oil or dairy-free butter.

Makes 16 pancakes

1¼ cups (125 g) lupin flour

¼ cup (20 g) oat fiber

1 tsp double-acting baking powder

½ tsp Himalayan salt

5 large eggs

¼ cup (60 ml) mild-flavored oil, melted coconut oil or melted butter, plus more for the pan

¼ cup (60 ml) water

4 tbsp (60 ml) lemon juice, or more as needed

Zest of 1 lemon

⅓ cup (82 g) whole milk ricotta cheese

½ cup (100 g) keto granulated sugar

½ tsp stevia extract or monk fruit extract

Sugar-free syrup, to serve

Lemon Ricotta Pancakes

Who doesn't love pancakes? This recipe gives a twist on the same-old pancakes. These fun-sized pancakes are a quick and easy breakfast with a unique zesty lemon flavor. They are perfect for a big breakfast with less mess.

In a large bowl, combine the lupin flour, oat fiber, baking powder, salt, eggs, oil, water, lemon juice, lemon zest, ricotta cheese, sugar and stevia extract. Stir well to blend.

Place a nonstick skillet over medium heat and add about 1 teaspoon of oil. Add about ¼ cup (60 ml) of batter, or less, depending on the size of your pan, to the skillet. Cook for 1 to 2 minutes on each side. Add more oil to the skillet between batches.

Serve with sugar-free syrup.

Recipe Notes:

- Silver dollar–size pancakes make for an easier flip.

- Pancakes can be made normal sized as well with good results.

- For the best results, use gram measurements and recommended brands on page 491.

Strawberry Cheesecake Glazed Donuts

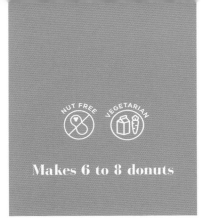

NUT FREE VEGETARIAN

Makes 6 to 8 donuts

The strawberry cheesecake filling in these donuts really takes this to the next level. Important note: You must use silicone donut molds in order for this recipe to turn out correctly.

Strawberry Filling

⅓ cup (80 ml) sugar-free honey

¾ cup (190 g) frozen strawberries

4 tbsp (56 g) butter

1 tsp vanilla extract

2 tbsp (18 g) keto powdered sugar

⅛ tsp Himalayan salt

Donuts

3 large eggs

¼ cup (60 ml) mild oil

½ cup (120 ml) water

¾ cup (75 g) lupin flour

¼ cup (20 g) oat fiber

1½ tsp (7 g) double-acting baking powder

½ tsp Himalayan salt

½ cup (100 g) keto granulated sugar

1 tbsp (15 ml) vanilla extract

3 oz (85 g) cream cheese

Glaze

½ cup (65 g) keto powdered sugar

2 tbsp (30 ml) sugar-free honey

2½ tbsp (38 ml) unsweetened full-fat coconut milk

1 tbsp (15 g) coconut oil

½ to 1 tsp powdered pink pitaya (for color)

Preheat the oven to 350°F (175°C). Grease six to eight silicone donut molds with oil. To make the strawberry filling, combine the honey, strawberries, butter, vanilla, sugar and salt in a saucepan and cook over medium heat, about 10 minutes, until the strawberries break down fully, whisking often. Set aside to cool.

To make the donuts, place the eggs, oil and water in a blender. Blend on high for 30 seconds. Add the lupin flour, oat fiber, baking powder, salt, sugar, vanilla and cream cheese and blend until smooth; you may need to scrape the sides of the blender once with a spatula. Pour the batter into the prepared molds, filling each mold about one-third or one-half full. Spoon the strawberry filling on top of the donut batter, using about 1½ teaspoons (7 ml) of filling per donut. Pour more batter into the molds on top of the strawberry filling, filling up each mold to the top; discard any extra batter. Bake for 23 to 26 minutes, until slightly golden. Allow the donuts to cool on the countertop or in the refrigerator for 15 minutes, then carefully remove them from the molds.

To make the glaze, combine the powdered sugar, honey, coconut milk, coconut oil and powdered pitaya in a small bowl and whisk until smooth. If the glaze clumps, blend with an immersion blender until smooth. When the donuts are completely cool, dunk one side of the donut in the glaze. Swirl the donut to ensure it is coated. Lift up the donut and allow the excess glaze to drip off. When the donut hole is clear of excess glaze, the donut is done dripping. Flip the donut over and place it on a plate or serving platter, glaze-side up. Repeat until all donuts are glazed. Keep the donuts in an airtight container in the refrigerator for up to 1 week.

*See image on pages 76–77.

Recipe Note:

For the best results, use gram measurements and recommended brands on page 491.

Substitution Note:

To make these *dairy free*, use coconut oil in place of butter and dairy-free cream cheese.

VEGETARIAN

Makes 6 to 8 donuts

Banana Cream Pie Glazed Donuts

The banana flavor really comes through well in these donuts— you won't believe there aren't any actual bananas baked in. Important note: You must use silicone donut molds in order for this recipe to turn out correctly. Lupin flour is sticky and will not come loose in any nonstick surface.

Donuts

3 large eggs

¼ cup (60 ml) mild oil, melted butter or melted coconut oil

¼ cup + 3 tbsp (105 ml) water

¾ cup (75 g) lupin flour

¼ cup (20 g) oat fiber

1½ tsp (7 g) double-acting baking powder

½ tsp Himalayan salt

½ cup (100 g) keto granulated sugar

1 tbsp (15 ml) vanilla extract

1 tbsp (15 ml) banana extract

3 oz (85 g) cream cheese

Glaze

½ cup (65 g) keto powdered sugar

2 tbsp (30 ml) sugar-free honey

1 tbsp (15 g) coconut oil

1 tbsp (15 ml) unsweetened full-fat coconut milk (from a can)

1 tbsp (15 ml) vanilla extract

Chocolate Drizzle

½ cup (84 g) keto-friendly dark chocolate chips

1 tsp coconut oil

Preheat the oven to 350°F (175°C). Grease six to eight silicone donut molds with oil.

To make the donut batter, place the eggs, oil and water in a blender. Blend on high for 30 seconds. Add the lupin flour, oat fiber, baking powder, salt, sugar, vanilla, banana extract and cream cheese and blend until smooth; you may need to scrape the sides of the blender once with a spatula. Pour the batter into the molds; discard any extra batter. Bake the donuts for 20 to 22 minutes, until slightly golden. Allow the donuts to cool on the countertop or in the refrigerator, then carefully remove them from the molds.

To make the glaze, combine the powdered sugar, honey, oil, coconut milk and vanilla in a small bowl. Whisk to blend.

To make the chocolate drizzle, in a small microwave-safe bowl add chocolate chips and coconut oil. Microwave on high for 30 seconds to 1 minute. Remove the bowl from the microwave and stir to combine; set aside.

When the donuts are cool, dunk one side of the donut in the glaze. Swirl the donut to ensure it is coated. Lift up the donut and allow the excess glaze to drip off. When the donut hole is clear of excess glaze, the donut is done dripping. Flip the donut over and place it on a plate or serving platter, glaze-side up. Repeat until all the donuts are glazed. Using a small spoon, drizzle the chocolate over the glazed donuts.

Keep the donuts in an airtight container in the refrigerator for up to 1 week.

*See image on pages 76–77.

Substitution Note:

To make these *dairy free*, use coconut oil and dairy-free cream cheese.

NUT FREE · VEGETARIAN

Makes 6 donuts

Margarita Lime Glazed Donuts

What's not to love about "adult" donuts? The adultness is only in the glaze: If you are making a batch for kiddos, just leave out the tequila. Important note: You must use silicone donut molds in order for this recipe to turn out correctly. Lupin flour is sticky and will not come loose in any nonstick surface. I discovered that silicone was the only way to have the donuts turn out every time. Allowing the cooked donuts to cool in the refrigerator for 10 to 15 minutes helps them come out of the silicone molds more easily.

Donuts

3 large eggs

¼ cup (60 ml) mild oil, melted butter or melted coconut oil

¼ cup + 3 tbsp (105 ml) water

¾ cup (75 g) lupin flour

¼ cup (20 g) oat fiber

1½ tsp (7 g) double-acting baking powder

½ tsp Himalayan salt

½ cup (100 g) keto granulated sugar

2 tbsp (30 ml) lime juice

Zest of 1 lime

Glaze

1 cup (132 g) keto powdered sugar

2 tbsp (30 ml) sugar-free honey

1 tbsp (15 g) coconut oil

2 tbsp (30 ml) tequila

1 tbsp (15 ml) lime juice

10 to 15 drops green food coloring (optional)

Optional Toppings

Unsweetened shredded coconut

Lime slices

Preheat the oven to 350°F (175°C). Grease six silicone donut molds with oil.

To make the donut batter, place the eggs, oil and water in a blender. Blend on high for 30 seconds. Add the lupin flour, oat fiber, baking powder, salt, sugar, lime juice and lime zest and blend until smooth; you may need to scrape the sides of the blender once with a spatula. Pour the batter into the molds; discard any extra batter. Bake the donuts for 20 to 22 minutes, until slightly golden. Allow the donuts to cool on the countertop or in the refrigerator, then carefully remove them from the molds.

To make the glaze, combine the powdered sugar, honey, oil, tequila, lime juice and food coloring (if using) in a small bowl. Whisk to blend.

When the donuts are completely cool, dunk one side of the donut in the glaze. Swirl the donut to ensure it is coated. Lift up the donut and allow the excess glaze to drip off. When the donut hole is clear of excess glaze, the donut is done dripping. Flip the donut over and place it on a plate or serving platter, glaze-side up. Repeat until all the donuts are glazed. Garnish with unsweetened coconut and lime slices. Keep the donuts in an airtight container in the refrigerator for up to 1 week.

Recipe Note:

For the best results, use gram measurements and recommended brands on page 491.

Substitution Note:

To make these *dairy free*, use coconut oil or mild oil options.

Pumpkin Spice and Chocolate Glazed Donuts

Makes 6 donuts

If you enjoy pumpkin bread, these donuts are for you. These donuts taste almost exactly like a carby version of pumpkin bread and then they are dipped in chocolate. I bet you won't have any leftovers of this donut! Important note: You must use silicone donut molds in order for this recipe to turn out correctly. Lupin flour is sticky and will not come loose in any nonstick surface. I discovered that silicone was the only way to have the donuts turn out every time.

3 large eggs

¼ cup (60 ml) mild oil, melted butter or melted coconut oil

4 tbsp (60 ml) water

4 tbsp (60 g) pumpkin purée

¾ cup (75 g) lupin flour

¼ cup (20 g) oat fiber

1½ tsp (7 g) double-acting baking powder

½ tsp Himalayan salt

½ cup (100 g) keto granulated sugar

1 tbsp (15 ml) vanilla extract

1 tbsp (8 g) ground cinnamon

1 tsp ground ginger

½ tsp ground nutmeg

¼ tsp ground cloves

Glaze

½ cup (84 g) keto-friendly dark chocolate chips

¼ tsp coconut oil

Cacao nibs, for topping

Preheat the oven to 350°F (175°C). Grease 6 silicone donut molds with oil.

To make the donut batter, place the eggs, oil and water in a blender. Blend on high for 30 seconds. Add the pumpkin purée, lupin flour, oat fiber, baking powder, salt, sugar, vanilla, cinnamon, ginger, nutmeg and cloves and blend until smooth; you may need to scrape the sides of the blender once with a spatula. Pour the batter into the molds; discard any extra batter. It may be helpful to use a spoon or to pipe the batter into the molds. Bake the donuts for 20 to 22 minutes, until slightly golden. Allow the donuts to cool on the countertop or in the refrigerator for 15 minutes, then carefully remove them from the molds.

To make the glaze, put the chocolate chips and coconut oil in a small microwave-safe bowl. Microwave on high for 30 seconds to 1 minute. Remove the bowl from the microwave and stir.

When the donuts are completely cool, dunk one side of the donut in the glaze. Swirl the donut to ensure it is coated. Lift up the donut and allow the excess glaze to drip off. When the donut hole is clear of excess glaze, the donut is done dripping. Flip the donut over and place it on a plate or serving platter, glaze-side up. Repeat until all the donuts are glazed. Garnish with cacao nibs. Keep the donuts in an airtight container in the refrigerator for up to 1 week.

Substitution Note:

To make these *dairy free*, use coconut oil.

NUT FREE VEGETARIAN

Makes 6 to 8 donuts

Blueberry Lemon Glazed Donuts

I just love blueberries and lemons together. These donuts are pretty easy to pull together. They are so delicious and pretty that they would make a great addition to brunch. Important note: You must use silicone donut molds in order for this recipe to turn out correctly. Lupin flour is sticky and will not come loose in any nonstick surface. I discovered that silicone was the only way to have the donuts turn out every time.

Donuts

3 large eggs

¼ cup (60 ml) mild oil, melted butter or melted coconut oil

4 tbsp (60 ml) water

¾ cup (75 g) lupin flour

¼ cup (20 g) oat fiber

1½ tsp (7 g) double-acting baking powder

½ tsp Himalayan salt

½ cup (100 g) keto granulated sugar

2 tbsp (30 ml) lemon juice

Zest of 1 lemon

6 to 8 tbsp (90 to 120 g) wild mini blueberries

Glaze

½ cup (65 g) keto powdered sugar

2 tbsp (30 ml) sugar-free honey

2 tbsp (30 ml) lemon juice

1 tbsp (15 g) coconut oil

Zest of 1 lemon

½ to 1 tsp sapphire wolfberry superfruit powder or purple food coloring (optional)

Preheat the oven to 350°F (175°C). Grease six to eight silicone donut molds with oil.

To make the donut batter, place the eggs, oil and water in a blender. Blend on high for 30 seconds. Add the lupin flour, oat fiber, baking powder, salt, sugar, lemon juice and lemon zest and blend until smooth; you may need to scrape the sides of the blender once with a spatula. Pour the batter into the molds, filling each mold about one-third to one-half of the way up. Spoon in the blueberries, using about 1 tablespoon (15 g) per donut. Pour the remaining batter on top of the blueberries and fill up each mold to the top; discard any extra batter. Bake the donuts for 26 to 30 minutes, until slightly golden. Allow the donuts to cool on the countertop or in the refrigerator for 15 minutes, then carefully remove them from the molds.

To make the glaze, combine the powdered sugar, honey, lemon juice, coconut oil, lemon zest and superfruit powder (if using) in a small bowl. Whisk to blend.

When the donuts are completely cool, dunk one side of the donut in the glaze. Swirl the donut to ensure it is coated. Lift up the donut and allow the excess glaze to drip off. When the donut hole is clear of excess glaze, the donut is done dripping. Flip the donut over and place it on a plate or serving platter, glaze-side up. Repeat until all the donuts are glazed. Keep the donuts in an airtight container in the refrigerator for up to 1 week.

Substitution Notes:

- To make these *dairy free*, use coconut oil.

- To make these *Paleo*, use real honey or maple syrup in the donuts. Swap powdered honey or powdered maple syrup in place of the keto powdered sugar in the glaze.

EGG FREE · DAIRY FREE · VEGETARIAN

**Makes 2 cups
(480 ml) each**

Dairy-Free Coffee Creamers in Four Flavors

Looking for a way to easily spice up your morning cup of joe? Look no further than our dairy-free keto coffee creamers. Here are four of my favorite flavors. Out of the two options I find that the macadamia nuts offer a closer experience to real cream in coffee. Another great option is to use raw unsalted cashews in place of the macadamia nuts, but cashews do run higher in carbs so keep that in mind. I found that monk fruit extract is the best option for sweetening coffee.

French Vanilla Coffee Creamer

1 (15-oz [444-ml]) can full-fat unsweetened coconut milk or 1 cup (240 ml) water + 1 cup (122 g) raw/unsalted macadamia nuts

1 tbsp (15 ml) vanilla extract

¼ tsp Himalayan salt

1 tbsp (15 ml) sugar-free honey or sugar-free maple syrup

¼ tsp monk fruit extract

Combine all the ingredients in a small bowl (or a blender if you are using the macadamia nuts). Whisk or process until totally smooth and creamy. Store in the refrigerator and use within 2 to 3 weeks.

Substitution Notes:

- To make this *Paleo*, substitute honey for the sugar-free honey.

- To make *nut free*, use the full-fat unsweetened canned coconut milk option.

Peppermint Mocha Coffee Creamer

1 (15-oz [444-ml]) can unsweetened full-fat coconut milk or 1 cup (240 ml) water + 1 cup (122 g) raw/unsalted macadamia nuts

1 tbsp (5 g) cocoa powder

¼ tsp vanilla extract

¼ tsp peppermint extract

¼ tsp Himalayan salt

1 tbsp (15 ml) sugar-free honey

¼ tsp monk fruit extract

Combine all the ingredients in a small bowl (or a blender if you are using the macadamia nuts). Whisk or process until totally smooth and creamy. Store in the refrigerator and use within 2 to 3 weeks.

Substitution Note:

To make this *Paleo*, substitute honey for the sugar-free honey. Omit the monk fruit extract.

Cherry Mocha Coffee Creamer

1 (15-oz [444-ml]) can unsweetened full-fat coconut milk or 1 cup (240 ml) water + 1 cup (122 g) raw/unsalted macadamia nuts

1 tbsp (5 g) cocoa powder

1½ tsp (7 ml) cherry extract

¼ tsp Himalayan salt

1 tbsp (15 ml) sugar-free honey or sugar-free maple syrup

¼ tsp monk fruit extract

Combine all the ingredients in a small bowl (or a blender if you are using the macadamia nuts). Whisk or process until totally smooth and creamy. Store in the refrigerator and use within 2 to 3 weeks.

Substitution Note:

To make this *Paleo*, substitute honey for the sugar-free honey. Omit the monk fruit extract.

Pumpkin Spice Coffee Creamer

1 (15-oz [444-ml]) can unsweetened full-fat coconut milk or 1 cup (240 ml) water + 1 cup (122 g) raw/unsalted macadamia nuts

¼ tsp vanilla extract

½ tsp ground cinnamon

¼ tsp ginger

¼ tsp nutmeg

¼ tsp Himalayan salt

1 tbsp (15 ml) sugar-free honey or sugar-free maple syrup

¼ tsp monk fruit extract

Combine all the ingredients in a small bowl (or a blender if you are using the macadamia nuts). Whisk or process until totally smooth and creamy. Store in the refrigerator and use within 2 to 3 weeks.

Substitution Note:

To make this *Paleo*, substitute honey for the sugar-free honey. Omit the monk fruit extract.

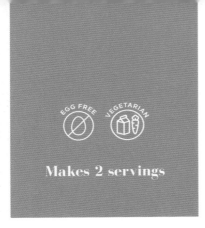

EGG FREE VEGETARIAN

Makes 2 servings

Pumpkin Spice Latte

This latte is delicious, easy to make and super reminiscent of the seasonal pumpkin spice latte you can find in nearly every coffee shop. It can be served hot or cold. I provided a range in amounts for the sweetener and cream. Start on the lower end and add more to reach your desired results. You can use heavy cream, or macadamia nuts or cashews. If you use the nuts, make sure to blend until they are fully broken down and creamy. Cashews are the higher-carb option here, so if you are trying to keep carbs as low as possible opt for the heavy cream or macadamia nuts.

1½ cups (360 ml) hot or cold coffee

½ cup (120 ml) heavy cream or ½ cup (66 g) raw unsalted macadamia nuts or raw unsalted cashews

1½ tsp (7 ml) vanilla extract

2 to 3 tbsp (30 to 45 ml) sugar-free honey

½ tsp pumpkin pie spice

Small pinch of salt

½ to ¾ tsp monk fruit extract

Toppings

Dairy-Free Whipped Topping (page 484)

Cinnamon

Add the coffee, cream, vanilla, honey, pumpkin pie spice and salt to a blender and process on high until frothy. Sweeten to taste with monk fruit extract.

Serve with unsweetened whipped cream or Dairy-Free Whipped Topping. Top with cinnamon.

Substitution Notes:

*   To make this *Paleo*, use honey or maple syrup and omit the monk fruit extract.

*   To make this *dairy free*, use the water and nuts option.

Makes 3 to 4 servings

1½ cup (360 ml) water

3 black tea bags

2 tsp (3 g) ground ginger

½ tsp ground black pepper

½ tsp ground cardamom

½ tsp ground cloves

¼ tsp ground nutmeg

¼ tsp Himalayan salt

2 cups (480 ml) canned unsweetened full-fat coconut milk (shaken)

1 tsp vanilla extract

3 tbsp (45 ml) sugar-free honey or maple syrup

¼ to ½ tsp stevia extract or monk fruit extract, to taste

1 tbsp (8 g) ground cinnamon

Dairy-Free Chai Latte

Chai lattes are my comfort drink. This spice mix is warm and inviting any time of year. This is a pretty straightforward chai mix and I can't wait for you to enjoy it. Serve with whipped cream or Dairy-Free Whipped Topping (page 484).

In a small saucepan, bring the water to a boil, then reduce to a simmer and add the tea bags, ginger, black pepper, cardamom, cloves, nutmeg and salt. Allow the tea to steep for 10 minutes along with the spices.

Remove the tea bags from the pan. Add the coconut milk, vanilla, sugar-free honey and stevia or monk fruit extract and stir to combine. Allow the mixture to warm on low for an additional 10 minutes. Turn off heat and let cool for 5 minutes, then whisk in the cinnamon. Strain through a fine-mesh strainer into glasses or a pitcher and serve.

Recipe Notes:

- To serve warm, keep the pan on the stove until your desired temperature is reached. To serve cold, fill a glass with ice and pour the warm chai into the glass. Add more ice as needed. When brewing tea, use one tea bag for each person you will be serving and then one extra bag for the pot. This will ensure enough flavor for everyone.

- If you prefer heavy cream instead, it can be used if you combine 1 cup (240 ml) of water with 1 cup (240 ml) of heavy cream—instead of using 2 cups (480 ml) of full-fat coconut milk.

- Cinnamon tends to thicken beverages when it's heated. Adding it at the end prevents this.

Substitution Note:

To make this *Paleo*, use regular honey instead of the sugar-free version and omit the stevia or monk fruit extract.

EGG FREE   VEGETARIAN

Makes 3 servings

Lavender Vanilla Latte

I live in Cleveland, Ohio, and in the spring a local chain called Phoenix Coffee makes an awesome lavender simple syrup you can have in your coffee. It's become one of my favorite treats that I look forward to getting. Once you make it, it will be on repeat in your home just as it is in ours. This batch of simple syrup will make about three batches of lavender lattes. For the very best experience, pick up a French press or Chemex (or both) and learn how to use these tools: No coffee machine can compare. If you prefer an iced coffee, use chilled coffee or cold brew instead, and serve with ice.

Lavender Simple Syrup

½ cup (120 ml) water

½ tsp lavender extract

½ tsp vanilla extract

¼ cup (60 ml) sugar-free honey or sugar-free maple syrup

2 tsp (10 ml) monk fruit extract

Pinch of Himalayan salt

Latte

1¼ cups (300 ml) hot strong coffee

¼ cup (60 ml) heavy cream or ¼ cup (33 g) unsalted macadamia nuts or unsalted cashews

4 to 6 tbsp (60 to 90 ml) lavender simple syrup

¼ tsp monk fruit extract

Dairy-Free Whipped Topping (page 484) or whipped cream, for serving (optional)

To make the lavender simple syrup, combine the water, lavender extract, vanilla, honey, monk fruit extract and salt in a small bowl and whisk until smooth. Store in a small jar in the refrigerator or at room temperature for several weeks.

To make the latte, add the coffee, cream, lavender simple syrup and monk fruit extract to a blender. Process on high until frothy. If you are using the nuts instead of heavy cream, you will need to run the blender until the nuts have fully broken down and are creamy. Pour into mugs, and top with the whipped topping, if desired.

Recipe Notes:

- I have tested out a lot of sugar-free sweeteners and have found that monk fruit extract tastes the best in coffee. I like stevia, and don't mind packets of stevia in coffee either, but monk fruit extract mimics the sweetness of real sugar the best when it comes to coffee.

- Liquid honey is the best option for the simple syrup, but if you can't find it online, the sugar-free maple syrup is the next best option. Macadamia nuts are lower in carbs than cashews. Choose them if you are looking to keep your carb count as low as possible.

Substitution Note:

To make this ***Paleo***, use real honey and omit the monk fruit extract.

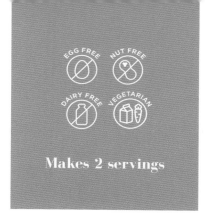

Makes 2 servings

Dairy-Free Matcha Frappuccino

Matcha for many years has been one of my favorite beverages, and with less caffeine than coffee, it is a great option for many people still looking for a burst of energy in the morning. It can be served hot or cold, but my favorite has always been in a frothy icy frap. Be sure to use a super creamy full-fat coconut milk from a can, not coconut milk labeled "light" or "cream." Any leftover milk can be stored in the refrigerator for up to a week.

1¼ cups (300 ml) unsweetened full-fat coconut milk (from a can), room temperature and shaken

¼ cup (60 ml) water

16 ice cubes

1 tbsp (15 ml) vanilla extract

3 to 3½ tsp (6 to 7 g) culinary-grade matcha (to taste)

½ tsp Himalayan salt

¾ to 1 tsp stevia extract or monk fruit extract (to taste)

Dairy-Free Whipped Topping (page 484) or keto chocolate syrup, for serving (optional)

Add the coconut milk, water, ice, vanilla, matcha and salt to a blender and blend on high until smooth. Add the stevia to taste, and blend again.

Serve immediately with whipped cream or chocolate syrup, if desired. Store leftovers in an airtight container in the refrigerator for 1 to 2 days.

Recipe Note:

For chocolate syrup, I use Lakanto or Nunaturals brand.

Substitution Note:

To make this *Paleo*, use regular honey or maple syrup in place of the stevia or monk fruit extract.

Main Dishes

Dinner can start to feel like a chore when you are following a diet. Every recipe in this chapter is packed with flavor and makes a meal you will look forward to eating. The sheet-pan dinners in particular deserve an honorable mention. You'll find sticking to keto a breeze thanks to this big, delicious and hearty chapter.

← See recipe on page 161.

Makes 8 to 10 servings

Brittany's Famous Cincinnati Chili

This recipe is probably the most-often-made recipe in our home and has been for many, many years. I make a big batch almost every weekend all through the fall and winter. I spent years perfecting the recipe, getting it just how we like it. It is traditionally served with spaghetti, and tastes amazing with gluten-free pasta. It can also be served with shirataki spaghetti noodles (just be sure to rinse them under warm water for a few minutes) or if you really want to go all out, make a batch of my Real Deal Low-Carb Fettuccine on page 251 to go with it!

3 tbsp (45 ml) avocado oil

1 large white or yellow onion, finely diced

1 tbsp (10 g) garlic powder

2 tbsp (16 g) ground cinnamon

4 tbsp (24 g) cumin

⅛ tsp cayenne (optional)

6 tbsp (48 g) chili powder

3 tbsp (15 g) unsweetened cocoa powder

½ tsp black pepper

½ tsp allspice

1 tbsp (18 g) Himalayan salt

2 lb (907 g) ground beef or ground sirloin

1 tbsp (18 g) Organic Roasted Beef Better than Bouillon

2 (6-oz [170-g]) cans tomato paste

2 tbsp (30 ml) apple cider vinegar

2 tbsp (30 ml) soy sauce

5 to 6 tbsp (75 to 90 ml) sugar-free honey or sugar-free maple syrup, to taste

For Serving

Shirataki noodles or Real Deal Low-Carb Fettuccine (page 251)

Shredded sharp cheddar cheese (optional)

1 white or yellow onion, chopped

In a large pot over medium heat, warm the avocado oil, then add the onion and cook until soft and translucent, about 5 minutes. Add the garlic powder, cinnamon, cumin, cayenne (if using), chili powder, cocoa powder, pepper, allspice and salt and stir well to combine. Cook until fragrant. Add 6 cups (1.5 L) of water to the pot, then add the ground beef, breaking it up as much as possible. Add the beef bouillon, tomato paste, vinegar and soy sauce. Stir well, then cover, leaving a small crack so the steam can release during cooking. Simmer, stirring occasionally, on low for 45 to 60 minutes, until the chili has thickened. Add sweetener to taste.

Serve the chili over noodles. Top with cheddar cheese (if using) and onion. Any leftovers can be stored, covered, in the refrigerator for 3 to 4 days.

Recipe Notes:

- For best flavor, dark cocoa powder is my favorite.

- Be sure to purchase the organic versions of Better than Bouillon when I call for them. The ingredients are substantially cleaner and the organic versions are dairy free.

- If you can't find or use Beef Better than Bouillon, use 3 cups (720 ml) beef broth plus 3 cups (720 ml) of water.

Substitution Notes:

- To make this *egg free*, use shirataki noodles.

- To make this *dairy free*, omit the cheese or use dairy-free cheese.

- To make this *Paleo*, use real honey or maple syrup.

Smoked Cracklin' Pork Belly Chili

EGG FREE · NUT FREE · PALEO

Makes 10 to 12 servings

This beanless chili is great for nights when you're in the mood for a one-pot meal or need a delicious meal for a large group. Top the chili with generous portions of crispy cracklin's to give this meal a balance of textures. Make the Smoky Cracklin' Pork Belly ahead of time from page 104 and use it as a garnish for this chili.

1 tbsp (15 ml) avocado oil

1 cup (160 g) chopped white onion

1 cup (100 g) chopped celery

1 green bell pepper, chopped

1 yellow bell pepper, chopped

1 orange bell pepper, chopped

4 cloves garlic, smashed

1 tsp dried oregano

1 tsp ground cumin

½ tsp ground cinnamon

1 to 1½ tbsp (7 to 13 g) smoked paprika

1 tbsp (8 g) chili powder

1 lb (454 g) ground beef

2 (15-oz [444-ml]) cans tomato sauce

2 (15-oz [425-g]) cans diced tomatoes

2 cups (280 g) Smoky Cracklin' Pork Belly (page 104)

Sour cream (vegan or regular), for serving

Diced avocado, for serving

Add the avocado oil to a large stockpot and warm over medium–high heat. Add the onion and cook for 5 to 10 minutes until the onions are translucent. Add the celery and bell peppers and stir to combine. Saute another 5 to 10 minutes. Add the garlic, oregano, cumin, cinnamon, paprika and chili powder and stir to combine. Add the ground beef to the pot and break it up, mixing it in well. Allow the ground beef to brown slightly, 5 to 7 minutes.

Add the tomato sauce and diced tomatoes to the pot, stir in well and cover. Lower the heat to simmer and allow the chili to cook for 10 minutes.

Serve the chili in bowls with Smoky Cracklin' Pork Belly as a garnish, along with sour cream and avocado.

Substitution Note:

To make this ***dairy free***, serve with dairy-free sour cream.

Smoky Cracklin' Pork Belly

Pork belly is one of those things you really have to try. Between the melt-in-your-mouth crispy texture of the pork and the smoky rub it's a win–win all around. Be sure to plan a day in advance for this recipe, as the 6-hour slow-cooking time in the oven and resting period cannot be skipped. It's an easy process however, so don't feel intimidated. Anyone can make this!

EGG FREE   NUT FREE   DAIRY FREE

Makes 1 lb (454 g) pork belly

1 (2-lb [907-g]) slab pork belly

3 tbsp (45 ml) sugar-free honey or maple syrup

1½ tsp (9 g) Himalayan salt

1 tsp black pepper

2 tsp (5 g) chili powder

1½ tsp (5 g) garlic powder

½ tsp cumin powder

2 tsp (5 g) smoked paprika

Preheat the oven to 200°F (95°C).

Brush the pork belly with the sugar-free honey. Mix together the salt, pepper, chili powder, garlic powder, cumin and smoked paprika in a small bowl, then evenly rub the spice mix on all sides of the pork.

Tear off a piece of parchment paper large enough to wrap around the pork belly. Place the pork belly on the parchment paper with the fatty side on top. Wrap the parchment paper around the pork belly. Then wrap the meat with two layers of aluminum foil, keeping track of the fatty side, which should remain on top. This will allow the fat to melt over the meat as it slowly cooks. Place the wrapped meat in a dry baking pan (I use a 7 x 7–inch [18 x 18–cm] square pan).

Place the pan in the oven and cook for 6 hours. Remove the pork from the oven and, keeping it wrapped, put it in the refrigerator to cool for 4 to 6 hours (or overnight).

After the pork has chilled, open the package and cut the pork into cubes of any size you wish. Place the pork and any fat left on the parchment into a dry frying pan. Fry the pork cubes over medium heat until crispy on all sides, 2 to 5 minutes.

Recipe Note:

To get the pork extra crispy, you can weigh down the meat by placing a second pot or large ramekin on top of the meat while it fries.

Substitution Note:

To make this **Paleo**, swap the sugar-free honey or maple syrup for regular honey/maple syrup.

EGG FREE · NUT FREE · DAIRY FREE · PALEO

Makes 12 servings

1 tbsp (15 ml) avocado oil

1 lb (454 g) spicy chorizo sausage links

1 large onion, minced

12 cloves garlic, minced

3 tbsp (24 g) chili powder

1½ tsp (3 g) smoked paprika

3 tbsp (9 g) dried oregano

2 tbsp (12 g) cumin powder

½ tsp Himalayan salt, plus more to taste

½ tsp black pepper

⅛ tsp cayenne (optional)

1 tbsp (8 g) ground cinnamon

1 lb (454 g) ground beef

1 (6-oz [170-g]) can tomato paste

2 (14.5-oz [411-g]) cans diced tomatoes

2 (14.5-oz [430-ml]) cans tomato sauce

2 to 3 bell peppers (different colors), chopped

Sour cream, for serving (optional)

Chopped cilantro, for serving (optional)

Chorizo and Beef Chili

I created this chili for my husband, Rich. Tex Mex, chorizo and chili are a few of his favorite things, so it made sense to combine them all into one meaty chili. For the best-tasting chili, I recommend getting the spicy chorizo links from Whole Foods. This recipe makes a large batch, but it freezes well if you can't finish it within a few days.

Add the oil to a large pot. Add the sausage links and cook over medium heat until seared on all sides and cooked through, 5 to 10 minutes. Remove the sausage from the pan and set aside to cool, reserving the oil in the pot. When the sausage is cool, use kitchen shears or a knife to cut the links into bite-size pieces.

Add the onion and garlic to the pot with the reserved oil from the sausage. If your pot needs a little more oil, add more here. Stir and cook the onion and garlic over medium heat for about 5 minutes. Add the chili powder, paprika, oregano, cumin, salt, pepper, cayenne and cinnamon and cook until fragrant. Add the ground beef and cook until the meat is brown, 8 to 10 minutes. Mix in the tomato paste, diced tomatoes and tomato sauce, then add the bell peppers and cooked sausage. Cover and simmer over low heat for 1 hour. Add more salt to taste. Serve with sour cream and chopped cilantro (if using).

Recipe Note:

Some brands of canned tomatoes are quite sour. To remedy this, you may need to add a little bit of real sugar. Start with a teaspoon and use as little as possible as this will make the carb count go up quickly.

Substitution Note:

To make this **vegetarian**, swap out the chorizo and ground beef for low-carb vegan alternatives.

Makes 6 to 8 servings

Creamy Tomatillo and Jalapeño Chicken Chili

If you're looking for a different type of comfort food to cozy up to tonight, give this recipe—which takes a zesty spin on chili—a try. This chicken chili is hearty and full of vegetables with a few staple Mexican ingredients thrown in. Feel free to alter the amount of jalapeño used if you're not so keen on spicy dishes. Serve this meal immediately after cooking or let it simmer on low until dinner is ready to be served.

10 tomatillos, peeled and sliced

1 tbsp (15 ml) avocado oil

1 yellow onion, diced

2 cups (200 g) diced celery

1 green bell pepper, diced

3 cloves garlic, smashed

2 tsp (12 g) + a pinch of Himalayan salt, divided

1 medium jalapeño (seeds removed), minced

1 tsp + a pinch ground black pepper, divided

1½ lb (680 g) ground chicken

2 tsp (5 g) smoked paprika, divided

1½ tsp (4 g) chili powder, divided

1 tsp ground cumin, divided

1 tsp dried oregano, divided

1 slice lime

1 cup (240 ml) chicken broth

1 (8-oz [227-g]) can mild green chiles, diced

1 (8-oz [227-g]) can hot green chiles, diced

1 cup (240 g) cream cheese (dairy or nondairy)

3 sprigs cilantro

½ cup (55 g) shredded white cheddar cheese (optional)

1 avocado, sliced, to garnish

Fill a small stockpot halfway with water and bring to a boil. Add the tomatillos and cook until the skins begin to blister, about 10 minutes. Drain the tomatillos and set them aside to cool, about 5 minutes. Add the cooled tomatillos to a food processor, and pulse for 30 seconds, or until smooth, then set aside.

Heat a large pot over medium–high heat, then add the avocado oil. Add the onion, celery, bell pepper, garlic and a pinch of salt, minced jalapeño and a pinch of pepper. Cook until the vegetables are tender, 5 to 7 minutes.

Season the ground chicken with 2 teaspoons (12 g) of salt, 1 teaspoon of black pepper, 1 teaspoon of the smoked paprika, ½ teaspoon of the chili powder, ½ teaspoon of the cumin and ½ teaspoon of the oregano. Add the seasoned chicken to the pot with the vegetables, mix well and cook until slightly brown, 5 to 7 minutes.

Add the blended tomatillos, lime slice, chicken broth, green chiles, cream cheese, cilantro sprigs and remaining paprika, chili powder, cumin and oregano to the pot, mixing well. Cook the chili, covered, on low for at least 20 minutes, or until dinner is ready to be served. Serve topped with cheddar cheese (if using) and sliced avocado.

Substitution Note:

To make this **vegetarian**, omit the chicken.

VEGETARIAN

Makes 8 servings

1 recipe Perfectly Flaky Piecrust (page 410)

3 tbsp (42 g) salted butter or butter-flavored coconut oil

2 large red onions, sliced

½ tsp fresh or dried thyme leaves

½ tsp Himalayan salt

½ tsp black pepper

5 cloves garlic, minced

2 tbsp (30 ml) dry vermouth

4 large eggs

1 tbsp (18 g) Organic Roasted Beef Better than Bouillon

1 cup (240 ml) heavy cream or room temperature unsweetened full-fat coconut milk (from a can)

1¼ cups (140 g) shredded Swiss cheese, divided

French Onion Quiche

Quiche is nothing new with the keto diet. It typically is not something that I really think about or crave. However, I do love French onion soup, so when the idea to merge quiche with the soup flavors popped into my head, I couldn't wait to get into the kitchen to try it. Be sure to take the time to allow the onions to fully caramelize; it's what makes the quiche so delicious.

Place the crust in a standard pie tin, cover and keep in the refrigerator while you prepare the filling.

Melt the butter in a skillet over medium-low heat. Add the onions, thyme, salt and pepper and slow-cook the onions for 20 minutes, or until fully caramelized, stirring every so often. About 15 minutes into the cook time add the minced garlic.

Turn off the heat and pour in the vermouth to deglaze the pan. Set aside to cool.

Preheat the oven to 375°F (190°C).

In a blender, combine the eggs, beef bouillon and cream. Blend on high for about 30 seconds, until frothy.

Place half of the onions on the bottom of the unbaked piecrust, spreading them out evenly. Add 1 cup (112 g) of the Swiss cheese and spread it out evenly on top of the onions. Pour in the egg mixture, then add the remaining onions to the top of the quiche, spreading them out evenly. Sprinkle with the remaining ¼ cup (28 g) of Swiss cheese. Place carefully on the middle rack of the oven. Bake for 20 minutes, then cover the quiche with foil and bake for an additional 20 minutes.

Remove the quiche from the oven and serve warm or cold. Store in the refrigerator, covered, for up to 1 week.

Substitution Note:

To make this **_dairy free_** or **_Paleo_**, use butter-flavored coconut oil and coconut milk instead of heavy cream. Omit the cheese.

Recipe Note:

If you can't find Organic Better than Bouillon, it can be omitted from the recipe. However, you will lose a punch of flavor and may find some additional salt is needed. A bit of extra Swiss cheese could also help make up for the loss of flavor.

Makes 4 to 6 servings

Chorizo with Chimichurri Sheet-Pan Meal

Sheet-pan meals are all the rage and for good reason. It's really nice to be able to just throw everything on a pan and know that the meal will be ready in 30 minutes. This meal is packed with flavor—the chimichurri sauce takes it right over the top.

Chorizo

6 chorizo links, sliced

1 medium red onion, sliced

1 green bell pepper, chopped

1 red bell pepper, chopped

6 oz (170 g) portobello mushrooms, sliced

3 cloves garlic, minced

½ tsp oregano

¼ tsp cumin

¼ tsp smoked paprika

2 tbsp (30 ml) lime juice

¼ cup (60 ml) avocado oil

½ tsp Himalayan salt

½ tsp black pepper

Chimichurri

1 shallot

4 cloves garlic

¾ cup (45 g) fresh cilantro

½ jalapeño, seeds removed

1 tbsp (15 ml) avocado oil

¼ cup (60 ml) water

¾ tsp Himalayan salt

½ tsp black pepper

½ fresh avocado

1 tsp lemon or lime juice

2 tbsp (30 ml) lime juice, for garnish

Preheat the oven to 400°F (205°C). Place the sliced chorizo on a sheet pan.

In a medium bowl, toss together the onion, bell peppers, mushrooms, garlic, oregano, cumin, smoked paprika, lime juice, avocado oil, salt and pepper. Then spread the vegetables onto the sheet pan with the chorizo and cook in the oven for 30 to 35 minutes.

To make the chimichurri, add all the ingredients to a food processor. Blend the ingredients until the mixture is smooth, then set aside.

When the chorizo is finished cooking, drizzle with the chimichurri and the lime juice. Store any leftovers in the refrigerator in a sealed container for 3 to 4 days. Serve with cauliflower rice or on its own.

Substitution Note:

To make this **vegetarian**, use vegetarian chorizo.

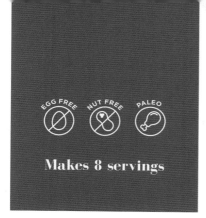

EGG FREE · NUT FREE · PALEO

Makes 8 servings

Homemade Ranch Rub Chicken and Cheddar Sheet-Pan Meal

This sheet-pan meal is to die for. Out of all the sheet-pan recipes in this book, this one is my personal favorite. The chicken is extremely tender and the seasoning pairs so well with the cheddar cheese. If you avoid dairy, this recipe is still worth making as the lemon and ranch seasoning will win your heart. This meal is easy to make and is a perfect comfort food, fall through winter.

Homemade Ranch Rub

1 tsp ground mustard powder

2 tbsp (6 g) dried dill

2 tbsp (6 g) dried oregano

2 tbsp (1 g) dried chives

1 tbsp (14 g) onion powder

2 tsp (6 g) garlic powder

1 tbsp (18 g) Himalayan salt

1 tsp black pepper

Chicken

8 bone-in chicken thighs

2 tbsp (30 ml) avocado oil

Veggies

1 medium head of broccoli, chopped

3 ribs celery, chopped (optional)

2 green bell peppers, chopped

1 small yellow onion, chopped

4 large carrots, chopped

1 small leek, sliced into ¼-inch (6-mm) pieces

2 tbsp (30 ml) lemon juice

¼ cup (60 ml) avocado oil

1 cup (112 g) grated sharp orange cheddar cheese

Salt and pepper, to taste

Preheat the oven to 400°F (205°C). Line an extra large sheet pan (or two standard-sized pans) with parchment paper.

To make the rub, in a medium bowl, stir together the mustard, dill, oregano, chives, onion powder, garlic powder, salt and pepper.

To make the chicken, in a large bowl, coat the chicken in the oil and sprinkle with all but 2 tablespoons (30 g) of the rub. Toss to coat. Let the chicken marinate for 30 minutes.

To make the veggies, in a separate bowl, toss the broccoli, celery, green peppers, onion, carrots and leek in the lemon juice, avocado oil and remaining 2 tablespoons (30 g) of the rub.

Place the chicken, skin-side up, on the prepared sheet pan and bake for 25 to 30 minutes, or until the chicken skin is slightly golden. Remove the pan from the oven and spread the vegetables on the pan with the chicken. Return the pan to the oven and cook for 15 to 20 minutes more, until the veggies are perfectly roasted and the chicken is fully cooked through.

When the chicken and vegetables are cooked, immediately sprinkle the cheddar cheese over the entire pan and put back into the oven for just 1 to 2 minutes, until the cheese has melted. Add salt and pepper to taste and serve.

Substitution Notes:

- To make this **dairy free**, omit the cheese.

- To make this **vegetarian**, use a vegan meat instead.

Makes 4 to 6 servings

Mediterranean Lamb Sheet-Pan Meal

If you enjoy lamb, this recipe will be a big hit. I chose a chop that is reasonably priced and easy to find. Not only is this dish delicious but it's beautiful, too. If lamb isn't your favorite meat, you can use pork chops instead. Just be sure to cook the pork to an internal temperature of 145°F (63°C).

Marinade

¼ cup (40 g) red onion, minced

½ tsp onion powder

¼ tsp cardamom powder

½ tsp coriander powder

1 tsp sumac

1 tbsp (15 ml) lemon juice

6 cloves garlic, minced

4 mint sprigs, chopped, plus more for garnish

1 tbsp (4 g) fresh parsley, minced

2 tsp (10 ml) sugar-free maple syrup or sugar-free honey

8 bone-in lamb shoulder chops

1 tbsp (15 ml) avocado oil

Veggies

1 eggplant, thickly sliced

2 zucchini, thickly sliced

1 red onion, sliced (optional)

1 tsp sumac

Avocado oil, for drizzling

1 tbsp (4 g) minced mint

1 tbsp (4 g) minced fresh parsley

Himalayan salt and pepper, to taste

Fresh rosemary, for garnish

Preheat the oven to 350°F (175°C). Line a sheet pan with parchment paper.

To make the marinade, in a large mixing bowl, combine the onion, onion powder, cardamom, coriander, sumac, lemon juice, garlic, mint, parsley and maple syrup. Add the lamb, coat it well with the marinade, then cover the bowl and refrigerate for at least 2 hours.

To make the veggies, place the eggplant, zucchini and onion on the prepared sheet pan and sprinkle with the sumac. Drizzle with a little oil.

Evenly coat a large skillet with 1 tablespoon (15 ml) of avocado oil over high heat. Add the lamb chops to the pan and sear on each side for 2 minutes (4 minutes total). Remove the lamb chops from the pan and place them on the sheet pan with the vegetables. Sprinkle the entire pan with the mint and parsley and bake for 15 to 20 minutes, or until the chops reach the desired doneness (see Kitchen Note).

When the meat and veggies are ready, remove from oven, sprinkle with salt and pepper and garnish with fresh rosemary.

Kitchen Note:

Doneness ranges for lamb are: **rare**—115 to 120°F (45 to 50°C); **medium rare**—120 to 125°F (50 to 52°C); **medium**—130 to 135°F (55 to 57°C); **medium well**—140 to 145°F (60 to 63°C); **well**—150 to 155°F (65 to 68°C).

Substitution Notes:

- To make this ***vegetarian***, use tofu, vegan chorizo or another vegan meat instead of the lamb.

- To make this ***Paleo***, replace the sugar-free maple syrup with regular maple syrup.

DAIRY FREE PALEO

Makes 4 servings

Harvest Turkey Meatballs with Cranberry Sauce Sheet-Pan Meal

There's nothing comparable to the flavors of fall. This recipe brings together the very best of those flavors in one healthy and delicious meal. You'll want to make this sheet-pan meal on repeat.

1 lb (454 g) ground turkey

1 large egg or ¼ cup (40 g) grated onion

½ cup (58 g) blanched almond flour

1 tbsp (15 ml) sugar-free maple syrup or sugar-free honey

2 celery ribs, finely chopped, divided

1 tsp dried oregano

4½ tsp (5 g) fresh or dried rosemary, chopped, divided

½ tbsp (5 g) garlic powder

1 tbsp (7 g) onion powder

¼ tsp ground sage

1 tsp Himalayan salt, plus more to taste

½ tsp black pepper, plus more to taste

1 eggplant, diced

2 to 3 cups (280 to 420 g) diced butternut squash

2 to 3 carrots, diced

1 cup (88 g) Brussels sprouts, halved

¼ cup (28 g) raw pecans, chopped

1½ tsp (2 g) dried oregano

3 to 4 tbsp (45 to 60 ml) avocado oil

Preheat the oven to 400°F (205°C). Line a sheet pan with parchment paper.

To make the meatballs, in a large bowl, combine the ground turkey, egg, almond flour, maple syrup, 1 celery rib, oregano, 3 teaspoons (4 g) rosemary, garlic powder, onion powder, sage, salt and pepper and mix well. Using a spoon or your hands, roll about 1½ tablespoons (20 g) of the ground turkey mixture into balls and place them on the prepared sheet pan.

To make the veggies, add the eggplant, squash, 1 celery rib, carrots, Brussels sprouts and pecans to the pan with the meatballs, then sprinkle the oregano and 1½ teaspoons (1 g) rosemary onto the vegetables. Drizzle the avocado oil over everything on the pan, then sprinkle a pinch or two of salt and pepper over the entire pan. Cook for 25 to 30 minutes, or until the meatballs are cooked through and the veggies are tender.

(continued)

Harvest Turkey Meatballs with Cranberry Sauce Sheet-Pan Meal (cont.)

Cranberry Sauce

1 cup (100 g) frozen cranberries

2 to 3 tsp (10 to 15 ml) lemon juice, to taste

2 tbsp (30 ml) sugar-free maple syrup or sugar-free honey

½ tsp tapioca or arrowroot starch

1 tsp dried or chopped fresh rosemary

Pinch of Himalayan salt

While the veggies and meatballs are roasting, make the cranberry sauce. In a small saucepan, combine the cranberries, lemon juice, maple syrup, tapioca, rosemary and salt and bring to a boil over medium–high heat. Cook for 7 to 10 minutes, until the sauce is reduced and thickened. If desired, transfer the sauce to a blender or food processor and process to create a smooth sauce.

Drizzle the cranberry sauce over the cooked meatballs and veggies on the sheet pan and serve.

Substitution Notes:

- To make this **egg free**, use grated onion in the meatballs.

- To make this **nut free**, use pumpkin-seed flour instead of almond flour.

- To make this **Paleo**, replace the sugar-free maple syrup with regular maple syrup. You will only need about half the syrup called for each time, as real maple syrup is sweeter than sugar free.

EGG FREE **NUT FREE**

Makes 6 drumsticks per recipe

Crispy Tandoori Drumsticks + Crispy Green Curry Drumsticks

One thing that will never go to waste in my house is Indian food leftovers. Tandoori chicken and green curry are both traditional Indian flavors that I wanted to bring to you in a simple and easy-to-prepare way. So naturally my thought was: drumsticks. These recipes can marinate in as little as 3 hours, but I recommend letting them marinate all day in the refrigerator.

Tandoori Drumsticks

1½ tbsp (9 g) tandoori seasoning (see Recipe Note)

1½ tsp (3 g) garam masala or curry powder

2 tsp (12 g) Himalayan salt

¼ tsp turmeric

¼ tsp cayenne pepper

¼ cup (60 g) unsweetened full-fat yogurt or unsweetened dairy-free yogurt

2 tbsp (30 ml) avocado oil

1½ tbsp (9 g) freshly grated ginger

3 cloves garlic, minced

Zest and juice of 1 lime

6 chicken drumsticks

In a small pan over low heat, add the tandoori seasoning, garam masala, salt, turmeric and cayenne pepper and toast the spices over low heat for 2 to 3 minutes until fragrant. Pour the spice blend into a food processor with the yogurt, avocado oil, ginger, garlic and the lime zest and juice and process to combine. Pour the marinade into a large glass bowl and add the drumsticks; toss to coat well. Cover the bowl and place in the refrigerator for 3 hours, or overnight.

Preheat the oven to 450°F (230°C), line a large baking sheet with foil and place a well-oiled wire rack in the pan. Place the marinated drumsticks on the rack on the baking sheet and place the pan in the oven for 45 minutes, flipping the drumsticks halfway through. At the end of the cook time, switch the oven to broil and cook for an additional 3 to 5 minutes, or until the drumsticks appear crispy. Remove the drumsticks from the oven and allow to cool slightly before serving. The drumsticks can be stored, covered, in the refrigerator for up to 3 days.

Recipe Note:

Tandoori seasoning blend is readily available in most grocery stores in the international foods aisle; however, if you cannot find it or choose to make your own, substitute the tandoori seasoning with 1½ teaspoons (3 g) paprika, 1½ teaspoons (3 g) ground cumin, 1½ teaspoons (3 g) ground coriander, 1½ teaspoons (2 g) ground ginger and ¼ teaspoon ground cloves.

(continued)

Green Curry Drumsticks

2 tbsp (32 g) green curry paste

1 tsp freshly grated ginger

2 tbsp (8 g) fresh cilantro

¼ tsp Himalayan salt

⅛ tsp cayenne pepper

¼ cup (60 g) unsweetened full-fat yogurt or unsweetened dairy-free yogurt

2 tbsp (30 ml) avocado oil

6 chicken drumsticks

In a food processor, blend the green curry paste, ginger, cilantro, salt, cayenne pepper, yogurt and oil and process until smooth. Pour the marinade into a large glass bowl and add the drumsticks; toss to coat well. Cover the bowl and place it in the refrigerator for 3 hours, or overnight.

Preheat the oven to 450°F (230°C), line a large baking sheet with foil and place a well-oiled wire rack in the pan. Place the marinated drumsticks on the prepared rack and place the pan in the oven for 45 minutes, flipping the drumsticks halfway through. At the end of the cook time, switch the oven to broil and cook for an additional 3 to 5 minutes, or until the drumsticks appear crispy. Remove the pan from the oven and allow the drumsticks to cool slightly before serving. The drumsticks can be stored, covered, in the refrigerator for up to 3 days.

Recipe Notes for BOTH: Use an Air Fryer

1. Prepare and marinate the chicken.

2. Preheat the air fryer to 400°F (205°C).

3. Place the chicken in the air fryer, making sure not to overcrowd. Cook for 10 minutes. If the chicken is not 165°F (74°C), add another 4 to 5 minutes.

Substitution Notes for BOTH:

• To make these recipes **dairy free** or **Paleo**, use unsweetened dairy-free yogurt.

• To make these recipes **vegetarian**, use paneer or tofu instead of chicken.

Makes 2 to 3 servings

One-Pot Honey Mustard Chicken with Celery Root

This recipe is simple but heavenly. It comes together in a flash and is extremely comforting. I'm not a mustard fan, but this dish does it for me. If you can't track down celery root (which I find to be the closest substitute for potatoes), low-carb vegetables such as cauliflower, rutabaga or parsnips are the next-best options.

3 tbsp (42 g) butter, ghee or butter-flavored coconut oil

1 large celeriac (celery root), peeled and diced

1 lb (454 g) chicken thighs

1½ tsp (3 g) dry mustard powder

1 tsp Himalayan salt

1 tsp black pepper

¼ tsp dried thyme

½ cup (120 ml) sugar-free honey or sugar-free maple syrup

¼ tsp stevia extract or monk fruit extract

¼ cup (60 ml) apple cider vinegar

In a large skillet over medium–high heat, melt the butter, then add the celery root and cook for 10 minutes, stirring regularly.

After 10 minutes, add the chicken, mustard, salt, pepper and thyme and cook the chicken on the first side for 4 minutes. Flip the chicken and add the honey, stevia extract and vinegar to the pan. Reduce the heat to medium and continue to cook for 10 more minutes, or until the chicken is cooked through, the celery root is tender and the sauce is thick.

Substitution Notes:

* To make this **vegetarian**, use extra-firm tofu or other vegan meat.

* To make this **Paleo**, use real honey and omit the stevia.

* To make **dairy free**, use butter-flavored coconut oil or nondairy butter of choice.

Makes 5 to 6 servings

Chicken Paprikash with Spätzle

This recipe may be the star of the book. The flavor is incredible. It was created by Kenna Dickman (who worked in my kitchen helping me write this book). She spent hours getting it just right. Chicken Paprikash is a Hungarian dish that features paprika. This recipe follows that tradition but also includes a few Americanized ingredients. The flavor is robust and subtly spicy. This is serious comfort food. One big note, use Hungarian imported sweet paprika and Hungarian hot paprika for the best results. American paprika just won't do—you will end up with little to no flavor.

Chicken

2 eggs, beaten

1 cup (116 g) blanched almond flour

1 tsp Himalayan salt

2 tsp (5 g) Hungarian sweet paprika

½ tsp ground black pepper

1 lb (454 g) chicken thighs

1 tbsp (14 g) butter or ghee

Sauce

1 tbsp (14 g) butter, ghee or butter-flavored coconut oil

1 large onion, diced

4 cloves garlic, minced

1 red or green bell pepper, diced

1 (14.5-oz [411-g]) can diced tomatoes

3 cups (720 ml) chicken broth

¾ cup (185 g) sour cream or unsweetened dairy-free yogurt

1 tsp Hungarian spicy paprika

1 tsp Himalayan salt

½ tsp ground pepper

2 tbsp (14 g) Hungarian sweet paprika

½ cup (58 g) blanched almond flour

1 recipe Low-Carb German Spätzle (page 255)

Chopped parsley, for garnish

To make the chicken, in a medium bowl, whisk the eggs until beaten. In a second medium bowl, mix the almond flour, salt, sweet paprika and black pepper to combine. Place one chicken thigh in the bowl with the eggs and coat both sides, then put it in the bowl with the flour mixture and coat both sides. Place the breaded chicken on a plate. Repeat until all the chicken is breaded. In a skillet, heat the butter over medium–high heat. Place the breaded chicken thighs in the pan and sear until golden brown on both sides, 2 minutes a side. Transfer the chicken to a clean plate. Repeat until all the chicken is browned.

To make the sauce, in a heavy-bottomed pot, melt the butter over medium–low heat. Add the diced onion and cook until the onion is translucent, 4 to 5 minutes. Add the garlic and cook an additional 2 minutes. Mix in the bell pepper, diced tomatoes and chicken broth and stir to combine. Increase the heat to high and bring the sauce to a boil.

While you are waiting for the sauce to boil, make the roux. In a medium bowl, mix the sour cream, Hungarian spicy paprika, salt, pepper, Hungarian sweet paprika and ½ cup (120 ml) of liquid from the pot. Mix to combine and then add to the mixture already on the stove. Once at a boil, add the breaded chicken thighs and reduce to a simmer. Cook, covered, for 35 minutes.

Remove the chicken from the pot and set aside. Add the almond flour to the sauce. Bring the sauce back to a low boil for 2 to 3 minutes, then reduce the heat and allow the sauce to thicken. When thickened, add the chicken back to the pot and serve with the spätzle and garnish with chopped parsley. Store leftovers in an airtight container in the refrigerator for up to 5 to 7 days.

Roasted Asiago and Artichoke-Stuffed Chicken

With nutty notes of Asiago and delicate artichokes, this juicy stuffed chicken is a simple answer for those who want a classic weeknight meal with a lot of flavor. If you prefer to make this recipe in an air fryer, use the cooking directions from the Air Fryer Chicken Cordon Bleu recipe on page 130.

Chicken

4 large boneless and skinless chicken breasts

1 tsp garlic powder

1 tsp onion powder

½ tsp herbes de Provence

½ tsp chives, dried

¼ tsp Himalayan salt

Black pepper, to taste

¼ cup (27 g) Asiago cheese, shredded

¼ cup (42 g) marinated and halved artichokes (from a jar)

1 egg

½ cup (60 g) ground pork rinds or blanched almond flour

½ cup (40 g) grated Parmesan

Hollandaise Drizzle

½ cup (113 g) butter

4 egg yolks

½ tsp Himalayan salt

¼ tsp cayenne pepper

¼ tsp black pepper

1 tsp lemon juice

Preheat the oven to 400°F (205°C). Line a sheet pan with parchment paper.

Place the chicken breasts in between wax paper and, using a mallet, pound until thin enough to roll. Season the chicken with the garlic powder, onion powder, herbes de Provence, chives, salt and pepper to taste. Lay the chicken down flat and place one-quarter of the Asiago cheese and one-quarter of the artichokes on each breast. Roll the chicken as tight as possible and secure with toothpicks; set aside.

In a small bowl, whisk the egg. In a separate medium bowl, mix together the ground pork rinds and grated Parmesan. Dip the rolled chicken into the egg, and then evenly coat in the pork rind-and-Parmesan mixture. Place the chicken on the prepared baking sheet and bake for 20 to 30 minutes, or until golden.

To make the hollandaise drizzle, in a small saucepan, melt the butter over medium heat. Place the egg yolks in a bowl and whisk, then add the salt, peppers and lemon juice and continue to whisk. Rapidly add the melted butter to the bowl containing the egg yolks and whisk. In the same saucepan you used to melt the butter, add about ¼ cup (60 ml) of water and heat over medium–high heat. Place the bowl containing the egg mixture over the simmering water and continue to whisk for a few seconds. Allow the sauce to rest; if the sauce becomes too thick, add a tablespoon (15 ml) of water. If you overheat your hollandaise sauce it will "break." Remove the pan from the stove when it reaches the perfect consistency.

Remove the cooked chicken from the oven and drizzle with the hollandaise sauce.

Substitution Note:

To make this **nut free**, use the pork-rind option for breading.

Air Fryer Chicken Cordon Bleu

Chicken Cordon Bleu is a favorite dish for many people, but the traditional recipe isn't keto friendly. Fortunately this recipe substitutes ground pork rinds and grated Parmesan for breadcrumbs, and it eliminates the need to fry on a messy stovetop by using an air fryer. Make this simple recipe when you're craving a delicious home-cooked meal but find yourself with little time to cook. If you wish to make this recipe in the oven, follow the baking directions in the Roasted Asiago and Artichoke–Stuffed Chicken recipe on page 129.

4 large boneless and skinless chicken breasts

1 tsp garlic powder

1 tsp onion powder

½ tsp herbes de Provence

¼ tsp Himalayan salt

Black pepper, to taste

4 thin slices ham

4 thin slices Swiss cheese

1 egg

½ cup (60 g) ground pork rinds or blanched almond flour

½ cup (40 g) grated Parmesan

1 recipe Hollandaise Drizzle (page 129)

Place the chicken breasts between sheets of wax paper and, using a mallet, pound them until they are thin enough to roll. Season with the garlic powder, onion powder, herbes de Provence, salt and pepper to taste. Lay the chicken down flat and place one slice of ham and Swiss cheese on each breast. Roll the chicken as tight as possible and secure with toothpicks; set aside.

In a small bowl, whisk the egg. In a separate medium bowl, mix together the ground pork rinds and grated Parmesan. Dip the rolled chicken into the egg, and then evenly coat in the pork rind-and-Parmesan mixture.

Place the chicken in the air fryer and cook for 20 minutes at 400°F (205°C), or set the air fryer to the chicken cooking option.

Remove the cooked chicken from the air fryer and drizzle with the hollandaise sauce.

Recipe Note:

Every air fryer is different, so some cook the chicken through a bit faster. Use your best judgment and take a peek at the chicken two-thirds of the way through the cooking time to check if it's done.

Substitution Note:

To make this **nut free**, use the pork-rind option for breading.

Makes 3 to 4 servings

Grilled Vietnamese Lemongrass Chicken

Lemongrass is one of my favorite flavors. It's become easier to find in stores than it once was and has become a staple in my refrigerator along with garlic and ginger. The key to lemongrass is knowing that when it cooks it doesn't get soft. When cooking with it, either finely grate it or leave it in large pieces that can be easily removed after cooking. To save time, you can also finely chop the lemongrass and put it in a small food processor. As long as you follow that rule, you can get all the awesome flavor every time you use it. This lemongrass chicken tastes great served in a salad, or with steamed or grilled veggies or cauliflower rice. This marinade can also be used with pork. This optional sauce tastes great over steamed or grilled veggies, or cauliflower rice.

Marinade

3 sticks lemongrass finely grated

1 tbsp (6 g) freshly grated ginger

5 cloves garlic, minced

Zest of ½ lime

1 large shallot, finely chopped

2 tbsp (30 ml) sugar-free honey or sugar-free maple syrup

3 tbsp (45 ml) lime juice

1 tsp fish sauce

1 tsp Himalayan salt

¼ tsp black pepper

1 lb (454 g) thin-cut chicken breasts or boneless chicken thighs

Sauce (optional)

¼ cup (60 ml) sugar-free honey or sugar-free maple syrup

2 tbsp (30 ml) sesame oil

1 tsp Roasted Chicken or Veggie Better than Bouillon

1 tbsp (15 ml) liquid aminos, coconut aminos or gluten-free soy sauce

¼ tsp black pepper

Himalayan salt, to taste (optional)

½ tsp tapioca starch (optional)

To make the marinade, whisk the lemongrass, ginger, garlic, lime zest, shallot, honey, lime juice, fish sauce, salt and pepper together. Place the chicken on a cutting board. With a meat tenderizer, pound the chicken until it's ½ inch (13 mm) thick. Place the prepared chicken in a container or bag with the marinade. Shake well to make sure all the meat is fully covered. Place the marinade and chicken in the refrigerator for a few hours.

Remove the chicken from the marinade and save the marinade for the sauce. Grill the chicken on a preheated grill for a few minutes on each side. You can also use a grill pan or sauté pan.

To make the sauce (if using), add the leftover marinade, 1 cup (240 ml) water, honey, sesame oil, bouillon, liquid aminos and pepper to a saucepan. Whisk over medium heat until the sauce has thickened. Add salt to taste if necessary. If the sauce is not thickening enough to your liking, whisk in the tapioca starch.

Substitution Notes:

- To make this **vegetarian**, use a meat substitute or tofu.

- To make this **Paleo**, use real honey or maple syrup.

Makes 4 servings

Al Pastor-Inspired Chicken and "Rice"-Stuffed Peppers

This recipe is a juicy take on traditional stuffed peppers by using pineapple extract tossed in ground chicken, plus plenty of mouth-watering seasonings. Feel free to drizzle queso (pages 278 and 281) or your favorite Mexican-blend cheese over the roasted poblano peppers to add a tantalizing twist.

1½ tsp (6 g) Himalayan salt, plus more to taste

1¼ tsp (5 g) black pepper

¼ tsp ground coriander

1 tsp ground cumin

¼ tsp ground cloves

2 tsp (2 g) dried oregano

1 tsp paprika

2 tbsp (30 ml) avocado oil

6 cloves garlic, minced

1 medium yellow onion, minced

1 lb (454 g) ground chicken

2 tbsp (30 ml) sugar-free honey or sugar-free maple syrup

2 tbsp (30 ml) pineapple extract

1 tbsp (6 g) orange zest

1 tbsp (15 ml) lime juice

10 oz (283 g) riced cauliflower

4 to 6 large poblano peppers, tops cut off and seeded

Shredded white cheddar cheese, for sprinkling (optional)

Preheat the oven to 400°F (205°C).

To make the spice blend, in a small bowl, combine the salt, pepper, coriander, cumin, cloves, oregano and paprika. Set aside.

Heat a large skillet over medium–high heat and warm the avocado oil. Add the garlic and onion, sauté for 3 to 5 minutes and then pour in the spice blend. Sauté until fragrant. Add the ground chicken and stir well to incorporate the spice blend. Cook for 10 minutes.

Add the honey, pineapple extract, orange zest and lime juice to the pan and stir, then add the cauliflower rice, and cook another 10 minutes, until the meat has cooked through and the cauliflower rice is tender. Add additional salt and pepper to taste. Stuff the chicken-and-cauliflower mixture evenly into the poblano peppers. Place each pepper on a piece of aluminum foil large enough to wrap the pepper. Sprinkle cheese on top of each pepper, then wrap each in foil.

Place the wrapped peppers in the oven and roast for 20 minutes. At the 15-minute mark, open each foil packet so the pepper can roast open faced. Sprinkle on a bit more cheese if desired. Serve hot. Store leftovers in the refrigerator for up to 3 to 4 days.

Recipe Note:

After the peppers have been stuffed and wrapped, they can be grilled at 400°F (205°C) for 15 to 20 minutes.

Substitution Notes:

- To make this **dairy free**, omit the cheese or the dairy-free queso from page 278 can be used instead.

- To make this **vegetarian**, use vegan ground beef or tofu.

Makes 3 to 4 servings

Indian Butter Chicken

Indian food was one of my passions when I was first learning to cook. I read book after book studying spices, wanting to soak it all in. Probably six times a year I make a huge feast of all of our favorite dishes: butter chicken, paneer korma, parathas, onion bhaji and naan. We eat way too much while watching a Bollywood movie. If my husband is having a rough week, Indian food is the one way to always cheer him up. It feels pretty special including this recipe that I was able to create completely on my own, thanks to many years of practice and learning which flavors all the unique spices can add to a dish. This dish is truly delicious and a must-make recipe.

8 tbsp (112 g) ghee or salted butter or butter-flavored coconut oil, divided

1 lb (454 g) chopped chicken thighs

2 tsp (8 g) garam masala

2 tsp (3 g) coriander powder

1 tbsp (6 g) freshly minced or grated ginger

⅛ tsp ground cardamom

⅛ tsp ground cinnamon

½ tsp Himalayan salt

1 tsp chili powder

1 (14.5-oz [411-g]) can diced tomatoes or plain tomato sauce

1 tbsp (30 ml) lemon juice

2 to 3 tbsp (30 to 45 ml) sugar-free honey or maple syrup

½ cup (120 ml) heavy cream or unsweetened full-fat coconut milk (from a can)

¼ cup (60 g) unsweetened yogurt (dairy or nondairy)

Cauliflower Rice (page 58), for serving

Heat a large skillet over medium–low heat and add 2 tablespoons (28 g) of ghee or salted butter. Add the chicken thighs to the pan, and immediately stir in the garam masala, coriander powder, ginger, cardamom, cinnamon, salt and chili powder.

Cook until the chicken is fully cooked, about 10 minutes, tossing often. Pour in the diced tomatoes, lemon juice, honey and 6 tablespoons (84 g) of ghee or salted butter. Cook for 10 minutes with the lid off, until the tomato juice has condensed by more than half, then stir in the heavy cream and plain yogurt. At this point you can serve the chicken, or you can boil the sauce down a little more if you prefer it thicker. Serve over cauliflower rice.

Recipe Note:

If you love the Indian dish chicken makhani, you can add up to 1 tablespoon (16 g) of tomato paste with the canned tomatoes to give this dish a stronger tomato flavor and deeper red color. If adding the tomato paste, I recommend an additional 1 to 2 tablespoons (15 to 30 ml) of the sugar-free honey or maple syrup.

Substitution Notes:

• To make this **dairy free**, use ghee or butter-flavored coconut oil, coconut milk and nondairy plain yogurt.

• To make this **Paleo**, use ghee, coconut milk and nondairy plain yogurt and use 1 to 2 tablespoons (15 to 30 ml) of real honey.

Makes 4 to 6 servings

Spicy Thai Basil Beef

Thai cuisine is always my go-to when I crave something different. The cuisine encompasses many citrus and spicy flavors, especially this recipe for Spicy Thai Basil Beef, also known as Pad Gra Prow. Don't hesitate to add additional Thai basil if you enjoy the herb; it'll only make for a tastier dish. This dish has quite the kick, so if you prefer things mild you can leave out the Chinese red peppers. The key to delicious Thai food is not overcooking the meat and veggies. Use your best judgment and stop cooking when the meat is just cooked through and the veggies are barely cooked through.

1 lb (454 g) strip steak, sliced into bite-size strips

1 tbsp (6 g) freshly grated ginger

½ tsp black pepper

1 cup (24 g) fresh Thai basil, minced

3 tbsp (45 ml) sesame oil

1 tbsp (15 ml) coconut aminos, liquid aminos or gluten-free soy sauce

1 tbsp (15 ml) lime juice

1 tbsp (15 ml) fish sauce

½ tsp tapioca or arrowroot starch

1 red onion, sliced

1 red bell pepper, sliced

3 Chinese red peppers (Tien Tsin), minced

5 cloves garlic, minced

2 tbsp (30 ml) avocado oil

Himalayan salt, to taste

Cauliflower Rice (page 58), for serving

In a large mixing bowl, toss the sliced strip steaks with the ginger, black pepper, Thai basil, sesame oil, coconut aminos, lime juice, fish sauce, tapioca, onion, bell pepper, Chinese red peppers and garlic; set aside.

Heat a wok or large skillet on high heat and add the avocado oil to the pan. When smoke begins to rise from the pan, add the steak-and-veggie mixture and sauté for 10 minutes for medium well (or more or less for your desired doneness). Add salt to taste. Serve with cauliflower rice.

Recipe Note:

Fresh Thai basil has a unique and delicious flavor that makes this dish so good. It can be found at most Asian markets.

Substitution Note:

To make this *vegetarian*, use extra-firm tofu instead of beef.

Makes 6 servings

Hungarian Beef Goulash with Dumplings

This recipe is comfort food at its best. Taking the time to sear the meat does wonders for the flavor and final cooked texture of the meat. Be sure to use Hungarian imported paprika or you will be missing some important flavor. This dish can be served as is, or mix in some sour cream when serving.

2 lb (907 g) beef loin or beef stew meat, cubed

3 tsp (18 g) Himalayan salt, divided

1½ tsp (3 g) ground black pepper, divided

1 tsp garlic powder

2 tbsp (28 g) butter, ghee or butter-flavored coconut oil, divided

2 large onions, diced

6 cloves garlic, finely chopped

2 red or green bell peppers, diced

2 cups (480 ml) beef broth

1 tsp caraway seeds

2 bay leaves

1 (14.5-oz [411-g]) can diced tomatoes

2 tsp (5 g) Hungarian sweet paprika

Dairy-Free Sour Cream (page 491), for garnish

Chopped chives or parsley, for garnish

1 recipe Czech Low-Carb "Bread" Dumplings (page 249)

To make the beef, place the meat in a medium bowl and season well with 2 teaspoons (12 g) of the salt, 1 teaspoon of the pepper and garlic powder, then set aside. Place a heavy-bottomed pot on the stove on medium heat and add 1 tablespoon (14 g) of butter. Working in batches, add some of the meat to the pan and sear for 2 minutes a side. Be sure to not crowd the pan. When all of the meat is seared, place it on a clean plate. Continue working in batches until all the meat is browned.

To make the sauce, add the remaining 1 tablespoon (14 g) of butter to the pan you used to sear the beef. Add the onions and as it releases its juice, scrape the bottom of the pan to release the brown bits from the meat. Cook the onion until translucent, 4 to 5 minutes. Add the garlic and bell peppers and cook for an additional 4 to 5 minutes. Next add the beef broth, caraway seeds, bay leaves, diced tomatoes, paprika, 1 teaspoon of salt and ½ teaspoon of black pepper. Stir to combine and bring to a boil, then add the meat and simmer for 45 minutes.

Serve, garnished with the sour cream, chives or parsley and Czech Low-Carb "Bread" Dumplings. Store in an airtight container in the refrigerator for 5 to 7 days.

Substitution Notes:

To make this *dairy free*, use ghee or buttered-flavored coconut oil.

To make this *nut free*, omit the dairy-free sour cream.

EGG FREE   NUT FREE

DAIRY FREE   PALEO

Makes 6 servings

Dublin Coddle Stew

When it comes to Saint Patrick's Day celebrations everyone thinks of corned beef, which is delicious no doubt, but I wanted to offer up another option. This stew will blow your taste buds. The flavor is to die for, and the meat is extremely tender. While it takes a few hours to finish the stew in the oven, I promise it's worth every moment. This "stew" isn't what you might expect, as it doesn't have any tomatoes. Trust me when I say that this is a must-make recipe—don't miss out!

1 tbsp (15 ml) avocado oil

1 lb (454 g) thick-cut bacon, chopped

1 lb (454 g) mild pork sausage in casings

1 large yellow onion, thinly sliced

4 large cloves garlic, minced

2½ cups (390 g) peeled and cubed celery root

6 carrots, peeled and chopped

1 tsp Himalayan salt

½ tsp black pepper

1 tsp caraway seeds

1 tsp organic Beef Better than Bouillon

1 cup (240 ml) boiling water

Cauliflower Rice (page 58), to serve

Preheat the oven to 300°F (150°C).

In a large skillet, warm the oil over medium heat. Add the bacon and cook until crispy, 10 to 15 minutes. Remove the bacon from the skillet with a slotted spoon and place on a paper towel to drain excess grease or oil. (Leave the bacon fat in the skillet.) Slice the sausage links into ½-inch (13-mm) pieces and brown the sausage in the same skillet. When the sausage starts to brown, about 10 minutes, add the onion and garlic. Cook for 3 to 4 minutes, or until the onion and garlic soften, then add the bacon back to the pan.

Transfer the sausage-and-onion mixture to a large, ovenproof pot. Add the bacon, celery root, carrots, salt, pepper, caraway seeds, beef bouillon and boiling water. Stir to combine. Place the pot into the preheated oven for 3 hours, stirring once every 30 to 60 minutes.

Serve on its own or with cauliflower rice. Store leftovers in the refrigerator for up to 3 to 4 days.

Recipe Note:

If the beef bouillon can't be found or used, you can use 1 cup (240 ml) of boiling beef broth instead and omit the boiling water.

NUT FREE

Makes 6 to 8 servings

Steak Fingers with Caramelized Onion Gravy

This recipe is a fun play on chicken fingers. We really enjoy eating these steak fingers dunked in my Caramelized Onion Gravy on page 193. This makes for a fun comfort-food meal.

1 cup (120 g) pork rinds, finely ground

½ cup (40 g) Parmesan, grated

½ tsp paprika

1 tsp chili powder

1 tsp onion powder

½ tsp garlic powder

¼ tsp cayenne powder

¼ tsp dried oregano

1 tsp Himalayan salt

½ tsp black pepper

1 lb (454 g) flank steak, thinly sliced

1 egg, whisked

Caramelized Onion Gravy (page 193), to serve

Preheat the oven to 400°F (205°C). Line a large sheet pan with parchment paper.

In a small mixing bowl, combine the pork rinds and Parmesan; set aside.

In a shallow bowl, mix together the paprika, chili powder, onion powder, garlic powder, cayenne, oregano, salt and pepper. Add the sliced steak and toss to coat it with all of the seasonings, then add the egg and mix well. Coat the seasoned steak with the pork rind-and-Parmesan mixture.

Place the steak strips on the prepared baking sheet. Be sure to leave space between the slices so that they are able to crisp properly. Bake the steak for 12 to 18 minutes, or until the steak is golden and cooked to your preferred doneness.

Serve with Caramelized Onion Gravy.

Recipe Note:

A full batch of gravy is more than you will need for the steak fingers, so feel free to cut the recipe in half or to freeze the extra portion of gravy for up to 1 month.

General Tso's Meatloaf

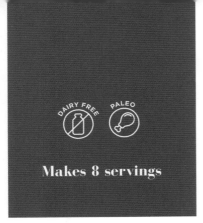

Makes 8 servings

This recipe takes a creative spin on the traditional American meatloaf. It is sweet with a little kick of spice and contains zesty notes of ginger that will wow your taste buds. If you prefer to keep it mild, the peppers can be omitted. Don't forget to garnish the loaf with sesame seeds and chopped green onions for a perfect presentation. If you want to add more veggies, you can also add a red, green or yellow chopped bell pepper to the meatloaf.

Meatloaf

1 lb (454 g) ground turkey or chicken

1½ tbsp (9 g) freshly grated ginger

1 tbsp (15 ml) liquid aminos, coconut aminos or gluten-free soy sauce

3 cloves garlic, minced

1 to 2 Asian spicy peppers (optional; see Recipe Note)

½ tsp Himalayan salt

1 tbsp (7 g) blanched almond flour

1 egg or ¼ cup (40 g) grated onion

General Tso Glaze

6 tbsp (90 ml) liquid aminos, coconut aminos or gluten-free soy sauce

2 tbsp (30 ml) rice vinegar

4 tbsp (60 ml) sugar-free honey or sugar-free maple syrup

2 tbsp (12 g) freshly grated ginger

Garnish

¼ cup (36 g) sesame seeds

¼ cup (24 g) green onions, chopped

Preheat the oven to 400°F (205°C). Spray a 9 x 5–inch (23 x 13–cm) loaf pan with cooking spray; set aside.

To make the meatloaf, in a large mixing bowl, combine the ground turkey with the ginger, liquid aminos, garlic, Asian peppers, salt, almond flour and egg; mix well.

To make the glaze, in a small saucepan, bring the liquid aminos, rice vinegar, honey and ginger to a simmer over medium heat and let cook until the sauce thickens, 5 to 10 minutes. Set the glaze aside.

Pack the ground turkey mixture into the prepared loaf pan. Coat the top of the loaf with half of the glaze. (Reserve the other half to use after baking.) Place the meatloaf in the oven and bake for 30 to 45 minutes, until the meatloaf is cooked through and there is no pink in the center.

Remove the meatloaf from the oven and drizzle on the reserved glaze, then garnish with the sesame seeds and green onions.

Recipe Note:

Asian spicy peppers are quite hot. You can omit them entirely for a milder meatloaf.

Substitution Note:

To make this **egg free**, use the grated onion option.

Makes 2 servings

2 (8-oz [227-g]) steaks

2 sprigs rosemary

6 cloves garlic, crushed

1 tbsp (18 g) Himalayan salt

1 tbsp (7 g) black pepper

2 tbsp (30 ml) olive oil

Sous Vide Steak Cooking Temperatures:

- **Rare:** 128°F (53°C)

- **Medium rare:** 130 to 134°F (55 to 57°C)

- **Medium:** 135 to 144°F (58 to 62°C)

Cooking Times:

- **1 inch (3 cm) or less thick steak:** 1 hour

- **More than 1 inch (3 cm) thick:** 2 hours

- **More than 2 inch (5 cm) thick:** 3 hours

Rosemary Garlic Sous Vide Steak

Talk about melt-in-your mouth good! One of the challenges with making steak just right is cooking it at the perfect temperature. It's hard to know if the inside is perfectly cooked without cutting open the steak, and then you end up losing a lot of the juices. The sous vide method is foolproof and ensures that the steak turns out literally perfect every single time. Once I learned this technique there was no turning back. The marinade is simple but is packed with flavor and pairs well with Cheesy Parsnip Latkes (page 194). If you wish, you can marinate the steaks up to 24 hours in advance. Feel free to double or even triple this recipe—the cooking time and method will remain the same.

Preheat a water bath to the temperature that matches the doneness you prefer (see sidebar).

Place the steaks in a resealable plastic bag with the rosemary sprigs, garlic, salt, black pepper and olive oil. Rub the ingredients into the steak and make sure a rosemary sprig is sitting on top of each steak.

Place the bag into the water, leaving an inch (3 cm) of the top of the bag open, allowing the water to press out the air. Once the air is pressed out, you can seal the bag or just clamp it against the side of the pot, making sure the steaks are fully submerged. Set a timer for the amount of time required per the thickness of your steak (see sidebar). Remove the steaks from the water bath, retaining the marinade.

Heat a frying pan over high heat. When the pan begins to smoke, carefully add the steaks and the marinade to the pan. (The juices may splatter a bit.) Sear the steaks on each side, then allow them to sit for a few minutes before serving. If your steak is thin, be careful not to sear for too long (30 seconds will do on each side) or else the steak will cook beyond your preference. If it is a thicker cut, you can do up to 1 minute on each side.

Recipe Note:

The sous vide portion of the cooking can be done in advance if you are planning for a group dinner. You can cook the steaks with the sous vide up to 2 to 3 days in advance and then let them rest in the refrigerator in their bag until you want to sear them. Just plan to sear right before serving. Doing this also gives the marinade some extra time to seep into the meat.

Smothered Pork Chops

What better way to indulge than with smothered pork chops? This belly-warming dish is simple to make and uses my savory keto-friendly gravy as an accompaniment. Pair the pork chops with sautéed green beans or a garlicky cauliflower mash.

Pork Chops

2 (4-oz [114-g]) pork chops, bone-in

1 tsp paprika

1 tsp onion powder

1 tsp garlic powder

1 tsp Himalayan salt

½ tsp black pepper

2 tbsp (30 ml) avocado oil

Gravy

4 tbsp (56 g) salted butter, ghee or butter-flavored coconut oil

1 cup (240 ml) heavy cream or unsweetened full-fat coconut milk from a can

½ cup (120 g) sour cream (optional)

1 tsp Worcestershire sauce

¼ tsp ground nutmeg

1 tsp garlic powder

1 tsp tapioca starch or arrowroot starch

2 tbsp (14 g) blanched almond flour

Salt and pepper, to taste

Preheat the oven to 375°F (190°C).

Season the pork chops with paprika, onion powder, garlic powder, salt and black pepper.

Heat a medium to large (ovenproof; see Recipe Note) skillet over medium–high heat, then add the avocado oil. Sear one side of the pork chops for 2 minutes, then flip. Sear the second side of the pork chops for 2 minutes, then move the pan to the preheated oven and cook for 20 minutes.

To make the gravy, while the pork chops bake, heat a small stockpot over medium heat.

Add the butter, heavy cream, sour cream, Worcestershire sauce, nutmeg, garlic powder, tapioca and almond flour to the small stockpot, stir and bring to a simmer. Whisk until thick and smooth, 2 to 5 minutes. Add salt and pepper to taste. Remove the gravy from the heat and set aside.

When the pork chops are finished baking, remove from the oven and serve smothered in gravy or serve the gravy alongside. Store any leftovers in a sealed container in the refrigerator for 3 to 4 days.

Recipe Note:

If you do not have an ovenproof skillet, after searing the pork chops, you can wrap them separately in aluminum foil and place them on a baking sheet to complete the oven cooking step.

Substitution Note:

To make this **dairy free**, use the coconut milk and omit the sour cream. Use ghee or butter-flavored coconut oil.

Makes 6 to 8 servings

Braised Bourbon Maple-Glazed Pork Roast

Although great for drinking, bourbon's savory and spicy flavor makes a great marinade for pork and beef alike. Accompanied by a few simple spices, this pork roast will win over everyone. Be sure to give the roast at least 3 hours to marinate in order to achieve the maximum amount of flavor and tenderness. You can add other veggies, such as parsnips or rutabaga to this dish.

Marinade

2 tsp (12 g) Himalayan salt

½ tsp black pepper

2 tbsp (20 g) garlic powder

2 cups (480 ml) bourbon or whiskey-bourbon

3 lb (1.4 kg) pork roast, bone-in

For the Roast

2 tbsp (30 ml) avocado oil

1 tbsp (2 g) dried or fresh thyme

1½ tbsp (23 g) Dijon mustard

1 tsp tapioca or arrowroot starch

1⅓ cups (320 ml) sugar-free maple syrup

½ tsp Himalayan salt

½ tsp black pepper

3 to 5 carrots, peeled and coarsely chopped

1 red onion, sliced

Cauliflower Rice (page 58) or mash, for serving (optional)

To make the marinade, in a large mixing bowl, combine the salt, pepper, garlic powder and bourbon. Add the pork roast and spoon the marinade over the meat. Cover the roast and refrigerate for at least 3 hours or up to 24 hours.

When you are ready to cook the meat, preheat the oven to 325°F (165°C) and heat a large Dutch oven over high heat. Add the avocado oil to the Dutch oven and place the roast, fat-side down, in the pan. Cook for 5 minutes on each side of the roast, or until the edges are visibly crisped. Set the seared roast aside in a separate pan, reserving the marinade.

Lower the stove temperature to medium–high and add the reserved marinade to the Dutch oven, along with the thyme, Dijon mustard, tapioca, maple syrup, salt and pepper and whisk, while bringing the mixture to a simmer for 3 minutes. Remove the Dutch oven from the heat and add the pork roast, carrots and red onion.

Brush the roast with the sauce from the pot and cover with the Dutch oven lid. Cook the pork roast, covered, for 45 minutes to an 1 hour, or until the internal temperature reaches 145 to 150°F (63 to 66°C). (The time will vary depending on the size of your roast.) Serve as is, or with cauliflower rice or mash (if using).

Substitution Note:

To make this **Paleo**, use ½ cup + 2 tablespoons (150 ml) of real maple syrup instead of sugar free.

EGG FREE · **DAIRY FREE**

Makes 2 to 3 servings

Citrus Pork with Thai Slaw

The dressing used in this recipe has been my favorite salad dressing for years. It also acts as a delicious marinade for your pork!

To make the marinade, whisk together the ginger, vinegar, oil, sesame oil, honey, lime juice and salt.

To make the slaw, in a serving bowl, toss the coleslaw mix, onion, cilantro and cashews together with the dressing.

To make the citrus pork, place the pork chops in a bag or an airtight container and add half of the citrus marinade. Shake well so the pork chops are completely coated. Place the pork chops in the refrigerator for a minimum of 1 hour or up to 24 hours (the longer they sit in the marinade the better the flavor will be).

When ready to cook, heat a frying pan over high heat and place the pork chops in the pan. Cook them for 2 to 3 minutes per side until there is no pink left (internally).

Use the marinade to dress your salad, and serve with the pork chops.

Substitution Note:

To make this **Paleo**, use real honey or maple syrup.

Citrus Marinade/Salad Dressing

2 tsp (4 g) fresh minced ginger

2 tbsp (30 ml) apple cider vinegar or rice vinegar

4 tbsp (60 ml) oil (grapeseed, macadamia oil, avocado oil or MCT oil)

1 tbsp (15 ml) sesame oil

3 tbsp (45 ml) sugar-free honey or sugar-free maple syrup or 2½ packets powdered stevia

1 tbsp (15 ml) lime or lemon juice

¼ tsp Himalayan salt (or more to taste)

Thai Slaw

1 (12-oz [340-g]) bag coleslaw mix

1 cup (160 g) chopped onion (red or white)

1 cup (50 g) freshly chopped cilantro

1 cup (135 g) roasted/salted cashews

Citrus Pork

2 or 3 pork chops

Makes enough
for 1 lb (454 g) meat
or tofu per recipe

Four Quick Marinades or Salad Dressings

These marinades are delicious and really simple to throw together. Coat meat or tofu with these marinades right before cooking or let them soak in all the flavor overnight. These sauces can also serve as a salad dressing or can be used for a quick stir-fry.

Honey Mustard

¼ cup (60 ml) sugar-free honey or sugar-free maple syrup

¼ tsp stevia extract or monk fruit extract

1 tbsp (16 g) yellow mustard

¼ cup (60 ml) avocado oil

¼ tsp Himalayan salt

¼ tsp black pepper

Mix all the ingredients together and place in a bag or container with 1 pound (454 g) of meat or tofu, or use as a salad dressing. The marinade will keep in a container in the refrigerator for up to 2 weeks.

Substitution Note:

To make this **Paleo**, swap real honey for the sugar-free honey and omit the stevia or monk fruit extract.

Thai Peanut

¼ cup (72 g) creamy peanut butter or SunButter

1 tsp sriracha

2 tbsp (30 ml) liquid aminos, coconut aminos or gluten-free soy sauce

2 tbsp (30 ml) sugar-free honey or sugar-free maple syrup

3 tbsp (45 ml) avocado oil

2 tbsp (30 ml) sesame oil

1 tbsp (6 g) freshly grated ginger

Mix all the ingredients together and place in a bag or container with 1 pound (454 g) of meat or tofu, or use as a salad dressing. The marinade will keep in a container in the refrigerator for up to 2 weeks.

Substitution Notes:

• To make this **nut free**, use unsweetened SunButter instead of peanut butter.

• To make this **Paleo**, swap real honey for the sugar-free honey.

Cilantro Lime

¼ cup + 1 tbsp (75 ml) avocado oil

1 tbsp (15 ml) water

2 tbsp (8 g) finely chopped fresh cilantro

1 tbsp (15 ml) lime juice

Zest of ½ lime

1½ tsp (3 g) cumin

¼ tsp garlic powder

¼ tsp Himalayan salt

⅛ tsp black pepper

2 tbsp (30 ml) sugar-free honey or sugar-free maple syrup

Mix all the ingredients together and place in a bag or container with 1 pound (454 g) of meat or tofu, or use as a salad dressing. The marinade will keep in a container in the refrigerator for up to 2 weeks.

Substitution Note:

To make this **Paleo**, swap real honey for the sugar-free honey.

Sugar-Free Teriyaki

¼ cup (60 ml) coconut aminos, liquid aminos or gluten-free soy sauce

1½ tsp (7 ml) Worcestershire sauce

2 tsp (10 ml) avocado oil

¼ tsp garlic powder

¼ cup (60 ml) sugar-free honey

¼ tsp stevia extract or monk fruit extract

2 tbsp (12 g) freshly grated ginger

Mix all the ingredients together and place in a bag or container with 1 pound (454 g) of meat or tofu, or use as a salad dressing. The marinade will keep in a container in the refrigerator for up to 2 weeks.

Substitution Note:

To make this **Paleo**, swap real honey for the sugar-free honey and omit the stevia or monk fruit extract.

Asian Pork Belly Tacos

This recipe is one of the stars of the book. You will need to plan ahead, as the pork belly takes 24 hours to make (although it's well worth the time, I promise). With the melt-in-your-mouth pork and the zesty beet ginger lime dressing and pickled onion and radish, you end up with an extremely flavorful taco. This recipe may seem intimidating but I promise each step is easy! You'll end up with the best tacos of your life.

Makes 4 to 6 tacos

1 recipe Crispy Asian Pork Belly (page 162)

1 recipe Beet Ginger Lime Yogurt Dressing (page 163)

Quick Pickled Red Onions and Radish (page 208)

Coconut wraps or grain-free tortillas (I recommend Siete brand)

Red cabbage, coarsely chopped

Scallions, chopped

Queso fresco (optional)

Lime wedges

Make the pork belly, beet ginger lime yogurt dressing and pickled onions and radish recipes.

Warm up the tortillas and load them up with all the fillings. Leftovers can be stored in the refrigerator for 3 to 4 days (although I can assure you, there will be none left).

Substitution Note:

To make this **_dairy free_** or **_Paleo_**, omit the queso fresco and use nondairy yogurt to make the beet ginger lime dressing.

(continued)

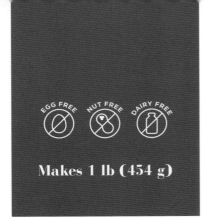

Makes 1 lb (454 g)

4 tbsp (60 ml) sesame oil

1½ tsp (5 g) garlic powder

¼ tsp crushed red pepper

1 tbsp (6 g) freshly grated ginger

3 tbsp (45 ml) sugar-free honey or maple syrup

1 tbsp (15 ml) lime juice

1⅛ tsp (7 g) Himalayan salt

1 to 2 lb (454 to 907 g) pork belly (unsliced)

Crispy Asian Pork Belly

In the world of meat, properly cooked pork belly is candy. The texture is like a meatier but melt-in-your-mouth bacon. Cooked too quickly and it ends up tough like overcooked pork chops, but if you give it time to slowly cook you will end up with one of the most delicious things that you could possibly eat. I tested out several cooking techniques for pork belly and this was the winner in every way. Just plan to start the meat 1 day in advance; it's not hard or complicated but does require a bit of planning ahead. Note that this recipe calls for 1 pound (454 g) of pork belly, but you can get away with making 2 pounds (907 g) using this marinade if you wish. This pork belly tastes amazing all on its own, but it can also be served on a salad, with roasted vegetables or in the Asian Pork Belly Tacos (page 161).

Preheat the oven to 200°F (95°C).

To make the marinade, whisk the sesame oil, garlic powder, red pepper, ginger, honey, lime juice and salt together.

Tear off a piece of parchment paper large enough to wrap around the pork belly. Cover all sides of the pork belly with the marinade. Place the pork belly on the parchment paper with the fatty side on top. Wrap the parchment paper around the pork belly. Then wrap the meat with two layers of aluminum foil, keeping track of the fatty side, which should remain on top. This will allow the fat to melt over the meat as it slowly cooks. Place the wrapped meat on a dry baking pan. Place in the oven and slow cook for 6 hours. After the 6 hours, place the pork (still wrapped) in the refrigerator to cool for 4 to 6 hours (or overnight).

When you are ready to finish cooking the pork, open the package and cut the pork into cubes of any size you wish. Place the pork and any fat and marinade left on the parchment paper into a dry frying pan. Fry the pork cubes over medium heat until crispy on all sides, about 5 minutes.

Recipe Note:

To get the pork extra crispy, you can weigh down the meat by placing a second pot or large ramekin on top of the meat while it fries.

Substitution Note:

To make this *Paleo*, swap the sugar-free honey or maple syrup for regular honey or maple syrup.

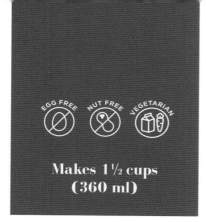

Makes 1½ cups (360 ml)

Beet Ginger Lime Yogurt Dressing

Truthfully I'm not a big fan of beets, but I do enjoy the beautiful color they add to recipes. This light and healthy sauce has zingy ginger and lime flavor and you really can't detect the beets aside from the beautiful color. I created it to serve on my Asian Pork Belly Tacos (page 161), but it also would work great as a salad dressing, or sauce poured over roasted vegetables or any type of meat or tofu.

1 small red beet, washed and peeled

8 cloves garlic

4 tbsp (60 ml) sesame oil, divided

1 tbsp (6 g) freshly grated ginger, divided

½ tsp salt, divided

1 cup (245 g) plain unsweetened yogurt (dairy or nondairy)

2 tsp (10 ml) lime juice

Zest of 1 lime

2 tbsp (30 ml) sugar-free honey or maple syrup

Preheat the oven to 400°F (205°C).

Peel and chop the beet. Place onto a square of aluminum foil. Add the garlic, 2 tablespoons (30 ml) of sesame oil, 2 teaspoons (4 g) of grated ginger and ¼ teaspoon of salt. Toss to coat the beet. Wrap the beet in foil and roast for 35 to 40 minutes.

Allow the beet to cool slightly, then add the contents of the foil packet to a small blender or food processor. Add the yogurt, lime juice, lime zest, 1 teaspoon of ginger, ¼ teaspoon of salt, 2 tablespoons (30 ml) of sesame oil and the honey. Purée until smooth. If your sauce is thicker than you wish, add water, a teaspoon or so at a time, to reach your desired thickness. Store in a sealed container in the refrigerator for 1 week.

Substitution Notes:

- To make this **Paleo**, swap the sugar-free honey for 1 tablespoon (15 ml) of real honey or maple syrup and use nondairy unsweetened yogurt.

- To make **dairy free**, use unsweetened dairy-free yogurt.

Makes 6 to 8 servings

1 tbsp (6 g) dried oregano

1 tbsp (6 g) chili powder

1 tbsp (6 g) ground cumin

¼ tsp ground cloves

1 tbsp (4 g) Himalayan salt

½ tsp black pepper

2 tbsp (30 ml) avocado oil

5 cloves garlic, minced

1½ cups (240 g) onions, chopped

3½ lb (1.6 kg) pork shoulder

1 (7.5-oz [222-ml]) can zero-sugar orange soda (such as Zevia brand)

¼ cup (60 ml) lime juice

2 tbsp (30 ml) sugar-free maple syrup or sugar-free honey

Tortillas, for serving

Lime wedges, for serving

¼ cup (15 g) chopped cilantro, for garnish

Instant Pot Pork Carnitas with Orange Soda

Words cannot describe how magical the flavor of these carnitas are. Rather than slow cooking pork shoulder, the Instant Pot® cuts the cooking time down to 30 minutes. Carnitas make for a great family weeknight meal or a noteworthy addition to your Taco Tuesday party. Refer to the Carnitas Taco Salad with Crispy Cassava Flour Tortilla Strips recipe (page 206) for a healthier alternative to these delicious pork carnitas.

To make the rub, combine the oregano, chili powder, cumin, cloves, salt and pepper in a small bowl. Rub the pork with the spices.

Preheat an Instant Pot to sauté mode and add the avocado oil. Add the garlic and onions and sauté for 5 minutes, or until the onions are light brown and tender. Add the pork shoulder to the pot and sauté for 5 minutes, browning each side of the pork. Add the orange soda, lime juice and maple syrup. Switch the Instant Pot over to high pressure–cooking mode; set the timer for 30 minutes.

When the cook time is complete, allow the Instant Pot to cool, then remove the pork. Allow the pork to cool until you can safely handle it, then pull apart the meat with a fork. Serve on warmed tortillas and garnish with lime and cilantro. Store leftovers in the refrigerator for up to 3 to 4 days.

Recipe Note:

This recipe cooks up juicy carnitas. If you prefer crisp carnitas (which I think are extra delicious), after the cook time, turn the Instant Pot back on to the sauté setting and allow the liquid to evaporate. After shredding the pork, transfer it to a baking pan and broil the shredded carnitas for 5 to 10 minutes in the oven. To save time, use the whisk attachment on a stand mixer to shred the pork.

Makes 2 servings

Masala Grilled Whole Red Snapper

Serving a whole fish is one way to get your friends and family members out of their comfort zone. While it can be off-putting to some, cooking a whole fish allows for more versatility and gives you the ability to pack the fish with the maximum amount of flavor. Feel free to swap out the red snapper for your favorite fish.

1 red onion, thinly sliced

1 green bell pepper, thinly sliced

1 red bell pepper, thinly sliced

1 yellow bell pepper, thinly sliced

½ lime, squeezed

1 tbsp (15 ml) coconut aminos, liquid aminos or gluten-free soy sauce

1 tbsp (16 g) tomato paste

1 tsp cumin

1 tsp ground ginger

2 sprigs thyme (or 1 tsp dried thyme)

6 sprigs cilantro, chopped

2 tsp (12 g) Himalayan salt

⅛ to ¼ tsp black pepper

3 tbsp (24 g) fish masala seasoning, divided

2 whole red snappers, cleaned and sliced open at the belly

Avocado oil, for greasing the foil

Preheat the grill to 375°F (190°C).

In a large bowl, mix together the onion, bell peppers, lime juice, coconut aminos, tomato paste, cumin, ginger, thyme, cilantro, salt and pepper; set aside.

Rub 1½ tablespoons (12 g) of the fish masala on the outsides of each of the fish; do not put any on the inside. Stuff each fish with half of the vegetable-and-spice mixture. Cut two large sheets of foil and cover one side of each sheet with avocado oil. Place one snapper in each sheet and wrap tightly, leaving the tail end outside the foil. Place both foil-wrapped fish on the grill and cook for 20 minutes.

After 20 minutes, open the foil and cook for an additional 5 to 10 minutes. Remove the cooked fish from the grill and serve.

Makes 4 servings

Fish

1 tbsp + 2 tsp (25 ml) avocado oil, divided

4 salmon filets

1½ tsp (8 g) Himalayan salt

1 tsp black pepper

⅓ cup (48 g) toasted sesame seeds, black or white

Cilantro Slaw

1 red cabbage, chopped

2 cups (265 g) diced cucumber

½ red onion, diced

¼ cup (15 g) cilantro, chopped

1 tbsp (15 ml) lime juice

Pineapple-Mint Dressing

1 tbsp (6 g) freshly grated ginger

4 large mint leaves

2 tbsp (30 ml) lime juice

2 tsp (10 ml) coconut aminos, liquid aminos or gluten-free soy sauce

2 tsp (10 ml) pineapple extract

¼ cup (60 ml) sugar-free honey

1 tbsp (15 ml) avocado oil

Sesame-Crusted Salmon with Cilantro Slaw and Pineapple-Mint Dressing

There are so many innovative ways to play with slaws. Unlike traditional coleslaw, this red cabbage–based slaw includes citrus, notes of cilantro, juicy cucumber, zesty lime and red onion. Top the slaw off with the sesame-crusted salmon to create a fulfilling meal, and drizzle the pineapple and mint dressing for a refreshing finish.

Preheat the oven to 375°F (190°C).

Heat a large skillet on medium–high heat with 1 tablespoon (15 ml) of the avocado oil. Pat the salmon filets dry, season with salt and pepper and brush each side with the remaining 2 teaspoons (10 ml) of avocado oil. Coat each filet with the toasted sesame seeds. When the skillet is fully heated, place each filet skin-side up and cook for 3 minutes. Flip the salmon filets over and move the skillet into the oven; cook for 10 minutes.

To make the slaw, in a large bowl, toss together the cabbage, cucumber, onion, cilantro and lime juice; set aside.

To make the dressing, add the ginger, mint, lime juice, coconut aminos, pineapple extract, honey and avocado oil to a food processor and blend until smooth; set aside.

Remove the cooked salmon from the oven and let cool, 3 minutes. Top the slaw with the salmon. Drizzle the dish with your desired amount of dressing and serve.

Substitution Note:

To make this **Paleo**, use real honey instead of sugar free.

Makes 2 servings

1 lb (454 g) tilapia (about 2 filets)

1 tbsp (15 ml) avocado oil

2 tsp (12 g) + a pinch of Himalayan salt, divided

½ tsp + a pinch of pepper, divided

2 tsp (10 ml) lemon juice, divided

1 tsp cumin, divided

½ tsp ground coriander

½ tsp paprika

⅛ tsp cayenne powder (optional)

Avocado oil spray

3 tsp (14 g) butter

¾ tsp cumin, divided

10 oz (283 g) riced cauliflower

½ cup (120 ml) red wine vinegar

3 tbsp (45 ml) avocado oil

1 tbsp (15 ml) sugar-free honey

¼ cup (15 g) cilantro, chopped

¼ cup (15 g) parsley, chopped

¼ cup (40 g) red onion, chopped

Mixed greens, to serve

1 yellow bell pepper, seeded and chopped, to serve

Grilled Tilapia with Moroccan Vinaigrette and Keto Couscous

Tilapia can seem somewhat limiting—it isn't one of the most durable fish to cook with, nor is it the most flavorful compared to others. Grilling tilapia, though, presents an opportunity to infuse a good amount of flavor and versatility in how you serve the fish. Serve alongside mixed greens and my grilled keto cauliflower couscous to prove to your family or guests that tilapia can actually be the star of the show.

Preheat the grill to 375°F (190°C).

Brush both sides of the tilapia filets with the avocado oil, then sprinkle with ½ teaspoon salt, ¼ teaspoon pepper, 1 teaspoon lemon juice, ¼ teaspoon cumin, coriander, paprika and cayenne. Spray two large sheets of foil with avocado oil and wrap the tilapia filets separately; set aside for grilling.

In a medium mixing bowl, combine the butter, 1½ teaspoons salt, ¼ teaspoon pepper, ¼ teaspoon cumin and riced cauliflower and mix well. Spray a large sheet of aluminum foil with avocado oil spray, then carefully place the cauliflower mixture in the middle of the sheet. Bring all four sides of the foil up around the cauliflower mixture to form a sealed pouch.

Place the foil-wrapped tilapia and the foil pouch filled with cauliflower onto the grill and cook for 10 to 15 minutes, until the fish is cooked through and falls apart easily when touched with a fork. Continue to cook the cauliflower for another 10 to 15 minutes, or until fully cooked.

In the meantime, put the vinegar, avocado oil, ½ teaspoon cumin, 1 teaspoon lemon juice, honey, cilantro, parsley, onion and a pinch of salt and black pepper in a food processor. Blend until smooth, then set aside.

Serve the tilapia on top of the cauliflower couscous with mixed greens and chopped yellow pepper and drizzle with the Moroccan vinaigrette or serve the dressing on the side.

Makes 6 to 8 servings

Savory Herb Butter Dutch Baby with Roasted Tomatoes, Garlic and Ricotta

This Dutch baby is a showstopper and is a fun way to eat a filling meal without all the excess carbs. The dried bouquet garni seasoning included in this recipe is easy to make from scratch or you can simply substitute your favorite herb mixture.

Roasted Tomatoes

16 grape tomatoes, halved

4 cloves garlic, minced

1 tsp oil of choice

Dutch Baby

¾ cup (75 g) lupin flour

¼ cup (20 g) oat fiber

1 tsp double-acting baking powder

¼ tsp Himalayan salt

3 large eggs

¼ cup (60 ml) mild-flavored oil, melted coconut oil or melted butter

½ cup + 1 tbsp (135 ml) water

Oil or butter, for pan

Herb Butter

4 tbsp (56 g) salted butter, ghee or butter-flavored coconut oil

1 tsp bouquet garni (page 174) or herbs de Provence

Toppings

1 cup (250 g) ricotta cheese or burrata

4 to 6 strips of prosciutto (optional) broken into smaller pieces

¼ cup (24 g) chopped green onions or 1 tbsp (4 g) fresh parsley, chopped

Preheat the oven to 425°F (220°C). Place the tomatoes, garlic and oil in a small baking pan; set aside.

To make the batter, combine the lupin flour, oat fiber, baking powder, salt, eggs, oil and water in a blender and process until smooth. Heat an oven-safe nonstick or well-seasoned cast-iron skillet over medium heat and add a little oil or butter. Pour in the batter, remove the skillet from the stovetop and transfer it to the oven. Place the tomato-and-garlic mixture in the oven as well. Bake for 20 to 25 minutes.

While they are baking, make the herb butter. Heat the butter and herbs in a small skillet or pan. Cook over medium heat until golden brown. Remove from the heat.

After 20 to 25 minutes, remove the fully-cooked Dutch baby and tomatoes from the oven. Brush half of the herb butter over the baked Dutch baby. Spread the ricotta on top, then add the roasted tomatoes and garlic. Add the prosciutto and garnish with green onions or parsley. Drizzle the remaining herb butter all over the top.

Substitution Notes:

- To make this *dairy free*, use Dairy-Free Ricotta Cheese (page 491). Substitute butter for vegan butter or butter-flavored coconut oil.

- To make this *vegetarian*, omit the prosciutto.

- To make this *Paleo*, use Dairy-Free Ricotta Cheese (page 491) and use your favorite Paleo pancake recipe instead, leaving out any sweetener.

(continued)

**Makes 4 teaspoons
(4 g)**

½ tsp dried rosemary

½ tsp dried thyme

½ tsp dried oregano

½ tsp dried basil

½ tsp dried dill weed

½ tsp dried marjoram

½ tsp dried sage

½ tsp dried tarragon

Homemade Bouquet Garni

If you can't find herbs de Provence or bouquet garni in stores, here is a spice blend mixture to make your own.

Stir together the rosemary, thyme, oregano, basil, dill, marjoram, sage and tarragon. Keep the mixture in an airtight jar or container for up to 1 year.

EGG FREE   NUT FREE   DAIRY FREE

Makes 1 ½ lb (680 g) meat per recipe

Mongolian Beef + Rogan Josh

Beef is a staple in many popular Asian dishes from Korean BBQ to Japanese and Chinese cuisine. Although not completely unheard of, most Indian dishes do not contain beef as cows are considered sacred in that culture. So these recipes are both interchangeable with lamb, if you prefer to avoid beef or just want to change up things. I personally love the warm and fragrant Indian spices with beef, which is why I made both of these dishes with it.

Mongolian Beef

1½ lb (680 g) skirt steak

2 tbsp (30 ml) sesame oil, divided

2 cloves garlic, minced

4 green onions, chopped

⅓ cup (80 ml) dry sherry wine

2 tbsp (30 ml) coconut aminos, liquid aminos or gluten-free soy sauce

2 tbsp (30 ml) sriracha

3 tbsp (45 ml) sugar-free honey or sugar-free maple syrup

2 tsp (6 g) toasted sesame seeds

Cauliflower Rice (page 58), for serving

Slice the skirt steak against the grain into thin strips and set aside. In a large wok over medium–high heat, heat 1 tablespoon (15 ml) of sesame oil. When the oil is hot, add the beef in two separate batches and stir-fry until the meat is cooked through, about 5 minutes for each batch.

Remove the beef from the wok and set aside. Reheat the wok and add an additional 1 tablespoon (15 ml) of sesame oil. When the oil is hot, add the garlic and green onions and cook for 2 to 3 minutes, then remove from the wok and set aside. Return the wok to the heat and add the sherry, coconut aminos, sriracha and honey. Bring the mixture to a boil and allow the sauce to thicken, about 5 minutes.

When the sauce has thickened, return the beef and cooked onions to the wok and toss to coat with the sauce. Sprinkle with the sesame seeds and serve immediately as is, or over cauliflower rice. Leftovers can be stored, covered, in the refrigerator for up to 3 days.

Substitution Notes:

- To make this **vegetarian**, use paneer or tofu.

- To make this **Paleo**, use 1 tablespoon (15 ml) of real honey.

(continued)

Rogan Josh

1½ lb (680 g) skirt steak

1 tbsp (14 g) ghee or butter-flavored coconut oil

2 onions, diced

3 cloves garlic, minced

½ cup (120 g) plain full-fat yogurt

1 tbsp (6 g) freshly grated ginger

1 tbsp (5 g) ground coriander

2 tsp (4 g) ground cumin

1 tsp ground cardamom

1 tsp turmeric

1 tsp chili powder

1 tsp Himalayan salt

½ tsp ground cloves

1 (14.5-oz [411-g]) can diced tomatoes

1 tsp garam masala

¼ cup (27 g) slivered almonds

Cauliflower Rice (page 58), for serving

Slice the skirt steak against the grain into thin strips and set aside.

In a large saucepan over medium heat, heat the ghee, then add the onions and garlic and cook until soft, about 5 minutes. Add the yogurt, ginger, coriander, cumin, cardamom, turmeric, chili powder, salt and cloves and stir well. Cook for 2 minutes, then stir in the tomatoes and cook for an additional 5 minutes. Add the sliced steak and stir to coat. Cover and cook on low for 45 minutes, covered, stirring occasionally.

Remove the lid and allow the sauce to simmer until it begins to thicken, about 15 minutes. Stir in the garam masala. Gently toast the almonds and sprinkle on top. Serve immediately as is, or over cauliflower rice. Leftovers can be stored, covered, in the refrigerator for up to 3 days.

Substitution Notes:

- To make this **nut free**, omit the almonds.

- To make this **dairy free** or **Paleo**, use unsweetened plain dairy-free yogurt.

- To make this **vegetarian**, use paneer.

Makes 3 to 4 servings

Indian Paneer Korma

This dish is another one of my household's favorites. It is usually made with golden raisins, but I chose to leave them out for the sake of keeping the carbs down. Instead, I recommend taking the time to really caramelize the onions, as their flavor and texture truly mimics the raisins. Doing this adds extra flavor, too. For a feast, serve this with Indian Butter Chicken (page 137), Rogan Josh (page 177), Indian Dosas with Aloo Gobi Filling (page 282), Simple Garlic Naan (page 229) and Cauliflower Rice (page 58).

3 tbsp (42 g) salted butter or ghee

1½ large onions, chopped

2 tbsp (12 g) fresh minced ginger

1¼ tsp (2 g) cardamom powder

2½ tsp (8 g) garlic powder

2 tsp (4 g) cumin powder

1½ tsp (8 g) Himalayan salt

1 cup (245 g) unsweetened yogurt

1¼ cups (300 ml) heavy cream

1 (1-lb [454-g]) package diced paneer

3 tbsp (45 ml) sugar-free honey

¼ cup (35 g) raw, unsalted cashews, lightly chopped (optional)

Cauliflower Rice (page 58), for serving

Heat a large skillet over medium–low heat. Add the butter and when it is melted, add the onions. Cook, stirring occasionally, for 20 to 25 minutes, until the onions are deep brown and caramelized.

During the last 5 minutes of cooking the onions, stir in the ginger, cardamom, garlic powder, cumin and salt and stir until fragrant. When the onions are caramelized, add the yogurt, heavy cream, paneer, honey and cashews. Simmer over medium heat for another 7 to 10 minutes to soften the paneer and cashews and to thicken the curry. Serve over cauliflower rice.

Substitution Note:

To make this **nut free**, omit the cashews.

Sides, Salads and Soups

Side dishes may seem boring until you turn the page. Your wildest keto dreams might just come true when you spot the French fries, poutine, samosas and empanadas. These dishes are so good, they deserve to be the star of the entire meal.

← See recipe on page 217.

EGG FREE   NUT FREE

DAIRY FREE   PALEO

Makes 2 servings

Shallot, Bacon and Sage Butternut Squash Mash

Adding bacon makes this a delicious upgrade to what might seem like a boring side dish. This is a perfect comfort-food side dish without all the starch.

2 lb (907 g; about 8 cups) diced butternut squash

3 tbsp (45 ml) olive oil, butter or butter-flavored coconut oil

5 slices bacon, finely chopped

2 shallots, chopped

¾ tsp powdered sage

1¼ tsp (7 g) Himalayan salt

¾ tsp black pepper

Preheat the oven to 375°F (190°C).

Place the butternut squash on one or two rimmed baking sheets and drizzle with the oil. Transfer to the oven and roast for 45 minutes.

Meanwhile, place the bacon and shallots in a skillet and sauté over medium heat, stirring often while the bacon cooks and the shallots caramelize. When the bacon and shallots are almost done, stir in the sage, salt and pepper. Cook until the bacon is crisp and onions are caramelized; remove from the heat.

When the squash is roasted, transfer it to a bowl. Using an immersion blender, purée the squash (or use a food processor). Then stir in the contents of the pan with the bacon-and-shallot mixture, including all of the bacon fat.

EGG FREE   NUT FREE   PALEO

Makes 2 servings

2 (12-oz [340-g]) bags frozen cauliflower or 1 head fresh cauliflower

½ cup (70 g) cubed pancetta

1 tsp crushed rosemary

2 tbsp (28 g) salted butter, ghee or butter-flavored coconut oil

½ to 1½ tsp (3 to 9 g) Himalayan salt, to taste

1 tsp garlic powder

1 tsp onion powder

Pancetta and Rosemary Cauliflower Mash

There are a few different mash recipes included in this book, but this one is my favorite. It has a light flavor but a nice crunch of pancetta. Pairing it with my Caramelized Onion Gravy (page 193) makes for a perfect side dish.

Place the frozen cauliflower in a saucepan and add water to cover. Bring to a boil over medium–high heat, and cook until fork tender, 10 to 15 minutes.

While the cauliflower is cooking, add the pancetta, rosemary, butter, salt, garlic powder and onion powder to a skillet. Sauté over low heat until the pancetta is a little crispy; set aside.

Strain the cauliflower and purée it using an immersion blender or food processor. Then stir in the contents of the skillet with the pancetta.

Recipe Note:

The amount of salt needed will depend on the size of your head of cauliflower. Therefore I recommend you add that to taste.

Substitution Note:

To make this **dairy free**, use butter-flavored coconut oil.

EGG FREE · DAIRY FREE

VEGETARIAN · PALEO

Makes 2 servings

Breaded Eggplant or Zucchini Fries

Eggplant is one of those veggies that I really love but often forget to cook. Zucchini can also be used in this recipe. These quick fries are simple to make and have great flavor. Truth be told, they are not as crispy as typical fries, as they are very low in starch, but in their own way they are still enjoyable. The longer you cook them the crispier they get, but they do shrink the more time they spend in the oven. I found 23 to 25 minutes to be the perfect amount of time but feel free to leave them in a little longer if you want them more well done.

Fries

1 large eggplant or 2 to 3 large zucchini

Coarse salt, for sprinkling (Himalayan or kosher)

Avocado oil spray

¾ tsp garlic powder

¼ tsp black pepper

Breading

5 tbsp (30 g) garbanzo bean flour

½ cup (58 g) blanched almond flour

1 tsp garlic powder

½ tsp cumin

½ tsp Himalayan salt

½ tsp paprika

Preheat the oven to 350°F (175°C). Line a rimmed baking sheet with parchment paper.

Using a mandoline or by hand, cut the eggplant or zucchini into the shape of fries (I make mine about ¼ inch [6 mm] thick). Lay them on a paper towel and sprinkle with a few big pinches of the coarse salt. Allow them to sit on the paper towel for 10 to 15 minutes, then press them dry by placing another paper towel on top and gently pushing down on the fries.

In a medium bowl, combine the garbanzo bean flour, almond flour, garlic powder, cumin, salt and paprika.

Place the fries on the prepared baking sheet. Liberally spray them with the avocado oil, tossing them gently to cover all sides with the oil. Sprinkle with the garlic powder and black pepper, then toss them in the breading mixture, turning to coat all sides. Return them to the baking sheet, then place the baking sheet on the middle rack of the oven and bake for 23 to 25 minutes, or longer if you prefer them well done. Remove the pan from the oven and add another sprinkle of salt if they need it.

Makes 2 servings

Rosemary Parsnip Fries

"Simple, with a flavor explosion" exactly describes this recipe. Parsnips make a great replacement for potatoes, and now you can enjoy flavorful fries without all the starch. These fries pair well with the Caramelized Onion Gravy to make great poutine (page 193). You can also use any leftover scraps of parsnips you might have after cutting out your fries to make Cheesy Parsnip Latkes (page 194).

2½ lb (1.1 kg) parsnips

3 tbsp (45 ml) olive oil

1 tbsp (2 g) fresh rosemary, finely chopped

1 large clove garlic, minced

5 sprigs rosemary (optional)

Himalayan salt, to taste

Black pepper, to taste

Preheat the oven to 450°F (230°C) and line a baking sheet with parchment paper.

Peel and cut the parsnips into fries and place them on the prepared baking sheet. Coat the fries with olive oil, rosemary and garlic, tossing until the parsnips are well coated.

Spread the parsnips out on the prepared baking sheet into an even layer and place the rosemary sprigs over the fries. Roast the fries for 10 minutes and then flip the fries, continuing to cook for 10 to 15 minutes, or until tender. Season with salt and pepper and serve.

Makes 2 servings

Chili Lime Parmesan Carrot Fries

I can't stop eating these fries. They have a sweet and spicy, zesty taste. You'll be amazed how similar they taste to sweet potato fries.

1 tbsp (8 g) chili powder

½ tsp cumin

¼ tsp cayenne pepper

¼ tsp garlic powder

¼ tsp onion powder

¼ tsp Himalayan salt

¼ tsp ground coriander

12 oz (340 g) carrots, peeled and cut into fries

2 tbsp (30 ml) olive oil or salted butter, melted

3 tbsp (15 g) Parmesan cheese (optional)

1 to 2 tbsp (3 to 5 g) minced fresh cilantro

Zest of ½ lime

Preheat the oven to 450°F (230°C). Line a baking sheet with parchment paper.

In a small bowl, combine the chili powder, cumin, cayenne, garlic powder, onion powder, salt and coriander.

Place the carrots on the prepared baking sheet and drizzle with the oil. Sprinkle the fries with the seasoning mix, stirring to ensure they are coated with the olive oil and seasonings. Place in the oven and bake for 5 minutes, flip the fries and place back into the oven for another 10 to 15 minutes, or until soft. (Heating times may vary depending on the size and thickness of the fries; be sure to keep an eye on them while they are in the oven.) Remove the fries from the oven and let cool briefly.

Sprinkle the fries with the Parmesan cheese, cilantro and lime zest.

Substitution Note:

To make these **dairy free** and **Paleo**, omit the cheese.

Parsnip Poutine

Makes 2 servings

Cheese curds, parsnip fries and keto gravy, yessss. I am here for it. The recipe is delicious and great for snacking, but without all the extra carbs to make you feel guilty. This is comfort food at its best.

Caramelized Onion Gravy

2 tbsp (28 g) salted butter or butter-flavored coconut oil

1 large onion, chopped

¼ tsp black pepper

½ tsp garlic powder

⅓ cup + 3 tbsp (60 g) blanched almond flour

1½ tbsp (24 g) Roasted Chicken Better than Bouillon

1½ cups (360 ml) water

¼ cup (60 ml) heavy cream or coconut cream

¼ to ½ tsp Himalayan salt

Poutine

1 batch Rosemary Parsnip Fries (page 189)

½ cup (125 g) cheese curds

To make the gravy, in a saucepan, melt the butter over medium-low heat, then add the onion. Cook for about 20 minutes, or until the onion is a beautiful golden brown color and is cooked through.

Add the black pepper, garlic powder, almond flour, bouillon, water and heavy cream and blend until smooth using an immersion blender. Turn up the heat to medium and whisk until thickened. Add salt to taste.

Pour the gravy over the fries and scatter the cheese curds over the top. Serve.

Substitution Note:

To make this ***dairy free***, use coconut cream in the gravy, dairy-free cheese and use butter-flavored coconut oil or vegan butter.

Makes 6 latkes

Cheesy Parsnip Latkes

These cheesy latkes are quick, easy and delicious. Normally latkes are made with potatoes, but to make this recipe keto I used parsnips and they are just so good. This recipe is a great way to use any raw parsnips you have left after cutting out your fries in my Rosemary Parsnip Fries recipe (page 189); you can just grate the leftover pieces. For the best results, make the latkes thin, so the parsnips cook through and end up crispy.

2 cups (300 g) grated parsnips

½ to 1 cup (55 to 110 g) shredded cheese, any flavor or variety (see Recipe Notes)

Himalayan salt and pepper, to taste

3 tbsp (45 ml) water + 1½ tsp (4 g) starch (tapioca, arrowroot or potato) *or* 1 egg (see Recipe Notes)

Chives (optional)

1 small diced onion (optional)

2 tbsp (30 g) coconut oil, divided

In a medium bowl, combine the grated parsnips and cheese. Season with salt and pepper (and any other spices that suit your fancy).

In a microwave-safe bowl, heat the water until it boils (roughly 1 minute). Quickly sift the starch into the bowl (to avoid clumping), then whisk it into the water until it forms a thick "goo." Stir the starch mixture into the parsnip mixture. If using chives or diced onion, stir them in as well. Using your hands, toss the ingredients together until they start to hold together fairly well. Divide the mixture into six equal-sized portions.

Heat a nonstick skillet over medium–high heat and add about ½ tablespoon (7 g) of the oil to the pan. When the oil is melted, add one to three mounds of latke mixture to the pan and flatten each into a patty. (How many you cook at a time depends on how large a pan you use. Make sure to always have oil in the pan when cooking the patties.) Cook the latkes for 3 to 4 minutes on each side. They should be golden brown, cooked through and firm to the touch. Repeat with the rest of the latke mixture.

Store leftovers in a sealed container in the refrigerator for up to 5 days.

Recipe Notes:

- You can use any kind of cheese you like best, including dairy free. You can vary the amount based on how cheesy you would like them to be—the higher amount yields a super-cheesy end result.

- The starch mixture or egg work equally well in this recipe.

Substitution Note:

To make this **dairy free**, use dairy-free cheese.

Makes 3 to 4 servings

Pork Banh Mi Kale Salad

Pork banh mi is a traditional Vietnamese street food served on a French baguette. To create a healthier alternative that almost anyone can enjoy, I've omitted the bread and substituted kale and cabbage. The peanut dressing adds a perfectly sweet touch to the pork loin, so be sure to serve the dressing alongside.

2 tbsp (30 ml) sugar-free honey or sugar-free maple syrup, divided

3 tbsp (45 ml) apple cider vinegar, divided

1 tsp garlic powder

1 tbsp (10 g) freshly grated ginger

¾ tsp Himalayan salt, plus more to taste

½ cup (120 ml) avocado oil, divided

1 (1-lb [454-g]) pork loin

1 cup (110 g) shredded carrots

Pinch of ground cinnamon

Black pepper, to taste

1 tbsp (15 ml) coconut aminos

1 tbsp (15 ml) lime juice

2 tbsp (30 ml) sesame oil

2 cloves garlic, minced

2 tbsp (36 g) creamy peanut or almond butter

3 cups (65 g) baby kale

3 cups (210 g) chopped Savoy cabbage

1 cup (135 g) diced cucumber

½ cup (80 g) diced red onion

2 to 3 radishes, thinly sliced

To make the marinade, whisk together 1 tablespoon (15 ml) honey, 1 tablespoon (15 ml) vinegar, garlic powder, fresh ginger, ¾ teaspoon salt and 2 tablespoons (30 ml) avocado oil. Place the pork in the marinade in a shallow container and place in the fridge for at least 30 minutes, or as long as overnight.

Meanwhile, to make the pickled carrots, add the shredded carrots, 2 tablespoons (30 ml) vinegar, 1 tablespoon (15 ml) oil, cinnamon and salt and pepper (to taste) to a bowl. Mix well, then set aside.

When the pork is done marinating, preheat the oven to 425°F (220°C). Place a 10-inch (25-cm) cast-iron skillet into the oven so that it can heat up with the oven. Once preheated and the pan is hot, add 1 tablespoon (15 ml) of oil to the pan. Place the pork into the hot pan and quickly close the oven. Roast for 10 minutes. Turn down the oven to 400°F (205°C). Carefully flip the pork and close the oven. Roast another 7 to 12 minutes, or until the pork reaches exactly 145°F (63°C), checking with an instant read thermometer. Remove the pork immediately from the hot skillet and let it rest for 10 minutes before slicing.

To make the dressing, in a medium bowl, whisk together the coconut aminos, ¼ cup (60 ml) avocado oil, 1 tablespoon (15 ml) honey, lime juice, sesame oil, garlic and peanut butter; set aside.

To make the salad, in a large bowl, combine the kale, Savoy cabbage, cucumbers, red onion and radishes. Drain the pickled carrots and add them to the salad. Season with salt and pepper. Slice the cooked pork to your preferred thickness and add to the salad. Drizzle the salad and pork with the peanut dressing or serve it on the side.

Substitution Note:

To make this **Paleo**, use real maple syrup instead of sugar-free maple syrup.

Makes 3 servings

Thai Noodle Steak Salad with Sesame Chili Dressing

This hearty salad would make any meat lover an undying fan of greens. With its Asian-inspired twist, the salad is packed with veggies, shirataki noodles and a juicy New York strip steak to top off things. Be sure to serve this with the sesame chili dressing for additional flavor.

Steak

1 tbsp (6 g) freshly grated ginger

2 tsp (6 g) garlic powder

2 tbsp (30 ml) coconut aminos, liquid aminos or gluten-free soy sauce

3 (8-oz [227-g]) New York strip steaks

Dressing + Salad

6 tbsp (90 ml) sesame oil

1 tbsp (15 ml) lime juice

3 tbsp (45 g) Thai red chili paste

¼ tsp stevia extract or monk fruit extract

3 cloves garlic, minced

¾ cup (180 ml) avocado oil

Himalayan salt and pepper

1 (1-lb [454-g]) bag kale

2 cups (140 g) shredded savoy cabbage

1 cucumber, spiralized

1 yellow bell pepper, sliced

1 red bell pepper, sliced

1 orange bell pepper, sliced

¼ cup (15 g) chopped cilantro, plus more for garnish

2 (8-oz [227-g]) bags shirataki noodles (optional)

¼ cup (36 g) crushed peanuts, for garnish

To make the steak, add the ginger, garlic powder and coconut aminos to a shallow container. Mix well, then add the steaks and allow them to marinate in the refrigerator for 30 to 45 minutes.

Meanwhile, to make the dressing, add the sesame oil, lime juice, Thai chili paste, stevia extract, garlic, avocado oil and a big pinch of salt and pepper to a food processor and blend until smooth; set aside.

To make the salad, in a large bowl, combine the kale, cabbage, cucumber, peppers and cilantro.

Heat a large oiled skillet over medium–high heat. When the pan begins to smoke, add the steaks (for medium rare cook 6 minutes on each side). Remove the cooked steaks from the pan and let rest for 5 to 10 minutes. Slice the steaks, and add them to the salad mixture.

If using the shirataki noodles, rinse them under cold water for a few minutes and toss into the salad. Garnish the salad with the peanuts and extra cilantro. Drizzle with the dressing or serve it on the side.

Substitution Notes:

- To make this **nut free**, omit the peanuts.

- To make this **Paleo**, use sunflower seeds instead of the peanuts, and use spiralized sweet potato noodles in place of the shirataki noodles. Omit stevia and monk fruit extract and sweeten with 1 to 2 tablespoons (15 to 30 ml) of honey or maple syrup in the dressing.

EGG FREE · DAIRY FREE · PALEO

Makes 3 servings

Tequila Lime Chicken Salad with Avocado Cilantro Dressing

You don't have to wait for a fiesta to cook with tequila. This boozy salad is packed with flavorful chicken and served with avocado dressing that has citrusy notes of cilantro. Spice up your normal lunch routine with this delicious salad.

Chicken

6 boneless chicken thighs

2½ tsp (6 g) cumin

2 tsp (4 g) adobo seasoning blend (with salt)

½ tsp smoked paprika

5 tbsp (75 ml) avocado oil, divided

¼ cup (60 ml) tequila

Avocado Cilantro Dressing

2 avocados, peeled and pitted

Juice of 2 limes

3 cloves garlic, minced

½ cup (120 ml) avocado oil

½ cup (25 g) chopped cilantro, plus more for garnish

¼ cup (60 ml) tequila

Pinch of salt

¼ tsp stevia extract or monk fruit extract

Salad

1 bag of arugula

1½ cups (225 g) cherry tomatoes, halved

2 red, yellow or orange peppers, thinly sliced

1 avocado, peeled, pitted and sliced

Salt and pepper, to taste

Toasted slivered almonds, for garnish

Using a meat tenderizer, pound the chicken thighs on a cutting board so that they are all about the same thickness.

To a bowl or shallow container, add the chicken, cumin, adobo, paprika, 1 tablespoon (15 ml) of avocado oil and tequila and mix well. Let the chicken marinate in the refrigerator for 1 hour or as long as overnight.

Meanwhile, to make the dressing, combine the avocados, lime juice, garlic, avocado oil, cilantro, tequila, salt and stevia extract in a food processor and blend until smooth. Set aside.

Heat up a cast-iron skillet over medium-high heat with 2 tablespoons (30 ml) of avocado oil. Once sizzling hot, add half of the chicken. Cook for 5 to 7 minutes depending on the thickness of the chicken. Then flip and cook the second side for another 5 to 7 minutes. Move the chicken to a cutting board. Add 2 more tablespoons (30 ml) of avocado oil to the skillet and repeat the process with the second half of the thighs. Give the chicken 10 minutes to rest and then cut into strips for the salad.

To make the salad, add the arugula, tomatoes, peppers and avocado in a bowl. Season with salt and pepper. Top the salad with the sliced chicken. Garnish the salad with the toasted almonds and extra cilantro. Drizzle with the dressing or serve it on the side.

Recipe Note:

If you use a salt-free adobo seasoning, just be sure to salt the chicken after cooking to taste.

Substitution Notes:

- To make **nut free**, omit the almonds.

- To make **Paleo**, omit stevia/monk fruit extract. Use about 1 tablespoon (15 ml), or more to taste, of real honey or maple syrup in the dressing instead.

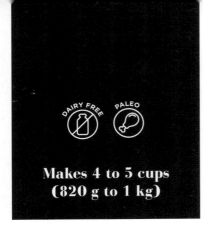

**Makes 4 to 5 cups
(820 g to 1 kg)**

Blueberry Lemon Poppy Seed Chicken Salad

This twist on traditional chicken salad comes together quickly and packs quite a flavor punch. A timesaver would be to buy precooked shredded chicken. Serve over a bed of your favorite greens and enjoy.

To make the chicken salad, in a large bowl, combine the chicken, celery, almonds, blueberries, white onion, garlic powder, salt and pepper. Stir to combine.

To make the mayonnaise, in a separate small bowl, combine the mayonnaise, lemon juice, lemon zest, poppy seeds and salt. Stir to combine.

Add the mayonnaise to the chicken salad and stir to combine. Serve on its own or over a bed of your favorite greens. Store the salad and dressing in airtight containers in the refrigerator for up to 2 weeks.

Substitution Note:

To make this *egg free*, use vegan mayonnaise.

Chicken Salad

2 cups (280 g) shredded chicken

1 cup (100 g) chopped celery

1 cup (92 g) sliced almonds

¾ cup (175 g) blueberries

1 cup (160 g) white onion, chopped (about one small onion)

½ tsp garlic powder

½ tsp Himalayan salt

½ tsp pepper

Lemon Poppy Seed Mayonnaise

½ cup (115 g) mayonnaise (vegan or regular)

3 tbsp (45 ml) lemon juice (1½ small lemons)

Zest of 1 small lemon

1 tbsp (9 g) poppy seeds

½ tsp Himalayan salt

Salad greens, for serving

EGG FREE DAIRY FREE

Makes 2 servings

Asian Chicken Salad with Tangerine Ginger Dressing

The tangerine extract really livens up this healthy salad—you can purchase it online. Combine it with ginger and you end up with a zesty and delicious dressing. I used chicken but feel free to use any protein of choice!

Tangerine Ginger Dressing

¼ cup (60 ml) avocado oil

½ tbsp (7 ml) coconut aminos, liquid aminos or gluten-free soy sauce

1 tsp tangerine extract

2 tsp (10 ml) toasted sesame oil

2 tbsp (30 ml) apple cider vinegar

¼ tsp ground mustard powder

2 tsp (4 g) freshly grated ginger

¼ tsp garlic powder

1 tbsp (9 g) sesame seeds

2 tsp (10 ml) sugar-free honey or sugar-free maple syrup

¼ tsp stevia extract or monk fruit extract

Salad

1½ cups (210 g) shredded chicken

4 cups (145 g) spring mix

1 cup (70 g) shredded red cabbage

1 cup (50 g) shredded carrots

1 green onion, chopped

½ cup (54 g) toasted almonds

To make the dressing, mix the avocado oil, coconut aminos, tangerine extract, sesame oil, vinegar, ground mustard, grated ginger, garlic powder, sesame seeds, sugar-free honey and stevia extract in a small bowl. Keep in the refrigerator until ready to serve.

To make the salad, in a bowl, combine the chicken, spring mix, cabbage, carrots, green onion and toasted almonds. Top with the dressing or serve the dressing on the side.

Substitution Notes:

- To make this **nut free**, omit the almonds.

- To make this **vegetarian**, swap the chicken for tofu or other protein replacement of choice.

- To make this **Paleo**, use real honey or maple syrup and omit the stevia or monk fruit extract.

Makes 4 servings

Carnitas Taco Salad with Crispy Cassava Flour Tortilla Strips

Carnitas have a ton of personality. They're packed with flavor and can be served in tortillas, on a salad or even in soups and stews. Using the Instant Pot Pork Carnitas with Orange Soda recipe (page 164) in this salad shows just how versatile the shoulder of pork can be. This salad also features crispy tortilla strips as a garnish to add a spin on the texture of a traditional salad, and a simple lime vinaigrette. For a sturdy salad, be sure to follow the crisping instructions listed in the Recipe Notes of the Instant Pot Pork Carnitas with Orange Soda recipe on page 164.

Salad

1 tbsp (15 ml) avocado oil

2 (6-inch [15-cm]) cassava flour tortillas, cut into strips

1 (6-oz [170-g]) bag baby spinach

2 large tomatoes, diced

1 bell pepper, chopped (any color)

3 to 6 slices pickled radish (page 208)

½ red onion, pickled (page 208, optional)

2 to 3 cups (500 to 750 g) cooked Instant Pot Pork Carnitas with Orange Soda (page 164)

Lime Vinaigrette

Juice of 1 lime

1 cup (240 ml) avocado oil

3 tbsp (45 ml) apple cider vinegar

Pinch of Himalayan salt

Pinch of black pepper

Pinch of ground cumin

1 bunch cilantro, chopped

Optional Garnishes

Crumbled queso fresco

¼ cup (15 g) chopped cilantro

Avocado slices

2 tbsp (20 g) diced red onion

1 lime, sliced

To make the salad, preheat a skillet with the avocado oil over medium heat. Add the tortilla strips and cook, continuously tossing, until the strips have turned light brown. Remove the tortilla strips from the skillet and set aside.

Line a large platter with the spinach, tomatoes, bell pepper, pickled radish and pickled onion (if using). Place the carnitas on top of the vegetables. Top with the crispy tortilla strips.

To make the dressing, add the lime juice, avocado oil, vinegar, salt, pepper, cumin and cilantro to a small bowl and whisk to combine. Drizzle the dressing on the salad or serve alongside the salad, along with your choice of optional garnishes.

Substitution Note:

To make this ***dairy free***, omit the optional queso fresco.

EGG FREE · NUT FREE · DAIRY FREE · VEGETARIAN

Makes 2 cups (300 g)

Quick Pickled Red Onions and Radishes

Pickled red onions and radishes are a staple that always live in my refrigerator. They add wonderful flavor and texture to a huge variety of recipes including salads, tacos—even roasted vegetables. Both versions can hang out in a sealed container in the refrigerator for about 2 weeks.

Red Onions

1 red onion, chopped

1 cup (240 ml) apple cider vinegar

¼ cup (60 ml) sugar-free honey or maple syrup

1 tsp Himalayan salt

1 cup (240 ml) water

Radishes

1 heaping cup (120 g) thinly sliced radishes (about 1 bunch)

½ cup (120 ml) apple cider vinegar

½ cup (120 ml) water

2 tbsp (30 ml) sugar-free honey or maple syrup

½ tsp Himalayan salt

Combine the ingredients for the pickles of your choice in a Mason jar. Let sit for 1 hour before using. Store in the refrigerator for up to 2 weeks.

Substitution Note:

To make this ***Paleo***, use 2 tablespoons (30 ml) of regular honey or maple syrup for the red onions, or 1 tablespoon (15 ml) of honey or maple syrup for the radishes.

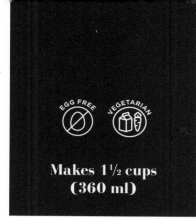

EGG FREE · VEGETARIAN

Makes 1½ cups (360 ml)

Keto-Friendly Salad Dressings in Three Flavors

Salad dressings are so easy to make at home with simple ingredients you may already have on hand. Here are three quick and easy keto-friendly salad dressings.

Ranch Dressing

NUT FREE

¾ cup (175 g) mayonnaise (regular or vegan)

¾ cup (180 ml) unsweetened full-fat coconut milk or heavy cream

2 tsp (2 g) dried dill

1½ tsp (1 g) dried chives

1 tsp garlic powder

½ tsp Himalayan salt

¼ tsp ground black pepper

Juice of ½ lemon

Whisk the mayonnaise, coconut milk, dill, chives, garlic powder, salt, pepper and lemon juice in a small bowl. Keep in an airtight container in the refrigerator for up to 2 weeks.

Substitution Note:

To make this **_dairy free_** and **_Paleo_**, use vegan mayonnaise.

(continued)

Maple Balsamic Dressing

¾ cup (180 ml) balsamic vinegar

½ cup (120 ml) avocado oil

½ cup (120 ml) sugar-free maple syrup

¼ tsp stevia extract or monk fruit extract (add more if desired)

½ tsp Himalayan salt

Juice of ½ lemon

Whisk the vinegar, oil, maple syrup, stevia extract, salt and lemon juice in a small bowl. Keep in an airtight container in the refrigerator for up to 2 weeks.

Substitution Note:

To make this *Paleo*, use real maple syrup and omit the stevia or monk fruit extract.

Lemon Poppy Seed Dressing

1 cup (240 ml) avocado oil

1 tbsp (9 g) poppy seeds

Juice of 1½ large lemons

Zest of 1 large lemon

3 tbsp (45 ml) sugar-free honey (add more if extra sweetener is desired)

¼ tsp stevia extract or monk fruit extract (add more if desired)

¼ tsp Himalayan salt

Whisk the oil, poppy seeds, lemon juice, lemon zest, honey, stevia extract and salt in a small bowl. Keep in an airtight container in the refrigerator for up to 1 month.

Substitution Note:

To make this *Paleo*, substitute honey for the sugar-free honey and omit the stevia or monk fruit extract.

Makes 4 to 6 servings per recipe

Spring and Summer Soups Four Ways

Soup is not the first thing most people typically think to eat during the warm spring and summer months, but I created some easy soup recipes that are so tasty you'll crave them on a hot summer day. Some of these recipes should be puréed, which can be done either in a Vitamix or standard blender, or with an immersion blender.

Avocado Basil and Lime Soup

3 cubed avocados

3 cups (720 ml) chicken or vegetable broth

3 tbsp (45 ml) lime juice

½ cup (12 g) fresh basil leaves, plus more for serving

¼ cup (60 ml) heavy cream or unsweetened full-fat coconut milk (from a can)

2 tbsp (30 ml) sugar-free maple syrup

1 tsp Himalayan salt

½ tsp chipotle chili powder (optional)

¼ tsp garlic powder

Zest of 3 limes

Lime wedges, for serving (optional)

In a large blender, pulse the avocados, broth, lime juice, basil, heavy cream, maple syrup, salt, chili powder, garlic powder and lime zest until smooth. Transfer the soup to a large bowl, cover and refrigerate for 3 hours or overnight. Serve chilled with optional basil leaves and lime wedges to garnish. Can be stored, covered, in the refrigerator for up to 3 days.

Substitution Notes:

- To make this **dairy free**, use full-fat coconut milk instead of heavy cream.

- To make this **vegetarian**, use the vegetable broth.

- To make this **Paleo**, use honey instead of sugar-free maple syrup.

Chilled Persian Yogurt Soup

2 cups (490 g) plain regular or dairy-free unsweetened yogurt

1½ cups (360 ml) ice water

¼ cup (6 g) fresh mint leaves

¼ cup (2 g) fresh dill weed

¼ cup (12 g) fresh chives

1 tsp Himalayan salt

½ tsp black pepper

½ tsp ground sumac berries, plus more for garnish

1 cup (130 g) peeled and diced cucumber, plus more for garnish

½ cup (50 g) chopped toasted walnuts

In a large blender, pulse the yogurt, water, mint, dill, chives, salt, black pepper and sumac until well combined. Transfer to a large bowl and mix in the cucumber and walnuts and stir well to combine. Cover and refrigerate for 3 hours or overnight. Serve chilled with optional sumac and cucumbers to garnish. Can be stored, covered, in the refrigerator for up to 3 days.

Substitution Notes:

- To make this **nut free**, omit the walnuts.

- To make this **dairy free** and **Paleo**, use unsweetened coconut milk yogurt.

Roasted Summer Vegetable Soup

1 quart (1.2 kg) cherry tomatoes

1 small zucchini, diced

1 small yellow squash, diced

1 tsp dried thyme

1 tsp garlic powder

2 tsp (12 g) Himalayan salt, divided, plus more to taste

1½ tsp (3 g) black pepper, divided, plus more to taste

Avocado or extra virgin olive oil

2 tbsp (30 g) coconut oil or butter

2 small onions, diced

8 cloves garlic, minced

¼ tsp cayenne pepper

4 cups (1 L) chicken or vegetable broth

1 cup (135 g) frozen peas

Parmesan cheese, for topping (optional)

Preheat the oven to 400°F (205°C) and line a large baking sheet with parchment paper.

Spread the cherry tomatoes, zucchini and yellow squash on the baking sheet and sprinkle with thyme, garlic, 1 teaspoon of salt, 1 teaspoon of black pepper and drizzle with avocado or extra virgin olive oil. Roast the vegetables for 30 minutes, then remove them from the oven and set aside.

Heat the coconut oil in a large saucepan over medium heat, then add the onions and garlic and cook for 3 to 5 minutes, or until tender. Add 1 teaspoon of salt, ½ teaspoon of black pepper and the cayenne pepper and stir well. Add the broth and bring the mixture to a low boil, then add the frozen peas and allow the soup to come back to a simmer. Add the roasted vegetables and remove the pot from the heat and serve. Add more salt and pepper to taste and sprinkle with Parmesan cheese (if using). This can be stored, covered, in the refrigerator for up to 3 days.

Substitution Notes:

- To make this **vegetarian**, use vegetable broth.

- To make this **Paleo** and **dairy free**, use the coconut oil and omit the cheese.

(continued)

Spinach and Artichoke Pesto Soup

Soup

2 tbsp (30 g) coconut oil

2 small onions, diced

2 cloves garlic, minced

1 tsp Himalayan salt

½ tsp black pepper

1 (12-oz [340-g]) bag frozen artichoke hearts

3 cups (720 ml) chicken or vegetable broth

Pesto

2 tbsp (30 ml) extra virgin olive oil

¼ cup (6 g) fresh basil leaves

¼ cup (6 g) baby spinach leaves

¼ cup (20 g) Parmesan cheese

¼ cup (34 g) toasted pine nuts, walnuts or almonds

1 clove garlic

½ tsp Himalayan salt

Heat the coconut oil in a large saucepan over medium heat, then add the onions and garlic and cook for 3 to 5 minutes, or until tender. Add the salt, pepper and artichoke hearts and cook until the artichokes are thawed and tender, 3 to 5 minutes. Add the broth and bring the mixture to a low boil.

While the soup comes to a boil, prepare the pesto. In a small food processor, pulse the olive oil, basil, spinach, Parmesan, pine nuts, garlic and salt until smooth. Spoon most of the pesto into the pot of soup, reserving a tablespoon or two (15 to 30 ml) for garnish. Using an immersion blender, purée the soup until smooth. Serve with the reserved pesto to garnish. Can be stored, covered, in the refrigerator for up to 3 days.

Substitution Notes:

- To make this **nut free**, omit the nuts from the pesto.

- To make this **vegetarian**, use vegetable broth.

- To make this **dairy free** and **Paleo**, omit the cheese from the pesto.

Fall and Winter Soups Four Ways

These recipes are perfect for savoring the flavors of fall and staying toasty on cold winter days.

Makes 8 to 10 servings per recipe

Roasted Pumpkin and Shallot Bacon Soup

5 large shallots, sliced

3 cups (420 g) cubed pumpkin or squash

8 cloves garlic, smashed

1 tsp fresh thyme leaves

1 tbsp (15 ml) avocado oil

1 lb (454 g) bacon, sliced

2 tsp (1 g) ground sage

1 to 2 tsp (6 to 12 g) Himalayan salt

1½ tbsp (12 g) ground cinnamon

1 tsp dried thyme

½ tsp dried rosemary

½ tsp cayenne pepper

1 tsp black pepper

1 tbsp (6 g) ground cumin

1 (10-oz [283-g]) can pumpkin purée

2½ cups (600 ml) coconut cream or heavy cream, plus more for garnish

4 cups (1 L) water

5 tbsp (75 g) Chicken Better than Bouillon

Toasted pumpkin seeds, for garnish

Preheat the oven to 450°F (230°C). Line a baking sheet with a large sheet of aluminum foil.

Spread the shallots, pumpkin, garlic and thyme on the baking sheet, drizzle with the oil and wrap the foil around the vegetables to form a makeshift pouch. Roast the vegetables for 20 to 25 minutes, or until the shallots begin to char.

In the meantime, heat a large stockpot over medium–high heat and add the sliced bacon; cook, stirring, until slightly brown, about 10 minutes. Remove the pot from the heat if the bacon finishes cooking before the roasted vegetables. Leave the bacon and the fat in the pot.

When the vegetables are fully roasted, turn the stove back on to medium heat and add the contents from the foil pouch to the pot; mix well. Add the sage, salt, cinnamon, thyme, rosemary, cayenne, black pepper and cumin and cook, stirring, for 3 minutes. Add the pumpkin purée, coconut cream, water and chicken bouillon to the pot; stir. Allow the soup to simmer over low heat for at least 30 and up to 60 minutes. Garnish the soup with toasted pumpkin seeds and additional coconut cream.

*Image on page 180.

Substitution Notes:

- To make this **dairy free** and **Paleo**, use coconut cream instead of heavy cream.

- To make this **vegetarian**, omit the bacon and use organic Better than Bouillon veggie flavor.

(continued)

Creamy Pumpkin Chicken Noodle Soup

¼ cup (60 g) butter-flavored coconut oil or butter

1 medium onion, finely chopped

1 cup (100 g) chopped celery

1 cup (128 g) chopped carrots

4 cloves garlic, minced

1 to 3 tsp (6 to 18 g) Himalayan salt

2 tsp (4 g) black pepper

1½ tsp (3 g) ground nutmeg

4 cups (1 L) chicken broth

2 cups (490 g) pumpkin purée

1 cup (240 ml) heavy cream or coconut cream

3 cups (420 g) shredded cooked chicken

2 (8-oz [227-g]) packages shirataki noodles or 2 batches Low-Carb Real Deal Fettuccine (page 251)

In a large skillet over medium heat, heat the oil, then add the onion, celery, carrots and garlic. Allow the vegetables to cook for 15 minutes, or until softened, stirring occasionally. Add the salt, pepper and nutmeg and stir to coat the vegetables, then cook for 1 minute. Add the broth, pumpkin and heavy cream, bring to a boil and reduce the heat to a simmer. Add the chicken and pasta. Stir to combine and remove from the heat.

Recipe Note:

Depending on the type of chicken broth you use, you may need more or less salt. Start with 1 teaspoon and add more to taste.

Substitution Notes:

* To make this *egg free* and *nut free*, use shirataki noodles instead of fettuccine.

* To make this *dairy free*, use butter-flavored coconut oil, coconut cream and shirataki noodles.

* To make this *vegetarian*, use vegetable broth and omit the chicken.

* To make this *Paleo*, use Paleo-friendly noodles.

(continued)

Green Curry and Lemongrass Soup with Chili-Mint Turkey Meatballs

Meatballs

1 lb (454 g) ground turkey

1 egg or ¼ cup (40 g) grated onion

3 cloves garlic, minced

1 scallion, minced

4 mint leaves, minced

1 tsp red chili paste

¼ cup (29 g) almond flour or finely ground pork rinds

¼ tsp Himalayan salt

1 tsp onion powder

Soup

1 tbsp (15 ml) avocado oil

1 medium yellow onion, minced

1½ cups (150 g) chopped celery

1 tbsp (6 g) fresh minced ginger

1 green bell pepper, chopped

¼ cup (64 g) green curry paste

1 tsp cumin

½ tsp ground coriander

1 tsp red pepper flakes

2 broccoli stalks, chopped into bite-size florets

1 red bell pepper, chopped

1 yellow bell pepper, chopped

2 Tien Tsin peppers (omit for mild soup)

1¼ cups (300 ml) unsweetened full-fat coconut milk

1 tbsp (16 g) Beef Better than Bouillon

1 tbsp (15 ml) fish sauce

1 lime slice, squeezed

1 stick lemongrass

Handful fresh Thai basil leaves

Salt, to taste

To make the meatballs, add the turkey, egg, garlic, scallion, mint, chili paste, almond flour, salt and onion powder to a large mixing bowl. Combine the mixture gently and set aside.

To make the soup, heat the oil in a large pot over medium heat. Add the onion, celery, ginger and green bell pepper and sauté for 2 minutes. Add the curry paste, sauté to allow the mixture to combine, then add the cumin, coriander and red pepper flakes. Sauté for an additional 2 to 3 minutes or until the ingredients are thickened.

Add the broccoli, red and yellow bell peppers and Tien Tsin peppers to the pot and sauté for 3 minutes. Add the coconut milk and bouillon, stirring to combine. Bring the soup to a boil, then add the fish sauce, 4 cups (1 L) water, lime juice, lemongrass and basil.

Form the meatballs into heaping tablespoon-sized balls. When the soup is at a boil, gently drop in the meatballs. Be careful not to stir the soup until they are fully cooked through, about 10 minutes. When the meatballs are cooked through, gently simmer for 30 minutes. Serve hot. Store leftovers in the refrigerator for up to 3 to 4 days.

Recipe Notes:

- If you prefer broccoli al dente, it can be added at the end to cook 5 minutes before serving.

- I used Thai Kitchen red and green chili paste. Some brands are very spicy—Thai Kitchen is mild and perfect for this soup.

Substitution Notes:

- To make this *egg free*, use grated onion instead of an egg in the meatballs.

- To make this *nut free*, use pork rinds instead of almond flour in the meatballs.

(continued)

Thai Pumpkin Ramen Noodle Soup

2 tbsp (30 ml) sesame oil

1 small onion, diced

3 cloves freshly minced garlic

1 to 2 Thai red peppers, thinly sliced (optional)

1 tbsp (6 g) freshly minced ginger

¼ cup (64 g) Thai red curry paste

2 tsp (5 g) ground nutmeg

2 tsp (5 g) smoked paprika

1 (14-oz [397-g]) can unsweetened full-fat coconut milk or 2 cups (480 ml) heavy cream

1 (14-oz [397-g]) can pumpkin purée

¼ cup (60 ml) sugar-free honey or sugar-free maple syrup

¼ tsp stevia extract or monk fruit extract

¼ cup (60 ml) coconut aminos, liquid aminos or gluten-free soy sauce

2 tbsp (30 ml) fish sauce

1 tsp lime juice

4 cups (1 L) chicken or vegetable broth

2 (8-oz [227-g]) packages shirataki noodles or 2 batches Real Deal Low-Carb Fettuccine (page 251)

In a large pot over medium heat, warm the oil, then add the onion, garlic, peppers and ginger and cook until the onion is tender, about 5 minutes. Add the curry paste, nutmeg, paprika, coconut milk, pumpkin, honey, stevia, coconut aminos, fish sauce and lime juice and stir well to combine. Then add the broth and bring to a rolling boil. Allow to boil for 3 minutes before adding the noodles. After adding the noodles to the pot, turn off the heat.

Recipe Note:

Add some shredded or diced chicken if you want a hearty protein punch. If gluten is your only dietary concern, use gluten-free ramen noodles.

Substitution Notes:

- To make this *egg free* and *nut free*, use shirataki noodles instead of fettuccine.

- To make this *dairy free*, use coconut milk and shirataki noodles.

- To make this *vegetarian*, omit the fish sauce and use vegetable broth.

- To make this *Paleo*, use Paleo-friendly noodles, use regular honey or maple syrup instead of the sugar-free version and omit the stevia or monk fruit extract.

Bread and Pasta

Bread and pasta are the things that people miss the most when watching their carbs. This chapter will give you back *all* of your favorites, but made in a healthier way. The recipes have been tested to perfection and will fulfill all your carby dreams.

← See recipe on page 230.

**Makes 5 to 6
flatbread rounds**

½ cup (84 g) coconut flour

¼ cup (29 g) blanched almond flour

1 tbsp (16 g) psyllium husk powder

½ tsp double-acting baking powder

¾ tsp Himalayan salt

2½ tbsp (37 ml) avocado or olive oil, divided

1 cup (240 ml) hot water

Perfect Easy Flatbread

You will be absolutely amazed at the perfect texture of this pita bread. It does not taste low carb. The texture is 100% bread and as an added bonus, this flatbread couldn't be easier to make. There are no extra steps required to work with yeast, or resting periods. Simply weigh out the ingredients using a kitchen scale, mix the dough, roll it out and cook it in a skillet. This bread remains soft and delicious for 4 to 5 days stored at room temperature. You can bend and roll this flatbread so it is great for sandwiches. It reminds me of pita bread, just a bit softer. The key to getting this bread just right is the temperature of the skillet. If it's not high enough, it won't puff up at all and will end up being somewhat fragile. For the best-tasting bread be sure to roll it out thin.

Combine the coconut flour, almond flour, psyllium husk powder, baking powder and salt in a medium bowl. Mix well, then add 1½ tablespoons (22 ml) of oil and the water. Stir together for 30 seconds, then knead the dough for another 2 minutes to make sure it's smooth, thick and isn't sticky.

Place a nonstick frying pan on the stove and preheat it over medium heat. Form the dough into a ball and cut it in half both ways to produce four evenly sized pieces of dough. Roll the first one out between two sheets of parchment paper. You want your dough to be thin, about 1/16 inch (1 mm). Using a 7-inch (18-cm or similar size) pot lid, cut the dough into a circle. (You can skip this step if you don't care about having perfectly round bread.) If using the pot lid, you will end up with extra dough; roll these scraps together and form additional bread rounds (you will be able to form one to two additional flatbreads).

Pour 1 tablespoon (15 ml) of avocado oil into the hot skillet. Add the first piece of rolled-out bread to the hot skillet and set a timer for 2 minutes. Flip the bread after 2 minutes and cook the other side of the bread for an additional 2 minutes. Remove from the pan and set aside to cool. Repeat these steps with the remaining bread dough.

Recipe Note:

Keep an eye on your bread. If your flatbread does not puff up at all, and breaks easily when bent, this means your heat needs to be turned up. If your flatbread burns in the first 2 minutes on the stove, this means your heat is too high.

Makes 3 pieces

1 cup (113 g) shredded mozzarella

1 cup (116 g) blanched almond flour

1 tbsp (16 g) psyllium husk powder

1 tsp garlic powder

½ tsp Himalayan salt

1½ tsp (7 g) double-acting baking powder

¼ cup (60 g) sour cream, or unsweetened yogurt or water

1 tsp apple cider vinegar

Butter or ghee, for topping

Chopped cilantro, for topping

Pan-fried chopped garlic, for topping

Simple Garlic Naan

This naan is so tasty. Due to the fact that it is starch free, it is not fluffy like traditional naan but it does have a nice texture and flavor—I really enjoy the crispy edges. The cheese in this recipe is a binder and gives the bread some crispiness. I made each piece of bread the size you'll find in a restaurant, but keep in mind that it is super filling due to the almond flour and psyllium. You could easily get away with making four smaller pieces instead of three if you wish. I like to top my naan with butter or ghee and chopped cilantro right as it comes out of the oven. You can also top the naan with minced garlic that has been toasted to perfection in ghee or butter. For the best results, use the sour cream option in the bread.

Preheat the oven to 500°F (260°C). Place a sheet of parchment paper on a standard or large-sized rimmed baking sheet.

Add the mozzarella, almond flour, psyllium husk powder, garlic powder, salt and baking powder to the bowl of a food processor. Process for about 1 minute.

Warm up the sour cream in the microwave for about 30 seconds and then pour it into the food processor with the dry ingredients. Add the vinegar, then process for another minute, until a thick dough forms.

Divide the dough into three or four equal-sized pieces. Press them out one at a time between two sheets of parchment until they are ¼ to ⅓ inch (6 to 10 mm) thick. Leave divots and fingerprints in the dough as this is what makes it look like traditional naan when it's baked. Carefully transfer each piece of dough to the prepared baking sheet and repeat with the remaining dough. When all the naan is on the baking sheet, quickly place the sheet into the hot oven. Bake for 5 minutes. Remove the pan from the oven, flip the naan to the other side using a spatula, then bake for another 5 minutes on the second side.

Remove the sheet from the oven, allow the naan to cool for a few minutes, then spread with butter or ghee and sprinkle with chopped cilantro and/or pan-fried garlic.

Substitution Note:

To make this ***dairy free***, the mozzarella cheese can be swapped out for diary-free mozzarella. Also, use unsweetened dairy-free yogurt.

Makes 8 biscuits

Fluffy and Flaky Biscuits

These biscuits have a fantastic texture and freeze well. Serve them with my Caramelized Onion Gravy (page 193) or in the Vanilla Bourbon Strawberry Shortcake with Mascarpone Whipped Cream (page 391). Making biscuits is not challenging, but it is very important that you do it right, so follow carefully.

1½ cups (150 g) lupin flour

½ cup (40 g) oat fiber, plus more for rolling

½ tsp Himalayan salt

1 tsp double-acting baking powder

1 stick chilled salted butter or chilled dairy-free buttery sticks

2 large eggs

1 tsp lemon juice or apple cider vinegar

⅓ cup (80 ml) unsweetened nondairy milk

Preheat the oven to 425°F (220°C). Line a baking sheet with parchment and set aside.

Add the lupin flour, oat fiber, salt and baking powder to the bowl of a food processor and pulse until mixed. Cut the chilled butter into tablespoon-sized pieces and add them to the food processor. Process again *just* until the butter has broken down into pea-sized pieces. Do not go any smaller or your biscuits will not be flaky. Pour the mixture into a mixing bowl.

In a smaller bowl, whisk together the eggs, lemon juice and milk. Pour the wet mixture into the dry and stir *just* until the dough comes together. Do *not* overmix or your biscuits will not be flaky.

Dust a little oat fiber (about ½ tablespoon [1.5 g]) onto a sheet of parchment paper. Place the dough on the parchment and gently roll it out until it is about 1 inch (3 cm) thick. Using a 1- or 2-inch (3- or 5-cm)-wide biscuit cutter, cut the biscuits and transfer them to the prepared baking pan. Bake for 12 to 14 minutes.

Substitution Note:

To make this ***dairy free***, use dairy-free butter and milk.

VEGETARIAN

Makes 9 cinnamon rolls

Cinnamon Caramel

4 tbsp (56 g) salted butter

½ cup (120 ml) sugar-free maple syrup

5 tbsp (75 ml) heavy cream

4 tbsp (55 g) keto brown sugar (I recommend Sukrin Gold for this recipe)

1 tbsp (8 g) ground cinnamon

Dough

3 tbsp (45 ml) heavy cream, plus more for brushing

1 tbsp (15 ml) real honey or maple syrup

1½ tsp (6 g) fast-acting instant yeast

2 cups (225 g) shredded mozzarella cheese

2 large eggs

1 tsp psyllium husk powder

1 tbsp (15 ml) vanilla extract

½ cup (46 g) garbanzo bean flour

¼ cup (29 g) blanched almond flour

¼ cup (20 g) oat fiber

½ tsp xanthan gum or guar gum

1½ tsp (7 g) double-acting baking powder

⅛ tsp Himalayan salt

Mild-flavored oil

Low-Carb Fluffy Cinnamon Rolls with Caramel Filling and Cream Cheese Frosting

This recipe was a beast to figure out but was well worth the extra effort. These rolls are fluffy and with the right amount of bready texture. Despite having cheese as part of the base, I can assure you that you do not taste it at all in the finished rolls. Typically when I make cinnamon rolls I just use butter, cinnamon and brown sugar in the filling, but I found that the sweetness got lost when the rolls were baked. The caramel is well worth the extra effort; it adds the right amount of sweetness and some gooiness to the finished cinnamon rolls.

To make the caramel, add the butter, maple syrup, heavy cream and sugar to a medium saucepan. Bring to a simmer over medium heat and cook until thickened, 15 to 20 minutes, whisking often. Remove the pan from the heat, let it cool for 5 minutes, then stir in the cinnamon. Set aside to cool fully.

Preheat the oven to 200°F (95°C). When it is preheated, turn off the oven—it will be used as a hot box to quickly proof the cinnamon rolls. Line a 7 x 7–inch (18 x 18–cm) baking pan with parchment paper.

To make the dough, in a small microwave-safe cup or bowl, whisk together the cream and honey. Place in the microwave for 5 seconds and heat until lukewarm. If it's hotter than that, be sure to let it cool or your yeast won't work. Add the yeast to the mixture and set aside for 5 to 10 minutes, allowing the yeast to activate.

Place the mozzarella cheese in a microwave-safe bowl and microwave on high for 1 minute. The cheese won't be fully melted. Add the partially melted cheese to the bowl of a food processor, then add the eggs and psyllium husk. Process until the cheese has broken down fully. Add the yeast/cream mixture and vanilla, then add the garbanzo bean flour, almond flour, oat fiber, xanthan gum, baking powder and salt. Process until a thick and sticky dough forms.

(continued)

Low-Carb Fluffy Cinnamon Rolls with Caramel Filling and Cream Cheese Frosting (cont.)

Cream Cheese Frosting

2 tbsp (30 ml) melted salted butter

2 oz (57 g) cream cheese

1 tbsp (9 g) keto powdered sugar

⅛ tsp stevia extract or monk fruit extract

½ tsp vanilla extract

1 tbsp (15 ml) heavy cream

Place a sheet of parchment paper on a counter and oil it heavily. Using a spatula, scrape all of the dough out of the food processor and onto the oiled parchment. Oil your hands and press/roll out the dough until it is about ½ inch (13 mm) thick.

Pour the caramel on top of the dough and smooth it out to cover the dough evenly. Using the ends of the parchment, gently roll up the dough into a tube and place it seam-side down on the parchment. Using a sharp knife or dental floss, gently cut the dough tube into slices 1 inch (3 cm) thick. (Clean your knife between each cut for the best results.) Lay the slices in the baking pan, leaving space between them. Brush the tops with heavy cream. Cover the pan with a towel, and place it in the warm (but turned off) oven for 45 minutes to allow the dough slices to rise. They should double to triple in size.

Remove the pan from the oven, and turn on the oven to 350°F (175°C). Preheat fully.

Remove the towel from the pan and place the pan in the hot oven. Bake for 17 minutes if you want them a little gooey in the middle or 19 minutes if you want them fully cooked through.

Meanwhile, to make the frosting, in a small bowl, whisk together the melted butter, cream cheese, powdered sugar, stevia, vanilla and heavy cream. (You can also use an immersion blender.)

As soon as the cinnamon rolls come out of the oven, drizzle the frosting over them. Serve warm. Leftovers can be stored in a sealed container at room temperature for up to 3 days.

Makes 8 slices

Nonstick spray

½ cup + 3 tbsp (165 ml) warm water

1 tbsp (15 ml) real honey or maple syrup

1 tbsp (12 g) fast-acting instant yeast

½ tsp psyllium husk powder

½ cup (58 g) blanched almond flour

½ cup (46 g) garbanzo bean flour

⅓ cup (26 g) oat fiber

¼ cup (48 g) palm shortening

1 tsp Himalayan salt

1 tbsp (22 g) xanthan or guar gum

1 tbsp (15 ml) apple cider vinegar

Low-Carb Chicago Deep-Dish Pizza

My husband was born in Chicago and he absolutely loves deep-dish pizza. He's gotten me on board and I love it now just as much as he does. As a result, I had to put in many hours to create an authentic crust for numerous diets—first came a classic gluten-free crust, then I came up with a Paleo version. This new version is the latest, and initially it felt impossible to take on, but I am quite happy with the results. To get the right amount of fluffiness, I introduced a bit of garbanzo bean flour. This does increase the carbs a bit but I promise it is well worth every net carb. As an added bonus, this recipe is egg free and can be made dairy free, which is a rare thing in the low-carb world of pizza.

Set the oven to 200°F (95°C), and when it has preheated, turn off the oven; it will be used as a hot box to proof the dough.

Line the bottom of a 9-inch (23-cm) springform pan with parchment paper and spray the bottom and sides with nonstick spray.

In a small bowl, mix the warm water, honey, yeast and psyllium husk powder; set aside.

To the bowl of a food processor add the almond flour, garbanzo bean flour, oat fiber, shortening, salt, xanthan gum and apple cider vinegar. Then add the water/yeast mixture and process until a dough forms.

Using oiled hands, gently press the dough into the prepared pan, making it thinnest on the bottom and thickest on the sides. Bring the dough about 1 inch (3 cm) up the sides of the pan. Cover the pan with a towel and place in the warm (but turned off) oven with the door left open a crack for 30 minutes.

Remove the proofed pizza dough, and turn the oven back on to 350°F (175°C). When the oven is preheated, place the dough (without any toppings) into the oven and parbake for 6 minutes.

(continued)

Low-Carb Chicago Deep-Dish Pizza (cont.)

Toppings

1 tbsp (15 ml) oil of choice

1½ cups (170 g) shredded mozzarella cheese (dairy or nondairy)

6 links cooked Italian sausage, skin removed and crumbled

1 (15-oz [425-g]) can tomato sauce or diced tomatoes (if using diced, drain out just a little bit of the water)

⅓ cup (25 g) Parmesan cheese, optional

Remove the pan from the oven and brush the crust with the oil. Add the mozzarella cheese and sausage and top with the sauce. Sprinkle the Parmesan cheese on top of the sauce. Bake for 15 minutes, then cover the pan with aluminum foil. Continue baking for another 10 to 15 minutes.

Remove from the oven and let cool briefly, then serve hot! Store leftovers in the refrigerator for up to 5 days.

Recipe Note:

Real honey or maple syrup is required to activate the yeast. The yeast ultimately eats the sugar—therefore the carbs don't count in the recipe!

Substitution Notes:

- To make this **dairy free**, use dairy-free mozzarella and Parmesan.

- To make this **vegetarian**, omit the sausage.

Boiled Low-Carb Bagels

If you do a quick Google search you will find many keto bagels that are lower in carbs than this recipe, and that are just baked, without yeast and the extra steps you'll find here. But I really wanted to think outside of the box and to make a traditional New York–style boiled bagel. I spent 17 years living in Rochester, New York, and to me there is no other way to cook a bagel. In order for the bagels to hold together they do need some starch, and cassava is our magical super flour in this case, keeping the bagels from turning to mush when boiled. I assure you, these are fluffy and the real deal, and are worth the few extra net carbs.

Makes 8 bagels

Nonstick spray

2 tbsp (30 ml) heavy cream

1 tbsp (15 ml) honey or maple syrup

1½ tsp (6 g) fast-acting instant yeast

2 cups (225 g) shredded mozzarella cheese

4 large eggs, divided

1 tsp psyllium husk powder

¾ tsp xanthan or guar gum

2 tsp (10 g) double-acting baking powder

6 tbsp (36 g) lupin flour

½ cup (61 g) cassava flour

¼ tsp Himalayan salt

Toppings of your choice

Set the oven to 200°F (95°C), and when it has preheated, turn off the oven; it will be used as a hot box to proof the dough.

Cover a baking sheet with a sheet of parchment paper and spray it with nonstick spray.

Add the heavy cream to a microwave-safe bowl or cup. Warm in the microwave for 10 to 15 seconds, until lukewarm. (It cannot be hot or it will kill the yeast.) Mix in the honey or maple syrup and the yeast and set aside.

Add the mozzarella cheese to a microwave-safe bowl and microwave on high for 1 minute so that it is partially melted on the edges of the bowl. Scrape the melted cheese into the bowl of a food processor. Add 3 of the eggs to the food processor and process until smooth. Add the psyllium husk powder, xanthan gum, baking powder, lupin flour, cassava flour and salt. At this point the yeast mixture should be a little bubbly. Add that to the food processor as well. Process until a super-thick, sticky dough forms and the ingredients are fully combined.

Generously oil your hands and a ⅓-cup (80-ml) measuring cup. Divide the dough into eight balls (about ⅓ cup [80 ml]) each). Shape each piece of dough into a perfectly smooth ball and then using an oiled finger, create a hole in the center of each. Keep in mind that the bagels will expand quite a bit, so the hole needs to be about ¼ to ½ inch (6 mm to 13 mm) wide. Place the formed bagels on the prepared baking sheet. Cover the bagels with a towel and place them in the warm oven (that has been turned off) and leave the oven door open a crack. Set a timer for 30 minutes.

(continued)

Boiled Low-Carb Bagels (cont.)

While the bagels are proofing, bring 10 cups (2.4 L) of water to a boil in a large pot. Remove the bagels from the oven, and turn it back on to 375°F (190°C) to preheat.

Using a slotted spoon, carefully lower two bagels at a time into the boiling water and boil them for 20 seconds on each side. Gently place them back on the baking sheet, being sure all water has drained. Repeat with the remaining bagels.

When all the bagels have been boiled, whisk together 1 egg and 1 teaspoon of water in a small bowl. Brush the egg wash over all the bagels, and add toppings of your choice if you wish.

Place the baking sheet into the preheated oven and bake for 20 to 22 minutes, until golden brown. Serve the bagels warm!

Store them in a sealed container at room temperature for 3 days. Heat up in the microwave or toast before serving for the best texture. They can also be stored in the freezer for up to 1 month.

Makes 8 pretzels

Boiled Low-Carb Soft Pretzels

Just like my Boiled Low-Carb Bagels (page 239) it was of utmost importance to me that my soft pretzels be boiled the traditional way. The baking soda water makes a big difference in giving them an authentic texture and flavor. With this comes the sacrifice of having a slightly higher carb count than other recipes you might find online. But, I can assure you, they are worth it, as you will end up with fluffy, chewy, authentic soft pretzels.

Nonstick spray

2 tbsp (30 ml) heavy cream

1 tbsp (15 ml) honey or maple syrup

1½ tsp (6 g) fast-acting instant yeast

2 cups (225 g) shredded mozzarella cheese

4 large eggs, divided

1 tsp psyllium husk powder

¾ tsp xanthan or guar gum

2 tsp (10 g) double-acting baking powder

6 tbsp (36 g) lupin flour

½ cup (61 g) cassava flour

¼ tsp Himalayan salt

½ cup (110 g) baking soda

Coarse sea salt or bagel seasoning blend, for topping

Set the oven to 200°F (95°C), and when it has preheated, turn off the oven; it will be used as a hot box to proof the dough.

Cover a baking sheet with a sheet of parchment paper and spray it with nonstick spray.

Add the heavy cream to a microwave-safe bowl or cup. Warm in the microwave for 10 to 15 seconds, until lukewarm. (It cannot be hot or it will kill the yeast.) Mix in the honey or maple syrup and the yeast and set aside.

Add the mozzarella cheese to a microwave-safe bowl and microwave on high for 1 minute so that it is partially melted on the edges of the bowl. Scrape the melted cheese into the bowl of a food processor. Add 3 of the eggs to the food processor and process until smooth. Add the psyllium husk powder, xanthan gum, baking powder, lupin flour, cassava flour and salt. At this point the yeast mixture should be a little bubbly. Add that to the food processor as well. Process until a super-thick, sticky dough forms and the ingredients are fully combined.

Generously oil your hands and a ⅓-cup (80–ml) measuring cup. Divide the dough into eight balls (about ⅓ cup [80 ml] each). Using oiled hands, roll out each ball to form 12-inch (30-cm) ropes about 1 inch (3 cm) thick. Gently fold the dough over itself to make a pretzel shape. Carefully place the formed pretzel on the prepared baking sheet. Repeat with all eight pieces. Cover the prepared pretzels with a towel and place them in the warm oven (that has been turned off) and leave the oven door open a crack. Set a timer for 30 minutes.

While the pretzels are proofing, bring 10 cups (2.4 L) of water to a boil in a large pot. Add the baking soda. Remove the pretzels from the oven, and turn it back on to 375°F (190°C) to preheat.

(continued)

Boiled Low-Carb Soft Pretzels (cont.)

Using a slotted spoon, carefully lower the pretzels in groups of two and boil for 25 to 30 seconds. Gently place the boiled pretzels back on the baking sheet, being sure all water has drained.

When all the pretzels have been boiled, whisk together 1 egg and 1 teaspoon of water in a small bowl. Brush the egg wash over all the pretzels, and sprinkle with the coarse salt.

Place the baking sheet in the preheated oven and bake for 20 to 22 minutes, until golden brown. Serve warm! Store in a sealed container at room temperature for 3 days. They can also be stored in the freezer for up to 1 month.

Recipe Note:

I have tried several brands of bagel seasoning and liked them all. However, the Balanced Bites Blend far surpassed the others in freshness and flavor. If you can get your hands on some, it will take these soft pretzels to another level.

Makes 9 full-sized buns or 12 slider buns

¾ cup (165 g) warm water

1 tbsp (16 g) honey or maple syrup

1 tbsp (12 g) fast-acting yeast

¾ cup (87 g) blanched almond flour

½ cup + 2 tbsp (50 g) oat fiber

½ cup + 2 tbsp (62 g) lupin flour

1 cup (150 g) flax meal

2 tbsp (32 g) psyllium husk powder

1½ tsp (5 g) xanthan or guar gum

1 tbsp (14 g) double-acting baking powder

¼ cup (48 g) vegetarian shortening, broken down into small pieces (I recommend Spectrum brand)

6 egg whites, chilled

2 tsp (6 g) cream of tartar

1 tsp Himalayan salt

1 tbsp (15 ml) apple cider vinegar

1 egg yolk

¼ cup (36 g) sesame seeds

Keto Hamburger Buns & Rolls

These dairy-free buns are surprisingly fluffy despite being low carb! This recipe can double as buns or rolls. For the best results, weigh all the ingredients.

Set the oven to 200°F (95°C), and when it has preheated, turn off the oven; it will be used as a hot box to proof the dough. Line a baking sheet with parchment paper.

Add the warm water, honey and yeast to a small bowl. Mix well, then set aside to allow the yeast to activate for about 10 minutes.

In a large bowl, mix the almond flour, oat fiber, lupin flour, flax meal, psyllium husk powder, xanthan gum and baking powder until well combined. Add the shortening and, using your fingers or a fork, combine the shortening and flour mixture until pea-sized pieces form; set aside.

In the bowl of a stand mixer or a large bowl, beat the chilled egg whites for 1 minute. Add the cream of tartar, salt and vinegar, then continue to beat until soft peaks form. Pour in the yeast mixture and half of the flour/shortening mixture. Using a spatula, carefully stir to blend, stirring just until the mixture is combined (the egg whites will collapse but that is okay). Add the second half of the flour/shortening mixture, and stir just until a smooth dough forms. Divide the dough into nine pieces for full-sized buns (about ⅓ cup [80 ml] each) or twelve pieces (about ¼ cup [60 ml] each) for sliders. Roll each piece of dough into a smooth ball and then press down just slightly (mimicking the shape of a hamburger). Place the dough on the prepared pan, spacing the pieces 1½ inches (4 cm) apart. Brush each piece of dough with a little water, then place a clean kitchen towel over the tray. Put the tray in the warm (but turned off) oven for 45 minutes to proof, leaving the door open a crack.

After the 45-minute proof, remove the tray from the oven and preheat the oven to 350°F (175°C). While the oven is preheating, whisk the egg yolk with 1 teaspoon of water. Gently brush the egg mixture over the buns and then sprinkle on the sesame seeds. Bake for 35 minutes until cooked through, firm to the touch and golden brown. Allow the buns to cool for 15 minutes and then slice in half with a bread knife and serve with your burger or sandwich of choice. Store in a sealed bag or container at room temperature for up to 4 days or store in a sealed container in the freezer for up to 1 month.

Perfect Low-Carb Chewy Gnocchi

NUT FREE VEGETARIAN

Makes 4 servings

Rich, my husband, has always loved gnocchi. I wanted to surprise him so I set out to learn how to make it, and in the last 14 years I have made it countless times. First with regular all-purpose flour, then gluten free, then grain free and now keto. To my surprise, the keto variation is his favorite and he thinks we need to package and sell this pasta. Making gnocchi is not challenging, and I highly recommend that you stop what you're doing and give this recipe a go right now!

2 cups (225 g) shredded mozzarella

2 large eggs

1¼ tsp (4 g) xanthan or guar gum

¼ tsp Himalayan salt

6 tbsp (36 g) lupin flour

6 tbsp (48 g) cassava flour, plus more for rolling

Oat fiber, for dusting

Place the mozzarella cheese in a microwave-safe bowl and microwave on high for about 1 minute. Stir the cheese and set aside for a few minutes to allow it to cool.

When the cheese is no longer extremely hot, add the eggs and xanthan gum to the bowl. Using an immersion blender, process until the mixture is smooth. (Note: This can also be done in a food processor.) Add the salt, lupin flour and cassava flour. Knead until the dough is smooth. The dough may still be a little bit wet and sticky at this point. Wrap the pasta dough in plastic wrap, or place in a sealed container and allow it to chill in the refrigerator for 1 hour.

When the pasta dough has chilled, it will be firm and easy to work with. Place a handful of oat fiber on your work surface. Cut the pasta dough into four equal pieces. One at a time, roll each section of pasta dough into a long snake-like shape, ½ to 1 inch (13 mm to 3 cm) thick. Slice each dough log into ½-inch (13-mm) pieces of dough. At this point the pasta can be cooked as is, or you can roll it on a gnocchi board or roll against a fork to get the classic grooved gnocchi appearance.

Bring a pot of water to a boil, and boil the pasta for 45 to 60 seconds. Remove from the pot and rinse under cold water. Serve with any sauce of choice.

Recipe Notes:

- This pasta can be stored in the refrigerator for several days prior to boiling, or it can be frozen. The pasta can be cooked from frozen, and will not require extra boiling time. Be careful not to overcook as the pasta may get soggy.

- The cheese does not need to melt entirely. After 1 minute, if it is only half melted that is okay—the recipe will still work.

Czech Low-Carb "Bread" Dumplings

2 tbsp (30 ml) heavy cream

1 tbsp (15 ml) real honey or maple syrup

2 tsp (8 g) fast-acting instant yeast

2 cups (225 g) shredded mozzarella

3 large eggs

1¼ tsp (4 g) xanthan or guar gum

¼ tsp Himalayan salt

6 tbsp (36 g) lupin flour

½ cup (61 g) cassava flour, plus more for rolling

Typically if you go to a Hungarian, Czech or European restaurant you will get to choose between spätzle or dumplings served with your meal. I love both, and was delighted when I finally figured out how to make both gluten free and much lower in carbohydrates than the regular versions. Truth be told, I don't think a half cup (61 g) of cassava flour is keto friendly, so consider this recipe a special-occasion treat. In order for the dumplings to hold up well when boiled, some starch was required. When made the authentic way, bread dumplings are made from mashed-up bread but I was able to mimic that texture exactly, without needing any bread. This recipe is dedicated to my Czech mother-in-law, Rosemary Wilder.

In a small microwave-safe bowl, combine the cream and honey. Microwave for 5 to 10 seconds, until lukewarm. (If it is too hot it will kill the yeast; if it is not warm enough the yeast will not activate.) Sprinkle in the yeast and mix. Set aside for 10 minutes until slightly foamy.

Set the oven to 200°F (95°C), and when it has preheated, turn off the oven; it will be used as a hot box to proof the dough.

Place the mozzarella cheese in a microwave-safe bowl and microwave on high for about 1 minute. Add the cheese to a food processor, then add the eggs and xanthan gum to the bowl. Process until the mixture is fully combined, then add the yeasted cream. Add the salt, lupin flour and cassava flour. Process until the dough is smooth. It may still be a little bit wet and sticky at this point. Place the dough into a bowl and cover with a towel to proof. Place the covered bowl into the warm oven. Leave the oven door open a crack and let the dough proof in the oven for 30 to 45 minutes.

After the dough has proofed, remove it from the oven. If it's a little sticky you can dust your work surface with more cassava flour. Cut the dough in half and gently roll each piece into 5- to 6-inch (13- to 15-cm) logs. Let the dough rest, and bring a pot of water to a rapid boil.

(continued)

Czech Low-Carb "Bread" Dumplings (cont.)

Add the dumpling dough logs carefully into the boiling water. Gently boil with a lid covering most of the pan (but allowing some steam to escape) for 6 to 8 minutes. Halfway through carefully flip the dumplings once.

Very carefully remove each piece of the boiled dough using two utensils to support it as much as possible and place on a cutting board. Allow the dough logs to cool for 20 to 30 minutes so they will firm up. Then, using a sharp knife (or dental floss) carefully cut each log into eight slices. Serve with the Chicken Paprikash with Spätzle (page 126) or Hungarian Beef Goulash (page 141).

Store in the refrigerator for 3 to 4 days.

Recipe Notes:

- When shaping the dough into logs, you can use oat fiber or cassava flour. The cassava contains carbs, but does give the dumplings the best texture possible. If you are trying to keep your carbs as low as possible, opt for the oat fiber instead—the dumplings will still turn out great.

- When forming into logs, do your best to make sure the dough is fully sealed; if not, knead it a little to smooth out any imperfections. Any tears in the dough will separate a bit during the boiling process.

Makes 4 servings

2 cups (225 g) shredded mozzarella

2 large eggs

1¼ tsp (4 g) xanthan or guar gum

¼ tsp Himalayan salt

6 tbsp (36 g) lupin flour

6 tbsp (48 g) cassava flour

Oat fiber, for dusting

Real Deal Low-Carb Fettuccine

I have made so many variations of pasta over the years—gluten free, vegan, grain free—and had much success. This recipe was the most challenging of them all, and took much trial and error. The end result is incredible—it tastes like real pasta. It will completely blow your mind!

The key to good pasta is starch, and I was able to work around that for the most part by using mozzarella cheese. I decided that including a bit of cassava flour was worth a slightly higher carb count. It makes the pasta easier to work with, and gives it the perfect texture, plus it allows the pasta to be boiled in water. I used a classic pasta crank machine to roll out my pasta, but feel free to just roll it out to the desired thickness by hand and to use a pizza cutter to cut it into strips.

Place the mozzarella cheese in a microwave-safe bowl and microwave on high for about 1 minute. Stir the cheese and set aside for a few minutes to allow it to cool.

When it is no longer extremely hot, add the eggs and xanthan gum to the bowl. Using an immersion blender, process until the mixture is smooth. (Note: This can also be done in a food processor.) Add the salt, lupin flour and cassava flour. Knead until the dough is smooth. It may still be a little bit wet and sticky at this point. Wrap the pasta dough in plastic wrap, or place in a sealed container and allow it to chill in the refrigerator for 1 hour.

After the pasta dough has chilled, it will be firm and easy to work with. Place a handful of oat fiber on your work surface. Cut the pasta dough into four equal pieces. Cover the dough in oat fiber and start putting it through the pasta press on the widest setting. Put some more oat fiber on the dough, and bend it over itself. Feed it through the machine again, and repeat as necessary until you end up with a smooth, rectangular piece of dough. You do not need to reduce the width of the pasta machine, as the largest width works perfectly for fettuccine. Alternatively, dust a piece of parchment with oat fiber, place the dough on it, and then cover with another sheet of parchment. Roll out to your desired thickness and cut the noodles with a pizza cutter. Repeat this process with the remaining three pieces of dough.

(continued)

Real Deal Low-Carb Fettuccine (cont.)

Carefully roll the prepared dough through the fettuccine setting on your pasta maker. Set aside the fettuccine on a sheet of parchment.

Bring a large pot of water to a rapid boil, and boil the pasta for 30 to 40 seconds. Remove from the pot and rinse under cold water. Serve with any sauce of your choice.

Recipe Note:

This pasta can be stored in the refrigerator for several days prior to boiling, or it can be frozen. The pasta can be cooked from frozen, and will not require extra boiling time. Be careful not to overcook this pasta as it may get soggy.

Makes 4 servings

2 cups (225 g) shredded mozzarella

3 large eggs

1¼ tsp (4 g) xanthan or guar gum

¼ tsp Himalayan salt

6 tbsp (36 g) lupin flour

6 tbsp (48 g) cassava flour

2 tbsp (10 g) oat fiber, plus more for dusting

Low-Carb German Spätzle

On my side of the family we have some German heritage, and on my husband's side there is a lot of Czech. Despite that, both he and I had never tried spätzle until about two years ago. Naturally we loved it. (Who doesn't?) I have come to love European comfort foods. I'm so thrilled to have figured out a healthier way to make this delicious pasta/dumpling. Make sure you have a spätzle maker (I snagged mine online). Make the Chicken Paprikash (page 126) or Hungarian Beef Goulash (page 141) to go with this recipe.

Place a pot of water on the stove, and let it come to a boil while preparing the dough.

Place the mozzarella cheese in a microwave-safe bowl and microwave on high for about 1 minute. Add the cheese to a food processor. Add the eggs and xanthan gum to the bowl. Process until the mixture is fully combined. Add the salt, lupin flour and cassava flour. Process until the dough is smooth. It may still be a little bit wet and sticky at this point. Remove the dough from the food processor and knead the oat fiber into it to make the dough less sticky.

Place the dough into the spätzle maker over boiling water (be very careful not to spill or dump the hot water on yourself). Every few seconds press down the dough farther as you grate it back and forth. During this process the dough will get sticky; add more oat fiber to it so that it does not stick to your hands.

Once all the spätzle has been grated in, cook it for about 30 seconds. Quickly pour it into a colander and rinse with cool water. Serve warm or store in the refrigerator for several days. (If storing in the refrigerator, I like mixing a little oil into it to keep it from sticking together.)

Recipe Note:

When melting the cheese, it does not need to melt 100%. Even if just partially melted it will work perfectly for this recipe.

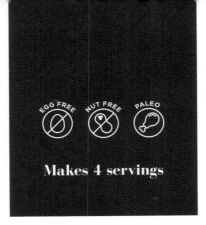

Makes 4 servings

2 lb (907 g) scallops

½ tsp Himalayan salt

½ tsp black pepper

6 tbsp + 1 tsp (90 g) salted butter, ghee or butter-flavored coconut oil, divided

2 lemon slices, squeezed

3 cloves garlic, minced

1¼ tbsp (2 g) bouquet garni (page 174), or preferred French herb mixture

2 (8-oz [227-g]) packages tofu shirataki, 1 batch Real Deal Low-Carb Fettuccine (page 251) or 2 spiralized zucchini or yellow squash

Lemon Herb Butter Scallop Scampi

This light but filling dish makes for a great summer meal when it's too hot to use the oven. Serve the scallop scampi on top of shirataki noodles, my Real Deal Low-Carb Fettuccine recipe (page 251) or your favorite spiralized vegetable noodle.

Pat the scallops dry with a paper towel to remove excess water, then sprinkle with the salt and pepper.

In a small saucepan over medium heat, melt 4 tablespoons (56 g) of butter, then add the lemon juice, garlic and bouquet garni. Bring the mixture to a simmer, then remove the pan from the heat and set aside.

Remove the tofu noodles from the packaging and rinse under cold water in a strainer. If you are using the Real Deal Low-Carb Fettuccine, follow the cooking directions in the recipe on page 251. If you are using spiralized vegetables, lay them out on a few layers of paper towels, then sprinkle them with a little kosher salt. Let them sit for 10 to 15 minutes, then press out the excess moisture. Sauté the spiralized vegetables in a pan with a teaspoon of your oil of choice over medium heat for a few minutes, until just cooked through.

When your preferred noodles are cooked, heat a large skillet over medium-high heat and add 2 tablespoons (28 g) butter or oil. Add the scallops to the skillet and sauté, about 5 minutes. Pour the butter mixture into the skillet containing the scallops and then add the noodles. Toss the ingredients together for 3 to 5 minutes. Serve hot.

Makes 8 to 10 servings

2 tbsp (28 g) salted butter or olive oil

2 large onions, chopped

1 lb (454 g) ground beef or ground sirloin

1 (28-oz [794-g]) can tomato purée

1 (28-oz [794-g]) can whole tomatoes

1 (28-oz [794-g]) can diced tomatoes

3 tbsp (30 g) garlic powder

1 tbsp (18 g) Himalayan salt

1 tsp black pepper

1 tbsp (2 g) dried parsley

1 tbsp (2 g) dried basil

1 tsp dried oregano

2 to 3 tbsp (30 to 45 ml) sugar-free honey or sugar-free maple syrup

Real Deal Low-Carb Fettuccine (page 251) or cooked zucchini noodles, to serve

"Marry Me" Sauce

When I met and moved in with my then-boyfriend, now-husband, I quickly learned that sauce was one of his favorites. At that point I didn't know how to cook a thing (in fact, he is the one who taught me how to cook chicken). But, being the Sicilian girl that I am, I figured I was up for the challenge. I spent a solid year making many variations and finally landed on what we jokingly refer to as "Marry Me Sauce". As soon as I mastered the recipe he proposed. Perhaps the two life events don't correlate, but knowing how much this man appreciates good food, I swear it's the sauce that landed me a lifetime commitment. I have made this recipe probably 300 times in the last 10 years and this is the very first time I'm putting this special and sacred part of our home into writing. I hope you enjoy it as much as we do.

In a large pot over medium heat, melt the butter, then add the onions and sauté for a few minutes, until the onions are translucent. Add the ground beef, break it up and continue stirring until the ground beef is fully cooked, about 8 minutes.

Add the tomato purée, whole tomatoes, diced tomatoes, garlic powder, salt, black pepper, parsley, basil and oregano. Depending on how sour your tomatoes are (I find organic canned tomatoes sometimes seem to have more acid), add the honey, starting with the smaller amount and adding a little at a time to taste as needed to balance out the flavor. Stir well, then cover the pot and simmer on low for an hour (or longer to develop the flavor further). Give it a final taste test and add a bit more salt if you want.

Serve over preferred noodles. Store in the refrigerator for up to 3 days or freeze for 1 month.

Recipe Note:

To really up the delicious factor, sauté some Italian sausage links in a skillet for a few minutes over high heat to sear and then add them to the pot to simmer in the sauce when you add the tomatoes. They will finish cooking while the sauce simmers. The combo of ground beef and sausage is about as good as it gets.

Substitution Notes:

- To make this **Paleo**, use 1½ tablespoons (23 ml) of real honey instead of the sugar-free honey and use the olive oil option.

- To make this **dairy free**, use the olive oil option.

**Makes 2 to 3 servings
per recipe**

Taco Spaghetti + Cilantro-Lime Avocado Pasta

If you own a spiralizer, these recipes are for you. Both use zucchini noodles. Although, if that's not your jam feel free to substitute shirataki noodles or even Real Deal Low-Carb Fettuccine (page 251). Both recipes make for fantastic weeknight meals.

Taco Spaghetti

1 tbsp (15 g) coconut oil

½ cup (80 g) chopped onion

1 tsp Himalayan salt, divided

½ lb (227 g) ground beef

1 tsp dried oregano

½ tsp black pepper

½ tsp ground cumin

½ tsp garlic powder

⅛ tsp cayenne pepper

1 (14.5-oz [411-g]) can diced tomatoes

1 (6.5-oz [184-g]) can sliced black olives, plus more for garnish

¼ cup (60 ml) beef broth

2 zucchini, spiralized

In a large skillet over medium–high heat, melt the coconut oil, then add the chopped onion and ¼ teaspoon of salt. Cook for 3 minutes, then add the ground beef and break it up into small pieces with a wooden spoon.

While the beef is cooking, add the oregano, ¾ teaspoon of salt, black pepper, cumin, garlic powder and cayenne pepper and stir to incorporate well. Cook the beef for 4 minutes, or until brown. Add the tomatoes, black olives and beef broth and allow the mixture to come to a simmer, then add the zucchini noodles and allow them to cook in the sauce for 3 to 5 minutes, or until tender.

Serve immediately, garnished with additional black olives if desired. Leftovers can be stored, covered, in the refrigerator for up to 3 days.

(continued)

Cilantro-Lime Avocado Pasta

1 large avocado, diced

½ small jalapeño, finely diced

¾ cup (40 g) fresh cilantro

1 tbsp (15 ml) lime juice

Zest of ½ lime

1 tsp garlic powder

¼ tsp Himalayan salt, plus more to taste

¼ tsp black pepper, plus more to taste

1 tbsp (15 g) coconut oil or butter

2 zucchini, spiralized

Lime wedges, for garnish

In a small food processor, pulse the avocado, jalapeño, cilantro, lime juice, lime zest, garlic powder, salt and black pepper until smooth and paste-like.

In a large skillet over medium–high heat, melt the coconut oil, then add the zucchini noodles, and a dash of salt and black pepper and allow to cook for 3 to 5 minutes, or until the zucchini noodles are tender.

When the noodles are tender, add the prepared avocado paste to the skillet and toss to coat. Serve immediately, garnished with lime wedges, if desired. Leftovers can be stored, covered, in the refrigerator for up to 3 days.

Makes 3 to 4 servings per recipe

Pasta Primavera + Pasta with Dairy-Free Vodka Sauce

These dishes are low carb/guilt free yet taste so indulgent. I'm usually not a big zucchini noodle person, but in these dishes I crave them all the time. The pasta primavera dish in particular really just tastes like the real thing to me. Note: if you prefer, you can use shirataki noodles or my Real Deal Low-Carb Fettuccine (page 251) instead of zucchini noodles. Note that zucchini noodles do thin out the sauce a bit.

Pasta Primavera

3 large carrots, peeled

1 large onion, chopped

1 yellow bell pepper, chopped

1 pint (300 g) cherry tomatoes, halved

1 yellow squash, chopped

¼ cup + 1½ tbsp (82 ml) olive oil, divided

½ tsp dried oregano

½ tsp dried basil

½ tsp dried thyme

½ tsp dried parsley

1 tsp black pepper

1 tsp Himalayan salt, plus more for taste

3 large zucchini

Shredded Parmesan or Romano cheese, for serving

Preheat the oven to 450°F (230°C). On a rimmed baking sheet, place the carrots, onion, pepper, cherry tomatoes and yellow squash, then drizzle the veggies with the ¼ cup (60 ml) of the olive oil and the oregano, basil, thyme, parsley, black pepper and salt. Place in the oven and roast for 30 minutes, stirring the vegetables a few times during the cook time.

While the veggies are roasting, spiralize the zucchini. Place the noodles into a skillet and sauté with 1½ tablespoons (22 ml) of olive oil and sprinkle with a little salt. Cook over medium heat for just a few minutes, until cooked through, being careful not to overcook as they will become soggy.

When the veggies are finished roasting, remove them from the oven and pour the contents of the pan into a large bowl. Toss with the zucchini noodles. Liberally sprinkle with the shredded cheese. Stays fresh in the refrigerator for up to 3 days.

Substitution Note:

To make this **dairy free** and **Paleo**, omit the cheese.

(continued)

Pasta with Dairy-Free Vodka Sauce

4 shallots, minced

2 tbsp (28 g) ghee, butter-flavored coconut oil or butter

½ cup (120 ml) plain vodka

1 cup (240 ml) tomato sauce

¾ cup (180 ml) unsweetened full-fat coconut milk

1¼ tsp (4 g) garlic powder

1 tsp onion powder

⅛ tsp red pepper flakes

1 tsp tapioca or arrowroot starch

Salt and pepper, to taste

3 large zucchini

1 tbsp (15 ml) avocado oil

In a saucepan over medium–low heat, combine the shallots and ghee and cook, stirring, until the shallots have caramelized. Pour in the vodka, tomato sauce, coconut milk, garlic powder, onion powder, red pepper flakes, tapioca and salt and pepper to taste. Whisk the sauce as it heats up and allow it to condense into a fairly thick tomato sauce. (You want it extra thick if using zucchini noodles as they will water it down.)

Spiralize the zucchini and sauté in a skillet over medium heat with the oil and a pinch of salt. Cook until the noodles are just tender (if you overcook they may get soggy). Toss the noodles with the vodka sauce and serve. Stays fresh in the refrigerator for up to 3 days.

EGG FREE **NUT FREE** **DAIRY FREE**

VEGETARIAN **PALEO**

Makes 6 servings

Dairy-Free Fettuccine Alfredo with Broccoli

This alfredo recipe is so amazing you will forget that it's dairy free! Pour this sauce over Real Deal Low-Carb Fettuccine (page 251) or gnocchi, add some broccoli and you've got a perfect light dish. Shirataki fettuccine-style noodles can also be used for this recipe, just be sure to give them a good rinse before mixing them with sauce.

1 cup (240 ml) unsweetened full-fat coconut milk (from a can)

2 tbsp (28 g) ghee or butter-flavored coconut oil

1 tsp tapioca or arrowroot starch

Himalayan salt, to taste

¼ tsp black pepper

1 tsp garlic powder

1 tsp onion powder

½ tsp mushroom powder (I recommend Nom Nom Paleo brand)

1 batch Real Deal Low-Carb Fettuccine (page 251) or 1 (8-oz [227-g]) bag tofu shirataki noodles

2 cups (310 g) broccoli, steamed

In a saucepan, combine the coconut milk, ghee, tapioca starch, salt, black pepper, garlic powder, onion powder and mushroom powder. Bring it to a low boil and make sure everything is well mixed.

Boil the fettuccine or pasta of your choice, drain and top with the alfredo sauce and broccoli. Serve or store in a sealed container in the refrigerator for up to 3 days.

Recipe Note:

If you can have dairy you can use heavy cream instead of coconut milk and butter instead of ghee.

Snacks and Appetizers

This chapter is a glorious one filled with some of my favorite bar foods, such as chips and dips, burgers, sliders and wings galore. This chapter also includes delicious handheld appetizers, such as frittata cups, empanadas and samosas, which are perfect for snacking while socializing during a party.

← See recipe on page 273.

EGG FREE   NUT FREE

DAIRY FREE   VEGETARIAN

Makes 6 to 8 servings

2 tbsp (6 g) dried dill

2 tbsp (3 g) dried parsley

1 tsp onion powder

1 tsp garlic powder

1 tsp ground mustard

¼ to ½ cup (60 to 120 ml) oil of choice

2 to 3 large zucchini

2 tsp (12 g) kosher salt

Ranch Dressing (page 209), to serve

Ranch Zucchini Chips

I could eat these zucchini chips all day long. When you get all the water out of the zucchini slices, they fry up just like kettle-cooked potato chips and give a satisfying crunch.

To make the seasoning, combine the dill, parsley, onion powder, garlic powder and mustard in a small bowl.

To make the chips, pour oil into a large skillet to a depth of 1 to 2 inches (3 to 5 cm). Heat the oil over medium-high heat.

Meanwhile, slice the zucchini with a mandoline on the thinnest setting, about ⅛ inch (3 mm). Place the sliced zucchini in a colander. Sprinkle with the salt, toss the zucchini and allow it to rest for 5 minutes. The salt will draw out the water in the zucchini and allow it to crisp.

Next, lay out some paper towels on a baking sheet. Working in batches, lay out the zucchini on the paper towels and press out any excess water. Then place the zucchini in a medium bowl. Add the ranch seasoning to the zucchini. Toss to coat evenly. You may not use all of the ranch seasoning.

Working in batches, add the zucchini chips to the skillet (see Recipe Notes). Fry the chips for 2 to 3 minutes a side, then flip and fry for another 2 to 3 minutes. The chips should curl at the edges and turn golden brown. Remove the chips from the skillet and place on a paper towel-lined baking sheet to dry. They will begin to crisp as they cool. Add extra ranch seasoning to taste and serve with some Ranch Dressing. These chips are best eaten the same day you make them.

Recipe Notes:

- Don't crowd the skillet: The zucchini chips should float easily and bubble along all sides.

- Start the timer after the last piece of each batch is placed in the skillet; also start the timer after the last piece has been flipped. Cooking time may vary depending on the size and thickness of the slices.

Substitution Note:

To make this *Paleo*, use avocado oil for frying.

EGG FREE · NUT FREE · DAIRY FREE · VEGETARIAN

Makes 2 to 3 cups (52 to 78 g)

1½ cups (150 g) lupin flour

1 tsp Himalayan salt

1 tsp cumin powder

¼ tsp black pepper

¾ tsp double-acting baking powder

6 tbsp (90 ml) oil (coconut, avocado or olive oil)

6 tbsp (90 ml) hot water

Keto Tortilla Chips

These chips are very quick to make and will hold up perfectly dipped in my Dairy-Free Chili con Queso (page 278) or Dairy-Free White Queso (page 281)—or whatever dip you prefer.

Preheat the oven to 375°F (190°C). Cut two sheets of parchment paper to fit the size of your baking sheets and have another piece of parchment paper on hand; set aside.

In a medium bowl, combine the lupin flour, salt, cumin, black pepper and baking powder. Add the oil and hot water. Stir with a spoon and then knead with your hands briefly to bring the dough together.

Divide the dough in half and roll each half out as thin as possible between two sheets of parchment, using one of the two pieces of parchment you cut to fit your baking sheet as the bottom sheet of parchment. Cut the dough into triangles using a pizza cutter, leaving the dough on the bottom sheet of parchment. Carefully transfer the parchment to the baking sheet. Bake for 7 to 9 minutes, until perfectly golden brown.

While the first batch is baking, roll out the second half of the dough using another of the sheets of parchment you precut as the bottom piece. Repeat the rolling and cutting instructions above. Bake the second tray after removing the first.

Store any leftovers in an airtight container for up to 4 days.

Keto Cheezits

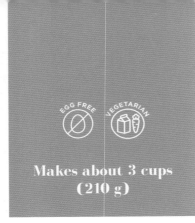

Years ago I created a cheezits recipe that was crunchy but used tapioca starch to get the crunch. Coming up with a lower carb version meant that I would need to rely on the cheese to get the crackers crisp—which worked! The texture is slightly different than cheezits from the store because they are low carb, but they are still quite delicious.

Makes about 3 cups (210 g)

¾ cup (87 g) blanched almond flour

½ cup (50 g) lupin flour

1 tsp double-acting baking powder

½ tsp Himalayan salt

1½ cups (170 g) shredded sharp cheddar

2 tbsp (30 ml) hot water

Preheat the oven to 315°F (157°C). Have on hand two baking sheets. Cut two sheets of parchment paper to fit the baking sheets and have another sheet of parchment paper on hand; set aside.

In a stand mixer, mix the almond flour, lupin flour, baking powder and salt until fully combined. Add the cheddar and water and continue mixing until a dough forms. Almond flour slowly releases fat and moisture as you mix it, so it may take longer than you would expect for the dough to come together.

Divide the dough in half. Roll out half of the dough between two sheets of parchment paper into a rectangle about 12 x 17 inches (30 x 44 cm) and about ¹⁄₁₆ inch (1 mm) thick. Using a knife or pizza cutter, cut the dough into ½-inch (13-mm) squares. (Do not separate the squares.) Slide the piece of parchment paper with the dough squares onto the baking sheet. Repeat the process with the second half of the dough.

Bake for 20 to 25 minutes. The exact time will vary depending on the thickness of your dough. When the crackers are done they will be firm and crispy. (Try a bite, they should be crispy all the way through.) Break the crackers along the seams you cut and let the crackers cool on the baking sheet. Store the cooled crackers in a sealed bag or container at room temperature for up to 1 week.

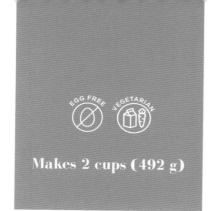

EGG FREE · VEGETARIAN

Makes 2 cups (492 g)

1 eggplant, cubed

½ red bell pepper, diced

1½ tbsp (22 ml) avocado oil, plus 1 tbsp (15 ml) (optional)

4 cloves garlic

1 tsp dried thyme

1 tbsp (15 ml) lemon juice

1 tbsp (8 g) za'atar spice

½ cup (120 g) Homemade Cashew Yogurt (page 492) or Greek yogurt

2 tbsp (30 g) tahini paste

Himalayan salt, to taste

Roasted Eggplant Za'atar Dip

Bring something different to your next gathering. This zesty dip is simple but a crowd-pleaser. Feel free to substitute the Greek yogurt for my Homemade Cashew Yogurt (page 492).

Preheat the oven to 400°F (205°C). Line a baking sheet with parchment paper.

Toss the eggplant, red bell pepper, oil and garlic together and then place on the prepared baking sheet. Roast for 20 to 30 minutes, or until the eggplant is golden brown. Remove the baking sheet from the oven and let cool.

Add the garlic, thyme, lemon juice, za'atar spice, yogurt, tahini and the cooled vegetables to a food processor and blend until smooth. Feel free to add a tablespoon (15 ml) of avocado oil to help the ingredients blend. Add salt to taste.

Serve hot or cold, with Ranch Zucchini Chips (page 270), Keto Tortilla Chips (page 273) or Keto Cheezits (page 274).

Substitution Note:

To make this **dairy free**, use dairy-free yogurt.

**Makes 3 to 4 cups
(759 g to 1 kg)**

Dairy-Free Chili con Queso

Fool your friends and family with this dairy-free queso recipe at your next get-together. The ooey gooey cheesy texture in this recipe makes a perfect healthy comfort food that will have all of your friends and family talking.

Homemade Almond Milk

3¾ cups (0.9 L) water

1½ packed cups (180 g) blanched almond flour

Queso

1½ cups (360 ml) Homemade Almond Milk (see Recipe Notes)

1 (10-oz [283-g]) can diced tomatoes with green chiles, strained

1 cup (240 g) refined coconut oil (see Recipe Notes)

5 tbsp (38 g) nutritional yeast

1 tsp onion powder

½ tsp garlic powder

½ tsp cumin

¾ tsp turmeric

1½ tsp (7 g) mushroom powder (see Recipe Notes)

Pinch of cayenne powder

Pinch of black pepper

½ to 1 tsp Himalayan salt (see Recipe Notes)

To make the almond milk, add the water and almond flour to a blender. Blend on high until completely smooth. Set aside.

To make the queso, pour 1½ cups (360 ml) of the almond milk into a saucepan (save any leftovers for another use; see Recipe Notes). Add the tomatoes, coconut oil, nutritional yeast, onion powder, garlic powder, cumin, turmeric, mushroom powder, cayenne, black pepper and salt to taste. Whisk over medium–low heat until the sauce reaches your preferred thickness. Be sure not to let the mixture boil or the sauce will break up and lose its gooey texture.

Serve warm with pork rinds or Ranch Zucchini Chips (page 270), Keto Tortilla Chips (page 273) or Keto Cheezits (page 274). Store any leftover queso in a sealed container in the refrigerator for up to 1 week. You can reheat it over medium–low heat in a saucepan or in the microwave, stirring it every 20 to 30 seconds until fully warmed. If you are Paleo, try this queso with cassava flour tortilla chips available in most health food stores.

Recipe Notes:

• Be sure to use the Homemade Almond Milk recipe provided with this recipe because homemade, unstrained almond milk has thickening properties you won't find with commercial varieties.

• The mushroom powder can be found at Whole Foods or on Nom Nom Paleo's website. If you are having trouble finding the mushroom powder, it can be left out, but you may need to increase the salt in the queso (to taste).

• Use ¾ cup (180 g) of coconut oil for a thicker queso. If the queso gets too thick, you can thin it out by adding 1 to 2 more tablespoons (15 to 30 ml) of water. Do not add more milk, as it will change the texture and flavor.

• If you want your queso thicker, blanched almond flour can be added 1 tablespoon (15 g) at a time. Whisk and gently simmer for a few minutes before adding more.

Makes 3 to 4 cups (720 to 960 g)

Homemade Almond Milk

3¾ cups (0.9 L) water

1½ packed cups (180 g) blanched almond flour

Queso

1½ cups (360 ml) Homemade Almond Milk (see Recipe Notes)

2 (4-oz [113-g]) cans diced green chiles, strained

1 cup (240 g) refined coconut oil (see Recipe Notes)

5 tbsp (38 g) nutritional yeast

1 tsp onion powder

½ tsp garlic powder

½ tsp cumin

1½ tsp (7 g) mushroom powder (see Recipe Notes)

Pinch of cayenne powder

Pinch of black pepper

½ to 1 tsp Himalayan salt (see Recipe Notes)

Dairy-Free White Queso

Just like the Dairy-Free Chili con Queso (page 278), this recipe will wow your party guests!

To make the almond milk, add the water and almond flour to a blender. Blend on high until completely smooth. Set aside.

To make the queso, pour 1½ cups (360 ml) of the almond milk into a saucepan (save any leftovers for another use; see Recipe Notes). Add the green chiles, coconut oil, nutritional yeast, onion powder, garlic powder, cumin, mushroom powder, cayenne, black pepper and salt to taste. Whisk consistently over medium–low heat until it's your preferred thickness.

Serve warm with pork rinds or Ranch Zucchini Chips (page 270), Keto Tortilla Chips (page 273) or Keto Cheezits (page 274). Store any leftover queso in a sealed container in the refrigerator for up to 1 week. You can reheat it over medium–low heat in a saucepan or in the microwave, stirring it every 20 to 30 seconds until fully warmed. If you are Paleo, try this queso with cassava flour tortilla chips available in most health food stores.

Recipe Notes:

- Be sure to use the Homemade Almond Milk recipe provided with this recipe because homemade, unstrained almond milk has thickening properties you won't find with commercial varieties.

- The mushroom powder can be found at Whole Foods or on Nom Nom Paleo's website. If you are having trouble finding the mushroom powder, it can be left out, but you may need to increase the salt in the queso (to taste).

- Use ¾ cup (180 g) of coconut oil for a thicker queso. If the queso gets too thick, you can thin it out by adding 1 to 2 more tablespoons (15 to 30 ml) of water. Do not add more milk, as it will change the texture and flavor.

- If you want your queso thicker, blanched almond flour can be added 1 tablespoon (15 g) at a time. Whisk and gently simmer for a few minutes before adding more.

Makes 8 dosas

Indian Dosas with Aloo Gobi Filling

This recipe is truly spot on. I feel confident it could be served at any Indian restaurant and no one would know that it was low carb. The texture of the dosas is perfect—crispy on the edges and soft enough to roll up. You may find it odd that there is mozzarella cheese in the base of the batter but I can assure you that you will not taste it in the finished recipe. It plays an important role in creating the crispiness of the dosas while also binding the batter together. Classic Aloo Gobi is made with cauliflower and potatoes. To reduce the carb count, I swapped potatoes for celery root and the results couldn't have been better. You will love everything from the perfect crepe-like bread to the buttery, flavor-packed filling. For the best results use the gram measurements.

Dosas

1 cup (116 g) blanched almond flour

1 cup (113 g) shredded mozzarella

½ cup (120 ml) heavy cream or half-and-half

5 egg whites

½ tsp Himalayan salt

⅛ tsp black pepper

2 tsp (8 g) ground cumin

To make the dosas, add the almond flour, mozzarella, cream, egg whites, salt, pepper and cumin to the bowl of a food processor. Process until the batter is completely smooth and thin. Preheat an 8-inch (20-cm) nonstick skillet (or very well-seasoned cast-iron skillet) over medium–low heat and preheat. Do not oil the skillet.

Pour 2 tablespoons (30 ml) of the dosa batter into the center of the preheated pan, then quickly pick up the pan and turn it so that the batter spreads thinly across the bottom into a circular shape. You can also give the pan a shake or tap it on the counter to help it spread. Note: If your batter is too thick to spread out easily, add a bit more cream (1 tablespoon [15 ml] or more as needed until it reaches the right consistency). You could also use a crepe pan and tool to spread the batter.

Let the batter cook for 30 to 60 seconds, until the edges are golden brown. Using a thin fish spatula, gently pull up the edges of the dosa until you can easily slide the spatula under the entire dosa and then flip. Cook for 30 to 60 seconds on the other side and then set aside on a plate. Repeat with the remaining batter to make seven more dosas.

(continued)

Indian Dosas with Aloo Gobi Filling (cont.)

Aloo Gobi Filling

1 large celery root or 2 small ones

Chicken or vegetable broth, or water, for boiling

3 cups (375 g) fresh or frozen cauliflower florets, roughly chopped

8 tbsp (112 g) salted butter or ghee

1½-inch (4-cm) piece of fresh ginger, finely minced or grated

2 tsp (4 g) cumin seeds

2 tsp (8 g) powdered coriander

¼ tsp turmeric

¼ tsp black pepper

1 to 1¼ tsp (6 to 7.5 g) pink Himalayan salt to taste

To make the filling, peel and cube the celery root. Place the cubes into a medium saucepan and add enough chicken or vegetable broth or water to cover. Bring to a gentle boil and cook for 10 minutes, until fork tender. Add the cauliflower to the pot and boil for another 5 minutes, until the cauliflower is also fork tender. Strain, and set the vegetables aside.

To the same saucepan you used for the vegetables, add the butter, ginger, cumin seeds, coriander, turmeric, pepper and salt. Cook the butter and spices over medium–low heat until the spices are toasted and fragrant and the butter is melted. Be careful not to burn the mixture. Add the vegetables back to the pot and stir everything together, then mash the vegetables until you reach your desired consistency. Keep the heat on and continue to cook the aloo gobi another 10 to 15 minutes, stirring every so often.

To serve, warm up the dosas in a small skillet with a little bit of butter (or microwave them). Place ¼ cup (60 g) of the aloo gobi filling into each dosa and serve hot. Store everything in the refrigerator, covered, for up to 3 to 4 days.

Substitution Notes:

- To make this **nut free**, swap the almond flour for finely ground pumpkin seed or sunflower seed flour.

- To make this **vegetarian**, use vegetable broth or water to boil the vegetables.

Frittata Cups Four Ways

NUT FREE

Makes 6 frittata cups per recipe

If you're looking for recipes that are easy and can be made ahead to keep your eating on track, look no further. Each of these frittatas is bursting with flavor. They are perfect to grab from the refrigerator to eat in the car on a busy morning. They make keto easier, which is a huge win in my book. When you're busy and hungry it can be hard to stick to a keto diet, so keeping a batch of these in the refrigerator really helps.

Pizza Frittata Cups

4 large eggs

½ cup (55 g) shredded mozzarella

¼ cup (35 g) chopped pepperoni

½ small onion, diced

3 tbsp (45 ml) tomato sauce

¼ tsp dried parsley

¼ tsp garlic powder

¼ tsp dried basil

¼ tsp Himalayan salt

Preheat the oven to 350°F (175°C). Lightly grease 6 wells of a muffin tin. Set aside.

In a medium bowl, whisk the eggs until frothy, then stir in the mozzarella, pepperoni, onion, tomato sauce, parsley, garlic powder, basil and salt. Pour into the prepared cups and bake for 40 to 45 minutes on the middle rack in the oven, until puffy and cooked through. Store in the refrigerator for up to 3 days, or freeze in a sealed container for up to a month.

Corned Beef Hash Frittata Cups

4 large eggs

½ small onion, diced

½ cup (70 g) cooked and chopped corned beef

½ cup (55 g) shredded mozzarella

½ tsp garlic powder

⅛ tsp black pepper

Preheat the oven to 350°F (175°C). Lightly grease 6 wells of a muffin tin. Set aside.

In a medium bowl, whisk the eggs until frothy, then stir in the onion, corned beef, mozzarella, garlic powder and black pepper. Pour into the prepared cups and bake for 40 to 45 minutes on the middle rack in the oven until puffy and cooked through. Store in the refrigerator for up to 3 days, or freeze in a sealed container for up to a month.

(continued)

Taco Frittata Cups

4 large eggs

½ small onion, diced

½ cup (115 g) cooked or raw ground beef

½ cup (50 g) chopped bell peppers

½ cup (55 g) shredded cheddar cheese

⅛ tsp cumin

¼ tsp Himalayan salt

¼ tsp chili powder

¼ tsp garlic powder

Pinch of cayenne

Preheat the oven to 350°F (175°C). Lightly grease 6 wells of a muffin tin. Set aside.

In a medium bowl, whisk the eggs until frothy, then stir in the onion, ground beef, peppers, cheese, cumin, salt, chili powder, garlic powder and cayenne. Pour into the prepared cups and bake for 40 to 45 minutes on the middle rack in the oven until puffy and cooked through. Store in the refrigerator for up to 3 days, or freeze in a sealed container for up to a month.

Greek-Style Frittata Cups

4 large eggs

½ small onion, diced

⅓ cup (80 g) feta cheese

¼ cup (34 g) chopped olives

½ cup (50 g) diced bell pepper (optional)

¼ tsp dried oregano

¼ tsp garlic powder

¼ tsp Himalayan salt

2 tsp (4 g) lemon zest

1 tbsp (15 ml) olive oil

Preheat the oven to 350°F (175°C). Lightly grease 6 wells of a muffin tin. Set aside.

In a medium bowl, whisk the eggs until frothy, then stir in the onion, feta, olives, bell pepper (optional), oregano, garlic powder, salt, lemon zest and olive oil. Pour into the prepared cups and bake for 40 to 45 minutes on the middle rack in the oven until puffy and cooked through. Store in the refrigerator for up to 3 days, or freeze in a sealed container for up to a month.

Substitution Note:

To make these *dairy free* and *Paleo*, omit the cheese.

Makes 24 empanadas and 12 samosas

Hearty Beef Empanadas + Celery Root Samosas with Cumin

These incredibly delicious appetizers are perfect for almost any crowd. Your friends and family will be blown away when you tell them these recipes are keto as they taste like the real deal in every way. These empanadas would taste delicious dipped in salsa too.

Empanadas

4 tbsp (54 g) butter or coconut oil

1 small onion, diced

2 cloves garlic, minced

1 lb (454 g) ground beef

½ tsp ground cumin

½ tsp Himalayan salt

½ tsp black pepper

½ tsp chipotle chili powder

½ tsp chili powder

⅛ tsp cayenne pepper

Oat fiber, for dusting

2 batches Perfectly Flaky Piecrust (page 410)

Melted coconut oil or butter, for brushing

Preheat the oven to 350°F (175°C). Line a baking sheet with parchment paper.

In a large skillet over medium heat, add the butter and when melted, add the onion and garlic and cook for 3 minutes, until soft. Add the ground beef to the skillet and cook until brown, 5 to 7 minutes, breaking up the meat with a wooden spoon. When the meat is cooked, add the cumin, salt, pepper, chipotle chili powder, chili powder and cayenne pepper; remove from the heat and stir to combine.

Dust a piece of parchment paper with oat fiber and roll out the piecrust dough to about ⅛ inch (3 mm) thick and cut into 3-inch (8-cm) rounds. Be cautious not to overuse the oat fiber or it will make your empanadas a bit dry. Just a small dusting should be all that you need. Place 1½ tablespoons (25 g) of filling into the center of each round of dough, then fold in half, crimping the edges shut with a fork.

Place the empanadas on the prepared baking sheet and brush each with a small amount of oil. Place the baking sheet in the oven and bake for 15 to 18 minutes, until golden brown and crispy. Serve immediately. Store in a sealed container in the refrigerator for up to 3 to 4 days.

(continued)

Samosas

1 large celery root, peeled and diced

4 tbsp (56 g) butter or coconut oil

1 small onion, diced

¼ cup (22 g) diced jalapeño pepper (seeds removed)

¼ cup (35 g) frozen peas

1 tbsp (6 g) freshly grated ginger

½ tsp Himalayan salt

½ tsp garam masala

Oat fiber, for dusting

1 batch Perfectly Flaky Piecrust (page 410)

Melted coconut oil or butter, for brushing

Preheat the oven to 350°F (175°C). Line a baking sheet with parchment paper.

To a medium saucepan, add the celery root and enough water to cover. Bring to a boil and cook until the celery root is fork tender, about 7 minutes, then drain and set aside.

In a large skillet over medium heat, melt the butter, then add the onion and jalapeño and cook until soft, about 5 minutes. Add the frozen peas, ginger, salt and garam masala, and cook for an additional 3 minutes. Turn off the heat and add the celery root to the pan, then mash with a potato masher and stir to combine.

Dust a piece of parchment paper with oat fiber and roll out the piecrust dough to about ⅛ inch (3 mm) thick and cut into 3-inch (8-cm) rounds. Place 1½ tablespoons (25 g) of filling into the center of each round of dough, then fold in half, crimping the edges shut with a fork. Place the samosas on the prepared baking sheet and brush each with a small amount of oil. Place the baking sheet in the oven and bake for 18 minutes.

Serve immediately with dipping sauce or side of your choice, or allow to cool and place in an airtight bag and freeze for up to 1 month.

Recipe Note:

Be cautious not to overuse the oat fiber or it will make your empanadas and samosas a bit dry. Just a small dusting will be sufficient in keeping the dough from sticking.

Substitution Notes:

- To make these recipes *dairy free*, use ghee or butter-flavored coconut oil.

- To make these recipes *Paleo*, use a Paleo piecrust such as my Paleo copycat "Pillsbury" crust on BrittanyAngell.com.

Burgers or Sliders in Six Flavors

Burgers are just one of those staples that will never go out of style. Everybody craves them—even vegetarians and vegans—so I also included a really delicious falafel burger. All six flavors are delicious, but I have to say my personal favorites are the Blackberry Brie Burgers as well as the Sausage Bourbon Bacon BBQ Burgers (page 295). Feel free to serve these with or without the buns. There is a keto bun recipe on page 245 or to keep things simple (and healthy), they all taste great wrapped in Boston lettuce.

Blackberry Brie Burgers

NUT FREE

Burgers

1 lb (454 g) ground beef

1½ cups (225 g) chopped blackberries

½ cup (80 g) finely minced onion

6 slices cooked bacon, chopped, plus more for serving

1 tsp Himalayan salt

½ tsp black pepper

1 (7-oz [196-g]) wheel of Brie, cut into 1-inch (3-cm) cubes (or ½-inch [13-mm] cubes for sliders)

Smoky Blackberry Sauce

1 cup (150 g) chopped blackberries

1 tbsp (16 g) tomato paste

1 tsp liquid smoke

2 tbsp (30 ml) sugar-free maple syrup

¼ tsp tapioca or arrowroot starch

In a medium bowl, mix together the ground beef, chopped blackberries, onion, bacon, salt and pepper. Gently mix until the mixture comes together. Do not overmix or your burgers will be tough. Form the mixture into 6 larger patties or 12 slider-sized patties. Press one cube of Brie into the center of each burger, covering it entirely with meat. Heat a skillet (cast iron preferably) until it is scalding hot and then place the burgers in the pan and cook for 2 to 4 minutes on each side (cook a total of 4 minutes for medium burgers, and 8 minutes total for well-done burgers).

Set the burgers aside to rest and make the smoky blackberry sauce. In a small saucepan over medium heat, combine the blackberries, tomato paste, liquid smoke, maple syrup and tapioca. Cook until the sauce becomes syrupy. Douse the burgers in the sauce, another slice of Brie and some bacon.

Recipe Notes:

- If you would like the sauce a bit sweeter, add ¼ teaspoon of stevia or monk fruit extract.

- Use fresh, dry blackberries for the best results.

Substitution Notes:

- To make this *dairy free*, omit the Brie.

- To make this *Paleo*, omit the cheese and substitute real maple syrup.

(continued)

Buffalo Chicken Burgers

1 lb (454 g) ground chicken or turkey

⅔ cup (106 g) chopped onion

½ cup (50 g) finely minced celery

1 tsp Himalayan salt

¼ to ½ cup (60 to 120 g) crumbled blue cheese (see Recipe Note), plus more for serving

1 tsp paprika

¼ tsp cayenne powder

¼ cup (60 ml) hot sauce, plus more for serving

Thin slices of celery, for serving

Lettuce, for serving (optional)

Sliced tomatoes, for serving (optional)

Gently mix the chicken, onion, celery, salt, cheese, paprika, cayenne and hot sauce until the mixture comes together. Do not overmix or your burgers will be tough. Form the mixture into 6 larger patties or 12 slider-sized patties. Heat a skillet (cast iron preferably) until it is scalding hot and then place the burgers in the pan and cook for 2 to 4 minutes on each side (cook for a total of 4 minutes for medium burgers, and 8 minutes total for well-done burgers).

Assemble the burgers with more blue cheese, a drizzle of hot sauce, the celery slices and the lettuce and tomato (if using).

Recipe Note:

Use the higher amount of blue cheese if you like a strong blue cheese flavor.

Substitution Note:

To make this *dairy free* and *Paleo*, omit the blue cheese.

Chicken Eggplant Basil Burgers

1 lb (454 g) ground chicken or turkey

2 cups (164 g) diced eggplant

½ cup (80 g) chopped onion

1 tsp garlic powder

1 tsp Himalayan salt

½ tsp black pepper

1 cup (24 g) fresh basil, finely chopped

Lettuce, for serving

Sliced onion, for serving

Sliced mozzarella or white cheddar cheese, for serving

In a medium bowl, mix together the chicken, eggplant, onion, garlic powder, salt, black pepper and basil. Gently mix until the mixture comes together. Do not overmix or your burgers will be tough. Form the mixture into 6 larger patties or 12 slider-sized patties. Heat a skillet (cast iron preferably) until it is scalding hot and then place the burgers in the pan and cook for 2 to 4 minutes on each side (cook for a total of 4 minutes for medium burgers, and 8 minutes total for well-done burgers).

Assemble the burgers with the lettuce, onion and cheese.

Recipe Note:

If you want to get fancy, grilled or sautéed eggplant sprinkled with salt makes a delicious topping.

Substitution Note:

To make this *dairy free* and *Paleo*, omit the cheese.

Sausage Bourbon Bacon BBQ Burgers

1 lb (454 g) Italian sausage (removed from casings if you are using links)

8 slices cooked bacon, chopped, plus more for topping

½ cup (80 g) minced onion

2 tbsp (32 g) tomato paste

½ tsp Himalayan salt

½ tsp black pepper

2 tbsp (30 ml) liquid smoke

¼ cup (55 g) keto brown sugar

¼ cup (60 ml) bourbon

2 tsp (10 ml) apple cider vinegar

Lettuce, for serving

Sliced onion, for serving

Sliced mozzarella or white cheddar cheese, for serving

In a medium bowl, mix together the Italian sausage, bacon, onion, tomato paste, salt, pepper, liquid smoke, sugar, bourbon and vinegar. Gently mix until the mixture comes together. Do not overmix or your burgers will be tough. Form the mixture into 6 larger patties or 12 slider-sized patties.

Heat a skillet (cast iron preferably) until it is scalding hot and then place the burgers in the pan and cook for 2 to 4 minutes on each side (cook for a total of 4 minutes for medium burgers, and 8 minutes total for well-done burgers).

Assemble the burgers with lettuce, onion, cheese and bacon.

Substitution Note:

To make this *dairy free* and *Paleo*, omit the cheese.

Jalapeño Popper Sausage Burgers

1 lb (454 g) Italian sausage

½ cup (80 g) minced onion

1½ jalapeños, minced (and seeded if you prefer less spicy burgers)

½ tsp Himalayan salt

½ tsp black pepper

2 cups (225 g) shredded mozzarella, plus more for serving

Lettuce, for serving

Sliced onion, for serving

Sliced or chopped cooked bacon, for serving

In a medium bowl, mix together the Italian sausage, onion, jalapeños, salt, pepper and mozzarella. Gently mix until the mixture comes together. Do not overmix or your burgers will be tough. Form the mixture into 6 larger patties or 12 slider-sized patties.

Heat a skillet (cast iron preferably) until it is scalding hot and then place the burgers in the pan and cook for 2 to 4 minutes on each side (cook for a total of 4 minutes for medium burgers, and 8 minutes total for well-done burgers).

Assemble the burgers with lettuce, onion, additional cheese and bacon.

Substitution Note:

To make this *dairy free* and *Paleo*, omit the cheese.

(continued)

Crispy Vegetarian Falafel

Falafel Burgers

1 (1-lb [454-g]) bag frozen cauliflower florets, thawed

1 tbsp (6 g) cumin

1½ tsp (9 g) Himalayan salt

2 tsp (5 g) garlic powder

2 tsp (5 g) onion powder

1 tsp paprika

6 tbsp (20 g) fresh chopped cilantro

2½ cups (290 g) blanched almond flour

½ cup (46 g) garbanzo bean flour

Avocado oil, for brushing

Lettuce, for serving

Sliced cucumbers, for serving

Sliced tomatoes, for serving

Dairy-free unsweetened yogurt, for serving

Crispy Coating

2½ tbsp (14 g) garbanzo bean flour

¼ cup (29 g) blanched almond flour

½ tsp garlic powder

¼ tsp cumin

¼ tsp Himalayan salt

¼ tsp paprika

Preheat the oven to 425°F (220°C) and line a baking sheet with parchment paper.

To make the burgers, add the cauliflower to a food processor and pulse until the cauliflower is the size of rice. Add the cumin, salt, garlic powder, onion powder, paprika and cilantro and pulse until mixed. Add the almond flour and garbanzo bean flour and pulse again to mix. Form the mixture into 8 to 10 full-sized patties or 15 mini sliders.

To make the crispy coating, in a small bowl, mix the garbanzo bean flour, almond flour, garlic powder, cumin, salt and paprika. Roll the patties in the coating. Place the coated burgers on the baking sheet and brush liberally with avocado oil on both sides. Bake on the middle rack of the oven for about 25 minutes, or until crispy and golden, flipping once while in the oven.

Assemble the burgers with lettuce, slices of cucumber and tomato and a drizzle of dairy-free unsweetened yogurt.

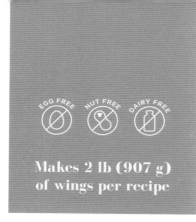

EGG FREE   NUT FREE   DAIRY FREE

Makes 2 lb (907 g) of wings per recipe

Nut-Free Thai "Peanut" Chicken Wings + Kung Pao Chicken Wings

Chicken wings are the ultimate party appetizer, tailgate food or the perfect side for pizza night. No one is ever mad when chicken wings are on the menu!

Thai "Peanut" Wings

¼ cup (60 ml) sesame oil

1 tsp Himalayan salt

1 tsp black pepper

1 tsp garlic powder

¼ tsp red pepper flakes

2 lb (907 g) chicken wings

3 tbsp (48 g) no sugar added SunButter or creamy peanut butter

2 tbsp (30 ml) sugar-free honey or sugar-free maple syrup

1 tbsp (15 ml) lime juice

1 tbsp (15 ml) coconut aminos, liquid aminos or gluten-free soy sauce

Chopped green onions, optional, for serving

Sunflower seeds or peanuts, for topping

Preheat the oven to 425°F (220°C). Line a baking sheet with foil and place a wire rack on top.

In a large bowl, combine the sesame oil, salt, black pepper, garlic powder and red pepper flakes. Toss the chicken wings, two at a time, in the oil/spice mixture to coat both sides. Place the wings on the wire rack in the prepared baking sheet and place in the oven for 15 minutes.

While the wings are cooking, prepare the sauce by combining the SunButter, honey, lime juice and coconut aminos in another large bowl. When the wings have baked for 15 minutes, remove them from the oven, toss them in the prepared sauce, then return them to the wire rack and bake in the oven for an additional 15 minutes.

Remove the wings from the oven and top with any remaining sauce and garnish with chopped green onions (if using), or serve the wings with leftover sauce on the side as a dip. Top with sunflower seeds or peanuts. Store any leftovers in an airtight container in the refrigerator for up to 3 days.

Substitution Note:

To make this *Paleo*, use real honey or maple syrup instead of sugar free.

(continued)

Kung Pao Wings

¼ cup (60 ml) sesame oil

1 tsp Himalayan salt

1 tsp black pepper

1 tsp onion powder

1 tsp garlic powder

¼ tsp red pepper flakes

2 lb (907 g) chicken wings

½ cup (120 ml) sugar-free maple syrup

¼ tsp stevia or monk fruit extract

1 tbsp (15 ml) sriracha

1 tbsp (15 ml) balsamic vinegar

1 tbsp (15 ml) coconut aminos, liquid aminos or gluten-free soy sauce

1 tsp tapioca or arrowroot starch

Preheat the oven to 425°F (220°C). Line a baking sheet with foil and place a wire rack on top.

In a large bowl, combine the sesame oil, salt, black pepper, onion powder, garlic powder and red pepper flakes. Toss the chicken wings, two at a time, in the oil/spice mixture to coat both sides. Place the wings on the wire rack in the prepared baking sheet and place in the oven for 15 minutes.

While the wings are baking, prepare the sauce by combining the maple syrup, stevia extract, sriracha, vinegar, coconut aminos and tapioca in a small pot over medium heat. Stir until it thickens, about 3 minutes. Transfer the sauce to a large heat-resistant bowl.

When the wings have baked for 15 minutes, toss them in the prepared sauce, return them to the wire rack and return the rack to the oven to bake for an additional 15 minutes. Remove the wings from the oven and top with any remaining sauce or serve the wings with any leftover sauce on the side as a dip. Store any leftovers in an airtight container in the refrigerator for up to 3 days.

Substitution Note:

To make this *Paleo*, swap the sugar-free maple syrup with molasses and omit the stevia or monk fruit extract.

DAIRY FREE **EGG FREE** **NUT FREE**

Makes 1½ pounds (680 g) per recipe

Air-Fryer Chicken Wings in Three Flavors

Make these wings for your next game night. The air fryer makes it a seamless process and produces crispy wings without the mess of a deep fryer. I learned that every air fryer does not work exactly the same. Use my cooking times as a starting point but use your judgment on when the wings are done.

Salt and Vinegar Chicken Wings

1½ lb (680 g) chicken wings or wing dings

Avocado oil spray

1 tsp garlic powder

1 tsp Himalayan salt

½ tsp black pepper

⅓ cup (80 ml) apple cider vinegar

1 tbsp (15 ml) sugar-free maple syrup or sugar-free honey

⅛ to ¼ tsp cayenne pepper (optional)

Pat the chicken wings fully dry with a paper towel. Spray the wings with the avocado oil, about 2 teaspoons (10 ml) worth. Season the wings with the garlic powder, salt and pepper.

Arrange the chicken inside the air fryer. If your air fryer has a basket to create two levels during cooking, you can cook all the wings at once. Insert half on the bottom portion and the other half on the top, leaving space between each piece of meat. If your air fryer doesn't have two levels, cook half of the wings at a time.

Set the timer for 20 minutes at 400°F (205°C). If cooking in two layers, remove the chicken halfway through the cooking time (10 minutes) and swap the meat on the top and the bottom for even cooking, then resume. (You don't need to do this if cooking in one layer.)

In a small mixing bowl, combine the vinegar, maple syrup and cayenne. Mix well and set aside.

Remove the wings from the air fryer, place in a large bowl and toss with the sauce until fully coated. Serve hot. Store in the refrigerator in a sealed container for up to 5 days.

Substitution Note:

To make this *Paleo*, use real maple syrup or honey instead of sugar free.

(continued)

Zesty Ranch Chicken Wings

PALEO

1½ lb (680 g) chicken wings or wing dings

Avocado oil spray

Homemade Ranch Rub

1 tsp ground mustard powder

2 tbsp (6 g) dried dill

2 tbsp (6 g) dried oregano

2 tbsp (1 g) dried chives

1 tbsp (14 g) onion powder

2 tsp (6 g) garlic powder

1 tbsp (18 g) Himalayan salt

1 tsp black pepper

Pat the chicken wings fully dry with a paper towel. Spray the wings with avocado oil, about 2 teaspoons (10 ml) worth. Mix the rub ingredients in a bowl. Season the wings with about 2 tablespoons (30 g) of the rub and save the rest. Toss to coat.

Arrange the chicken inside an air fryer. If the air fryer has a basket to create two levels during cooking, you can cook all the wings at once. Insert half on the bottom portion and the other half on the top, leaving space between each piece of meat. If your air fryer doesn't have two levels, cook half of the wings at a time.

Set the timer for 20 minutes at 400°F (205°C). If cooking in two layers, remove the chicken halfway through the cooking time (10 minutes) and swap the meat on the top and the bottom for even cooking, then resume. (You don't need to do this if cooking in one layer.) Remove the wings from the air fryer and serve hot. Store in the refrigerator in a sealed container for up to 5 days.

(continued)

Asian Sesame-Crusted Chicken Wings

1½ lb (680 g) chicken wings or wing dings

Avocado oil spray

½ tsp garlic powder

½ tsp onion powder

Salt and pepper, to taste

2 tbsp (18 g) toasted sesame seeds, divided

¼ cup (60 ml) sesame oil

1 tbsp (15 ml) coconut aminos, liquid aminos or gluten-free soy sauce

2 tbsp (30 ml) sugar-free maple syrup or sugar-free honey

Green onions or scallions, for garnish

Pat the chicken wings fully dry with a paper towel. Spray the wings with avocado oil, about 2 teaspoons (10 ml) worth. Season the wings with the garlic powder, onion powder, salt, pepper and 1 tablespoon (9 g) of the toasted sesame seeds and toss well to coat.

Arrange the chicken inside the air fryer. If your air fryer has a basket to create two levels during cooking, you can cook all the wings at once. Insert half on the bottom portion and the other half on the top, leaving space between each piece of meat. If your air fryer doesn't have two levels, cook half of the wings at a time.

Set the timer for 20 minutes at 400°F (205°C). If cooking in two layers, remove the chicken halfway through the cooking time (10 minutes) and swap the meat on the top and the bottom for even cooking, then resume. (You don't need to do this if cooking in one layer.)

In a bowl, combine the sesame oil, coconut aminos, syrup and the remaining tablespoon (9 g) of sesame seeds; set aside.

Remove the wings from the air fryer, place in a large bowl and toss with the sauce until fully coated. Serve hot garnished with green onions or scallions. Store in the refrigerator in a sealed container for up to 5 days.

Recipe Note:

If you prefer a thicker sauce, ⅛ teaspoon of xanthan or guar gum can be added to the sesame oil, coconut aminos and syrup mixture.

Substitution Note:

To make this *Paleo*, use real maple syrup or honey instead of sugar free.

Meatballs Five Ways

Who doesn't love meatballs? This is a great appetizer for a crowd. Each of these recipes is infused with tons of flavors that your guests will love.

Makes 16 to 20 meatballs per recipe

Jalapeño Goat Cheese Ground Beef Meatballs

1 lb (454 g) ground beef

¾ cup (87 g) blanched almond flour or 1 large egg

¼ cup (40 g) grated onion

1¼ tsp (8 g) Himalayan salt

1 tsp black pepper

1 tsp garlic powder

¼ cup (35 g) crumbled goat cheese

2 medium jalapeños, seeds removed and diced

Preheat the oven to 375°F (190°C). Line a baking sheet with parchment paper.

In a large mixing bowl, stir together the ground beef, almond flour, onion, salt, black pepper and garlic powder until well combined. Fold in the goat cheese and jalapeños. Divide the meat into 16 equal-sized portions and form into balls.

Place the meatballs on the prepared baking sheet and bake for 15 to 20 minutes, until the meatballs are golden brown and there is no pink in the middle. Store in an airtight container in the refrigerator for up to 3 days.

Substitution Notes:

- To make this *egg free*, use the almond flour option.

- To make this *nut free*, use the egg option.

- To make this *dairy free* or *Paleo*, omit the cheese.

(continued)

Santa Fe Ground Turkey Meatballs

1 lb (454 g) ground turkey

¾ cup (87 g) blanched almond flour or 1 large egg

¼ cup (40 g) grated onion

1 tsp Himalayan salt

1 tsp black pepper

2 tsp (7 g) garlic powder

2 small jalapeños, seeds removed and diced

½ yellow bell pepper, finely diced

½ red bell pepper, finely diced

Preheat the oven to 375°F (190°C). Line a baking sheet with parchment paper.

In a large mixing bowl, stir together the ground turkey, almond flour, onion, salt, pepper and garlic powder until well combined. Fold in the diced peppers. Divide the meat mixture into 20 equal-sized portions and form into balls.

Place the meatballs on the prepared baking sheet and bake for 15 minutes. Store in an airtight container in the refrigerator for up to 3 days.

Substitution Notes:

- To make this *egg free*, use the almond flour option.

- To make this *nut free*, use the egg option.

(continued)

Tequila Lime Ground Turkey Meatballs

1 lb (454 g) ground turkey

½ cup (58 g) blanched almond flour or 1 large egg

¼ cup (40 g) grated onion

1 tsp garlic powder

1 tsp Himalayan salt

½ tsp black pepper

½ tsp ground cumin

½ tsp ground coriander

½ tsp chili powder

¼ cup (60 ml) tequila

Zest of 2 limes

Preheat the oven to 425°F (220°C). Line a baking sheet with parchment paper.

In a large mixing bowl, stir together the turkey, almond flour, onion, garlic powder, salt, pepper, cumin, coriander, chili powder, tequila and lime zest and mix until well combined. Divide the meat mixture into 20 equal-sized portions and form into balls.

Place the meatballs on the prepared baking sheet and bake for 15 minutes. Store leftovers in an airtight container in the refrigerator for up to 3 days.

Substitution Notes:

- To make this *egg free*, use the almond flour option.

- To make this *nut free*, use the egg option.

(continued)

Sweet and Sour Ground Pork Meatballs

Meatballs

1 lb (454 g) ground pork

¾ cup (87 g) blanched almond flour or 1 large egg

2 tbsp (30 ml) pineapple extract

¼ cup (40 g) grated onion

1 tsp Himalayan salt

½ tsp black pepper

1 tsp garlic powder

½ tsp ground ginger

½ tsp mustard powder

½ tsp ground cinnamon

Sauce

1½ tbsp (22 ml) pineapple extract

⅔ cup (160 ml) rice vinegar

2 tbsp (30 g) tomato paste

½ cup (120 ml) sugar-free honey

¼ tsp stevia extract or monk fruit extract

½ tsp Himalayan salt

¼ tsp black pepper

Preheat the oven to 375°F (190°C). Line a baking sheet with parchment paper.

To make the meatballs, in a large mixing bowl, stir together the pork, almond flour, pineapple extract, onion, salt, pepper, garlic powder, ginger, mustard and cinnamon until well combined. Divide the meat mixture into 16 equal-sized portions and form into balls. Place the meatballs on the prepared baking sheet and bake for 15 minutes.

To make the sauce, add the pineapple extract, vinegar, tomato paste, honey, stevia extract, salt and pepper to a blender and blend until smooth. Transfer to a medium saucepan and cook over medium heat for 10 to 15 minutes, until heated through. Toss the cooked meatballs in the sauce and serve. Store leftovers in an airtight container in the refrigerator for up to 3 days.

Substitution Notes:

- To make this *egg free*, use the almond flour option.

- To make this *nut free*, use the egg option.

(continued)

Pizza-Style Ground Italian Sausage Meatballs

1 lb (454 g) ground Italian sausage

½ cup (58 g) blanched almond flour or 1 large egg

¼ cup (40 g) grated onion

⅔ cup (120 g) diced tomato (fresh or canned)

½ cup (56 g) shredded mozzarella cheese, plus more for topping

1 cup (140 g) chopped pepperoni

2 tsp (2 g) dried oregano

1 tsp garlic powder

1 tsp Himalayan salt

½ tsp black pepper

Preheat the oven to 425°F (220°C). Line a baking sheet with parchment paper.

In a large mixing bowl, stir together the sausage, almond flour, onion, tomatoes, mozzarella, pepperoni, oregano, garlic powder, salt and pepper until well combined. Divide the meat mixture into 20 equal-sized portions and form into balls.

Place the meatballs on the prepared baking sheet and bake for 15 minutes. Remove from the oven, top with additional shredded mozzarella cheese, return to the oven and bake for an additional 5 minutes. Store leftovers in an airtight container in the refrigerator for up to 3 days.

Recipe Note:

If you enjoy green peppers or olives on your pizza, feel free to chop up some and add them in too.

Substitution Notes:

- To make this *egg free*, use the almond flour option.

- To make this *nut free*, use the egg option.

- To make this *dairy free* and *Paleo*, omit the cheese.

Deviled Eggs
Three Ways

*Deviled eggs are a spring favorite. You can color the whites to
add a festive flair (see the individual recipes for instructions).
The directions for hard boiling the eggs are below. But if the
thought of peeling hard-boiled eggs feels like too much work,
purchase preboiled and peeled eggs at your local grocery store.*

Green Goddess Deviled Eggs

6 eggs

Filling

3 tbsp (44 g) mayonnaise
(regular or vegan)

½ tsp mustard (yellow or
Dijon)

1 tsp garlic powder

1 tsp white balsamic or
champagne vinegar

2 tbsp (6 g) finely chopped
chives, plus more for garnish

2 tbsp (3 g) finely chopped
tarragon, plus more for garnish

1 avocado, peeled, pitted and
roughly chopped

Himalayan salt and pepper, to
taste

Coloring (optional)

1 large beet, peeled and
roughly chopped

2 cups (480 ml) water

Fill a medium saucepan with 4 to 6 cups (950 ml to 1.4 L) of
water and bring to a boil. You should have enough water to fully
submerge the eggs. When the water is boiling, add the eggs and
reduce to a simmer. Simmer the eggs, uncovered, for 15 minutes.
Remove the saucepan from the heat and let stand an additional
15 minutes. When there is about 5 minutes left in the standing
time, create an ice bath for the eggs. Fill a medium bowl with
cold water and ice and set aside. When the eggs are finished,
remove them from the hot water with tongs or a slotted spoon
and place them immediately in the ice bath. Allow the eggs to
sit in the ice bath for 5 minutes, then remove them from the
cold water and allow them to dry. Peel the eggs and cut each
in half lengthwise. Using a small spoon, remove the yolks from
the whites and place the yolks in a medium bowl. Set the whites
aside.

To make the filling, in a blender, purée the egg yolks with the
mayonnaise, mustard, garlic powder, vinegar, chives, tarragon
and avocado until smooth and creamy, adding salt and pepper
to taste. Refrigerate the filling, covered, for 15 minutes or until
you are ready to fill the egg whites.

To color the egg whites (if desired), add the chopped beet and
water to a medium saucepan and bring to a boil. Reduce the
mixture to a simmer and cover the pan for 15 minutes. Decrease
the heat to the lowest setting, then add the egg whites to the
pan along with the beets (see Recipe Notes, page 319). Leave
the egg whites in the pan for 15 to 30 minutes, until the desired
color is reached. Remove the egg whites to a plate or cutting
board to cool. Dry off the egg whites with a paper towel.
Spoon some of the yolk mixture into each egg white. Garnish
with additional chives and tarragon. Store any leftovers in the
refrigerator for up to 1 week.

(continued)

Thai Green Curry Deviled Eggs

6 eggs, boiled and halved, yolks and whites separated (see directions on page 316)

Filling

1 tsp avocado oil

1½ tbsp (24 g) Thai green curry paste

3 tbsp (44 g) mayonnaise (regular or vegan)

½ tsp mustard powder

1 tsp garlic powder

¼ cup (15 g) chopped cilantro, plus more for garnish

3 scallions, chopped, plus more for garnish

Coloring (optional)

2 cups (180 g) chopped red cabbage

2 cups (480 ml) water

To make the filling, in a small skillet over medium heat, warm the avocado oil, then add the curry paste. Allow the paste to cook until just golden, about 5 minutes, then remove from the heat and set aside. In a blender, purée the egg yolks, curry paste, mayonnaise, mustard powder, garlic powder, cilantro and scallions until smooth and creamy. Refrigerate, covered, for 15 minutes or until you are ready to fill the egg whites.

To color the egg whites (if desired), add the chopped red cabbage and water to a medium saucepan and bring to a boil. Reduce the mixture to a simmer and cover for 15 minutes. Decrease the heat to the lowest setting and add the egg whites to the pan (see Recipe Notes below). Leave the egg whites in the pan for 15 to 30 minutes, until the desired color is reached.

Remove the egg whites to a plate or cutting board to cool. Dry off the egg whites with a paper towel. Spoon some of the yolk mixture into each egg white. Garnish with additional cilantro and scallions. Store any leftovers in the refrigerator for up to 1 week.

Recipe Notes:

- Leave the beets in the saucepan after you add the egg whites; they will continue to give off their color throughout the coloring process.

- This coloring will stain, so be careful when adding or removing the egg whites from the pan.

- The longer you leave the whites in the mixture, the darker the color.

- You may need to work in batches depending on how many eggs you would like to make.

(continued)

Pecorino Prosciutto Deviled Eggs

6 eggs, boiled and halved, yolks and whites separated (see directions on page 316)

Filling

3 tbsp (44 g) mayonnaise (regular or vegan)

½ tsp mustard powder

2 tsp (7 g) garlic powder

½ tsp white balsamic or champagne vinegar

3 tbsp (15 g) shredded Pecorino Romano sheep's milk cheese, plus more for garnish

¼ tsp black pepper

¼ tsp Himalayan salt

2 thin slices prosciutto, for garnish

Coloring (optional)

1 cup (240 ml) red wine

2 cups (480 ml) water

To make the filling, in a blender, purée the egg yolks with the mayonnaise, mustard powder, garlic powder, vinegar, Pecorino, pepper and salt until smooth and creamy. Refrigerate, covered, for 15 minutes or until you are ready to fill the egg whites.

To color the egg whites (if desired), add the red wine and water to a medium saucepan and bring to a boil. Reduce the mixture to a simmer, uncovered, for 15 minutes. Decrease the heat to the lowest setting and add the egg whites to the pan (see Recipe Notes on page 319). Leave the egg whites in the pan for 15 to 30 minutes, until the desired color is reached.

Remove the egg whites to a plate or cutting board to cool. Dry off the egg whites with a paper towel. Spoon some of the yolk mixture into each egg white. Garnish with slices of prosciutto and additional shredded cheese. Store any leftovers in the refrigerator for up to 1 week.

Substitution Notes:

- To make these **dairy free** and **Paleo**, omit the cheese.

- To make these **vegetarian**, omit the prosciutto.

Makes 8 taco cups

Taco Cups

Taco Tuesday just got better! These taco cups are perfect for taco parties and even great for kids. You can achieve these professional looking cups with just a few simple steps. They are quick to make and fun to eat.

Preheat the oven to 450°F (230°C).

Cut ½ inch (13 mm) off each side of a tortilla and fold the remaining square tortilla into the well of a muffin pan. Repeat this process to make 8 tortilla cups. Bake for 3 minutes.

To make the taco seasoning, combine the chili powder, garlic powder, onion powder, oregano, paprika, salt and pepper in a small bowl.

Add the ground beef to a skillet over medium heat, and cook for 10 minutes, adding the taco seasoning as the meat cooks. Place a heaping tablespoon (14 g) of the seasoned ground beef into each prebaked taco cup, then top with about 2 tablespoons (15 g) of the shredded cheese. Return the pan to the oven for 5 minutes, or until the cheese melts. Garnish with your choice of optional garnishes.

Taco Cups

1 bag almond flour tortillas (I recommend Siete brand)

1 tbsp (8 g) chili powder

¼ tsp garlic powder

¼ tsp onion powder

¼ tsp dried oregano

½ tsp paprika

1 tsp Himalayan salt

1 tsp black pepper

8 oz (227 g) ground beef

1½ cups (170 g) shredded sharp cheddar cheese

Optional Garnishes

Sliced avocado

Sliced tomato

Chopped cilantro

Lime juice

Sour cream

Substitution Notes:

- To make this *nut free*, use cassava flour tortillas.

- To make this *dairy free* and *Paleo*, omit the cheese.

- To make this *vegetarian*, use tofu or vegan ground beef.

Bars, Brownies and Cookies

Bars, brownies and cookies are loved by all, and are perfect for grab-and-go snacks. All of these recipes freeze beautifully and can be kept frozen for a treat when a craving strikes. If you have an egg allergy, this chapter in particular holds many recipe options for you.

← See recipe on page 355.

Makes 12 bars

Banana Chai Chocolate Bars

If you are in the mood for some banana bread, then look no further than these keto-friendly banana chai bars. The banana extract is an excellent substitution for real bananas. The warm chai spices will have your kitchen smelling so good, you may not be able to stop yourself from gobbling them all up. As a bonus this recipe is egg free.

3 packed cups (348 g) blanched almond flour

½ cup (100 g) keto granulated sugar

¾ cup (100 g) macadamia nuts, roughly chopped, divided

1 tbsp (14 g) double-acting baking powder

¼ tsp Himalayan salt

1 tbsp (15 ml) banana extract

5 tbsp (75 ml) unsweetened full-fat coconut milk

1 tsp vanilla extract

2 tsp (5 g) ground cinnamon

1½ tsp (3 g) ground cardamom

1 tsp ground ginger

¼ tsp ground nutmeg

Chocolate Glaze

½ cup (84 g) keto-friendly chocolate chips

1 tsp coconut oil

Preheat the oven to 350°F (175°C) and line an 8 x 8–inch (20 x 20–cm) baking pan with parchment paper.

In a large mixing bowl, combine the almond flour, sugar, ½ cup (66 g) macadamia nuts, baking powder, salt, banana extract, coconut milk, vanilla, cinnamon, cardamom, ginger and nutmeg. Mix thoroughly until the ingredients form a crumbly dough. Crumble the dough mixture into the baking pan, then press down evenly. Sprinkle ¼ cup (33 g) of macadamia nuts on top and press them lightly into the dough. Bake for 15 to 20 minutes, until the edges are golden brown. Make sure to allow the bars time to cool before cutting or they may crumble.

To make the chocolate glaze, put the chocolate chips and coconut oil in a small bowl. Microwave for 30 to 60 seconds. Stir until the chocolate is fully melted and drizzle on the bars.

Store in a sealed container at room temperature for 3 to 5 days. They can also be frozen for up to 1 month.

Recipe Note:

Be sure to press the bars down a decent amount so they hold together.

Substitution Note:

To make this **Paleo**, use coconut palm sugar, granulated maple sugar or granulated honey in place of the keto sugar.

Makes 12 bars

Lemon Poppy Seed Bars with Dragon Fruit Glaze

This recipe is so quick and easy. It will be ready to go into the oven in minutes. It triples as breakfast, dessert or an afternoon snack.

Lemon Poppy Seed Bars

3 packed cups (348 g) blanched almond flour

½ cup (100 g) keto granulated sugar

1 tsp double-acting baking powder

¼ tsp Himalayan salt

2 tbsp (18 g) poppy seeds

4 tbsp (60 ml) lemon juice

Zest of 1 lemon

Dragon Fruit Glaze

½ cup (66 g) keto powdered sugar

½ tbsp (7 ml) lemon juice

½ tsp pink pitaya superfruit powder (optional, see Recipe Notes)

2 tbsp (30 ml) water

Preheat the oven to 350°F (175°C) and line an 8 x 8-inch (20 x 20-cm) baking pan with parchment paper.

In a large mixing bowl, stir together the almond flour, sugar, baking powder, salt and poppy seeds until they form a dough. Mix in the lemon juice and lemon zest. Press the mixture evenly into the baking pan and bake for 20 to 25 minutes, until the edges are golden brown.

While the bars are baking, in a small bowl, whisk together the powdered sugar, lemon juice, superfruit powder and water until smooth.

Remove the bars from the oven and allow them to cool for 15 to 20 minutes. If you don't let the bars cool they will crumble. Drizzle the glaze over the slightly cooled bars.

Store in a sealed container at room temperature for 3 to 5 days. They can also be frozen for up to 1 month.

Recipe Notes:

- The pink pitaya superfruit powder is optional. If you do not use it, reduce the amount of water to 1½ tablespoons (22 ml).

- Be sure to press the bars down a decent amount before baking so they hold together.

Substitution Note:

To make this **Paleo**, you can use coconut sugar, palm sugar, granulated maple sugar or granulated honey in place of keto granulated sugar. Use powdered honey in the glaze.

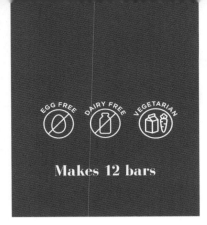

Makes 12 bars

Mixed Berry Bars with Lemon Glaze

The lemon in this recipe brings out the sweet flavors of the berries for a moist, delectable bar.

Mixed Berry Bars

3½ packed cups (406 g) blanched almond flour

½ cup (100 g) keto granulated sugar

1 tbsp (14 g) double-acting baking powder

¼ tsp Himalayan salt

2 tbsp (30 ml) unsweetened dairy-free milk

2 tbsp (30 ml) lemon juice

Zest of 1 lemon

½ cup (70 g) raspberries (fresh or frozen), halved

½ cup (75 g) blackberries (fresh or frozen), halved

Lemon Glaze

½ cup (66 g) keto powdered sugar

½ tbsp (7 ml) lemon juice

1½ tbsp (22 ml) water

Preheat the oven to 350°F (175°C). Line an 8 x 8–inch (20 x 20–cm) baking pan with parchment paper.

In a large mixing bowl, stir together the almond flour, sugar, baking powder, salt, dairy-free milk, lemon juice and lemon zest until pea-sized crumbles form. Add about one-quarter of the dough mixture to the pan, then add a layer of the halved raspberries and blackberries. Add another quarter of the dough mixture, allowing it to stay crumbly. Continue alternating the dough mixture and berries until all are used, ending either with a dough layer or berry layer. Press down lightly on the layers to form the bars. Bake the bars for 20 to 25 minutes, until the edges are golden brown. Allow the bars to cool fully to avoid crumbling.

While the bars are baking, in a small bowl, whisk together the powdered sugar, lemon juice and water until smooth.

Remove the bars from the oven and allow them to cool for 15 to 20 minutes. Drizzle the glaze over the slightly cooled bars.

Store in a sealed container at room temperature for 3 to 5 days. They can also be frozen for up to 1 month.

Recipe Notes:

- If you wish, up to one more cup (140 g) of berries can be added to the layers or the top.

- Be sure to press the bars down a decent amount before baking so that they hold together nicely.

Substitution Note:

To make this **Paleo**, use coconut sugar, palm sugar or granulated maple sugar in place of keto granulated sugar. Use powdered honey in the glaze.

Makes 12 bars

3 packed cups (348 g) blanched almond flour

½ cup (100 g) keto granulated sugar

1 tbsp (14 g) double-acting baking powder

¼ tsp Himalayan salt

¾ cup (100 g) macadamia nuts, chopped, divided

½ cup (37 g) unsweetened coconut flakes

1 tsp matcha powder

5 tbsp (75 ml) unsweetened dairy-free milk

1 tsp vanilla extract

½ cup (115 g) Homemade Dairy- and Sugar-Free White Chocolate (page 334)

Coconut Matcha Macadamia Bars with White Chocolate Glaze

These bars turn the perfect shade of green and taste amazing. They can easily be made ahead for breakfast, eaten as a snack or served as a dessert with coffee or tea.

Preheat the oven to 350°F (175°C) and line an 8 x 8-inch (20 x 20-cm) baking pan with parchment paper.

In a large mixing bowl, combine the almond flour, sugar, baking powder, salt, ½ cup (66 g) of macadamia nuts, coconut flakes, matcha powder, dairy-free milk and vanilla. Mix thoroughly until the ingredients form a crumbly dough. Place the dough mixture into the baking pan, pressing down evenly. Sprinkle ¼ cup (33 g) of macadamia nuts on top and press lightly into the dough. Bake for 15 to 20 minutes, until the edges are golden brown.

Allow the bars to cool for 10 to 15 minutes, until they are warm but not hot. Put the white chocolate in a microwave-safe bowl and microwave for 30 seconds to melt the chocolate. (You may need to microwave it an additional 15 to 30 seconds to achieve a pourable texture.) Using a spoon, drizzle the melted chocolate over the slightly cooled bars. Allow the bars to cool fully before slicing or they may crumble.

Store in a sealed container at room temperature for 3 to 5 days. The bars can also be frozen for up to 1 month.

Recipe Notes:

- Up to 1 tablespoon (15 g) of matcha powder can be used for more matcha flavor.

- Be sure to press down the bars enough before baking so that they hold together well.

Substitution Note:

To make this **_Paleo_**, use granulated honey in place of the keto granulated sugar.

Makes 3¾ cups (700 g)

Homemade Dairy- and Sugar-Free White Chocolate

This white chocolate is a unique variation that took some trial and error to figure out. The key is that liquid and oil do not mix, so be sure your nuts are completely dry and the utensils are dry as well. You can make this white chocolate ahead of time and store it in the refrigerator in a sealed container for several weeks.

2½ cups (545 g) unsweetened cocoa butter

2 cups (264 g) roasted macadamia nuts (salt free, or rinsed and fully dried)

½ vanilla bean, seeds scraped out

¼ cup (30 g) unsweetened coconut milk powder (optional)

¼ cup (30 g) keto powdered sugar

⅛ tsp Himalayan salt

Line an 8 x 8–inch (20 x 20–cm) baking pan with parchment paper.

Place the unsweetened cocoa butter in a microwave-safe bowl and melt in the microwave for 1 to 2 minutes. Pour the melted cocoa butter into the bowl of a food processor, then add the nuts, vanilla bean seeds, coconut milk powder (if using), powdered sugar and salt. Process until the mixture is completely smooth. Pour the mixture into the prepared pan. Place the pan in the refrigerator to cool and solidify for 30 minutes.

Break into chunks and store in a container in the refrigerator. Use within 3 to 4 weeks.

Substitution Note:

To make this **Paleo**, use powdered granulated honey or powdered maple sugar instead of the keto powdered sugar.

**Makes about 6 cups
(1.4 kg)**

Sugar-Free Marshmallows

Soft, fluffy and really easy to make, these marshmallows are the real deal. You'll find them used in ice cream recipes and bars in this book. Just keep in mind that due to the fact that they are not made with real sugar, they will not act the same as real marshmallows if you roast them—they will melt quickly.

½ cup (65 g) keto powdered sugar, for dusting

1 cup (240 ml) water, divided

2 tbsp (18 g) gelatin

1 cup (240 ml) sugar-free honey or sugar-free maple syrup

2 tsp (10 ml) vanilla extract

⅛ tsp Himalayan salt

Line an 8 x 8-inch (20 x 20-cm) pan with parchment and dust with about half of the powdered sugar.

In a large bowl, sprinkle the gelatin over ½ cup (120 ml) of water and set aside.

Add the honey, ½ cup (120 ml) of water, vanilla and salt to a small saucepan and heat over medium heat until the mixture is combined. Continue to stir, measuring the temperature with a candy thermometer, until the mixture reaches 175°F (80°C). Pour the hot mixture into the bowl with the gelatin mixture. Using a hand mixer or stand mixer, whip for 5 to 8 minutes, until the mixture is fluffy and thick but not too thick to handle.

Pour the warm mixture into the prepared pan and dust with the remaining powdered sugar. Press down on the mixture so that it is flat. Let cool at room temperature or in the refrigerator.

When cool and set, lift the mixture out of the pan using the parchment paper, then slice into marshmallows. Store in a sealed bag or container at room temperature. Dust with extra powdered sugar as needed to prevent stickiness.

Recipe Note:

The power of hand/stand mixers varies, as a result you might need up to 10 to 15 minutes of mixing to reach the proper thickness for the marshmallows. Stop when your marshmallows are thick but not too thick to smooth into your prepared pan.

Substitution Note:

To make this **Paleo**, use real honey or maple syrup. Use powdered honey or powdered maple syrup in place of the powdered sugar.

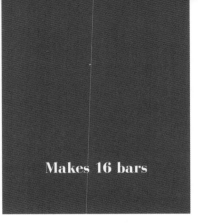

Peanut Butter Butterscotch Marshmallow Bars

Makes 16 bars

These bars only lasted two days in my house before they were all gone. This mixture of peanut butter, marshmallows, butterscotch extract, coconut flakes and peanuts makes for an extremely decadent dessert.

Cookie Base

1 cup (256 g) peanut butter

⅓ cup (65 g) keto granulated sugar

1 large egg

1 tsp vanilla extract

¼ tsp Himalayan salt

Butterscotch Sauce

½ cup (120 ml) sugar-free honey or sugar-free maple syrup

½ tsp stevia extract or monk fruit extract

¼ cup (60 g) butter-flavored coconut oil

2 tsp (10 ml) vanilla extract

10 oz (283 g) cocoa butter chips (unsweetened)

½ cup (120 ml) heavy cream or coconut cream (skimmed off the top of a can)

Pinch of Himalayan salt

1 tsp butterscotch extract

1 cup (75 g) unsweetened coconut flakes

1 cup (150 g) roasted and salted peanuts

½ recipe Sugar-Free Marshmallows (page 335)

Preheat the oven to 350°F (175°C) and line a 9 x 9-inch (23 x 23-cm) pan with parchment paper.

To make the cookie base, in a medium bowl, mix the peanut butter, granulated sugar, egg, vanilla and salt to form a smooth dough. Place the dough in the prepared pan and press down firmly. Bake for 15 to 20 minutes, until the cookie base is golden brown and firm to the touch.

To make the sauce, in a saucepan over medium-low heat, stir together the honey, stevia extract, coconut oil, vanilla, cocoa butter chips, cream, salt and butterscotch extract until completely melted, stirring frequently while the mixture melts. Bring the mixture to a boil and allow it to simmer for 10 minutes, or until the mixture thickens. Remove the butterscotch sauce from the heat and fold in the coconut flakes and peanuts; set aside.

When the cookie base is out of the oven, cover the top with marshmallows and bake again for 1 to 2 minutes, or until the marshmallows begin to puff up. Remove the pan from the oven and pour the butterscotch sauce over the marshmallows and refrigerate for 8 to 12 hours until solid. When fully set, cut into 16 bars and serve. Store in an airtight container in the refrigerator for up to 1 week or in the freezer for up to 1 month.

Substitution Note:

To make this ***dairy free***, use coconut cream in place of the heavy cream in the butterscotch sauce.

EGG FREE · DAIRY FREE · VEGETARIAN

Makes 12 bars

1 cup (180 g) grated zucchini

3¾ packed cups (439 g) blanched almond flour

¾ cup (150 g) keto granulated sugar

1 tbsp (14 g) double-acting baking powder

½ cup (50 g) chopped walnuts

1 tbsp (8 g) ground cinnamon

2 tsp (10 ml) vanilla extract

¼ tsp Himalayan salt

Keto Caramel (page 359), for drizzling (optional)

½ cup (50 g) toasted walnuts, for topping (optional)

Zucchini Walnut Bars

These bars are hearty, healthy and egg free. While this recipe can be enjoyed as dessert, it is also a great egg-free stand-in for muffins.

Preheat the oven to 350°F (175°C) and line an 8 x 8-inch (20 x 20-cm) baking pan with parchment paper.

Thoroughly dry the grated zucchini by pressing it with a few layers of paper towels. You may have to do this step a few times. Set aside.

In a large mixing bowl, mix the zucchini, almond flour, sugar, baking powder, walnuts, cinnamon, vanilla and salt with your hands until it forms a thick dough. Crumble the dough into the prepared baking pan and gently press down. Bake for 20 to 25 minutes, until lightly browned on the edges. If desired, drizzle with the Keto Caramel and top with walnuts. Allow the bars to fully cool before slicing or they may crumble.

Store in a sealed container at room temperature for 3 to 5 days. They can also be frozen for up to 1 month.

Recipe Note:

Be sure to press the bars down a bit before baking so they hold together.

Substitution Note:

To make this *Paleo*, use coconut sugar or granulated honey in place of keto granulated sugar.

Makes 12 bars

Apple Cinnamon Bars

The scents of apples and cinnamon are synonymous with the fall for me. They make a magical pair in these bars. This recipe will blow your mind.

Preheat the oven to 350°F (175°C). Line an 8 x 8-inch (20 x 20-cm) pan with parchment paper.

To make the bars, in a large mixing bowl, combine the almond flour, sugar, baking powder and milk. In a separate bowl, mix the chopped apples with the lemon juice and cinnamon. Mix the apples into the dough. Crumble the dough into the prepared baking pan with your hands and press down.

Bake for 45 minutes, or until lightly brown on top. Allow the bars to cool completely before cutting. Drizzle with Keto Caramel and top with spiralized apple (if using).

Store in a sealed container at room temperature for 3 to 5 days. They can also be frozen for up to 1 month.

Bars

3½ packed cups (406 g) blanched almond flour

½ cup (100 g) keto granulated sugar

1 tbsp (14 g) double-acting baking powder

3 tbsp (45 ml) canned unsweetened full-fat coconut milk, room temperature (shaken)

2 cups (180 g) chopped green apples

2 tsp (10 ml) lemon juice

2 tsp (5 g) ground cinnamon

Keto Caramel (page 359), for topping (optional)

Spiralized apple or apple slices, for topping (optional)

Recipe Notes:

- The peel of the apple can be left on or removed.

- I limited the amount of apple used to keep the carb count as low as possible—feel free to up the amount to 3 to 4 cups (540 to 720 g) for more apple flavor.

Substitution Note:

To make this **Paleo**, use coconut sugar in place of keto granulated sugar.

EGG FREE DAIRY FREE VEGETARIAN

Makes 12 bars

¼ cup (60 g) butter-flavored coconut oil

½ cup (128 g) peanut butter

⅓ cup (80 ml) sugar-free honey or sugar-free maple syrup

¼ tsp stevia extract or monk fruit extract

1 tsp vanilla extract

1 tsp almond extract (or more vanilla extract)

½ tsp Himalayan salt (optional)

2 cups (300 g) salted and roasted peanuts

¾ cup (105 g) salted and roasted sunflower seeds (or cashews)

½ cup (45 g) salted and roasted sliced almonds

Sweet and Salty Peanut Granola Bars

If you like Payday candy bars, then you will love these keto sweet-and-salty peanut granola bars. These no-bake bars solidify in the freezer and taste ahh-mazing.

Line an 8 x 8-inch (20 x 20-cm) pan with parchment paper; set aside.

In a large bowl, combine the coconut oil and peanut butter. (If your coconut oil is cold, warm it in the microwave for 20 to 30 seconds first.) Add the honey, stevia extract, vanilla, almond extract and salt (if using). Stir to combine. Add the peanuts, sunflower seeds and almonds and stir to coat them evenly with the peanut butter mixture.

Pour the mixture into the prepared pan and place it in the freezer for 25 to 30 minutes. Remove the pan from the freezer and using the parchment paper, lift the bars out of the pan and onto a cutting board. Cut the bars into 1-inch (3-cm) rectangles. Serve immediately.

Store in an airtight container in the refrigerator for up to 1 week.

Recipe Note:

Depending on how much salt you like, you may find the salt from the peanuts alone is enough. I would recommend mixing everything up and giving it a taste and adding in the ½ teaspoon of salt if you want it!

Substitution Note:

To make this **Paleo**, use real honey or maple syrup and omit the stevia.

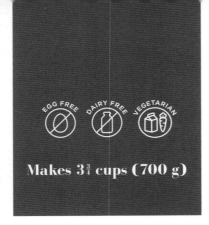

EGG FREE · **DAIRY FREE** · **VEGETARIAN**

Makes 3¼ cups (700 g)

1 batch Homemade Dairy- and Sugar-Free White Chocolate (page 334)

1 tsp pink pitaya superfruit powder or pink food coloring

1 tsp blue spirulina powder

1 tsp purple food coloring

1 tbsp (15 g) all-natural sprinkles (optional)

Keto Unicorn Bark

Nothing will get you in touch with your inner teenager quite like unicorn bark! You can use your favorite food coloring to color the white chocolate. I found that the superfruit powders worked well but may not be as vibrant as other food colorings. For fun, try adding a little cotton candy extract to the recipe!

Line a 7 x 11-inch (18 x 28–cm) or similar sized pan with parchment paper.

Separate the white chocolate into four bowls. Place each bowl in the microwave on high for 2 to 3 minutes, or until the chocolate is completely melted. Pour the chocolate from one bowl into the prepared pan.

To one of the three remaining bowls of melted chocolate, add the pink pitaya superfruit powder or pink food coloring. Mix to combine and set aside, keeping the spoon in the bowl. Repeat with the blue spirulina powder or blue food coloring in another bowl and the purple food coloring in the last bowl, keeping a spoon in each bowl.

Using the spoon, drizzle the pink-colored chocolate into the pan of white chocolate in large circles. Repeat with the blue- and purple-colored chocolate until all of the colored chocolate mixtures are used.

Using a clean knife, swirl the colors together in the pan. You will need to remove the knife and wipe it clean every few swipes so that the colors do not mix too much.

Add the sprinkles on top (if using). Place the pan in the refrigerator to cool and solidify, about an hour. When solid, break into chunks and store in a container in the refrigerator for up to 4 weeks.

Substitution Note:

To make this **Paleo**, be sure to make the Paleo version of the Homemade Dairy- and Sugar-Free White Chocolate (page 334).

EGG FREE · VEGETARIAN

Makes 8 bars

¾ cup (100 g) macadamia nuts

⅓ cup (80 g) coconut butter

¼ cup (60 ml) coconut cream or heavy whipping cream

2 tbsp (30 ml) sugar-free maple syrup or sugar-free honey

2 tbsp + 2 tsp (40 g) coconut oil, divided

3 tbsp (25 g) coconut flour

1 recipe Keto Caramel (page 359)

½ cup (75 g) roughly chopped salted toasted peanuts

1½ cups (252 g) dark chocolate chips (dairy or nondairy)

Recipe Notes:

- The bars do not have to be fully covered with chocolate; another option is to melt only ¾ cup (125 g) of dark chocolate with 1 teaspoon of coconut oil using the same process. Use a spoon to drizzle the melted chocolate over the frozen bars. This will cut the carb count down, and will be a less messy process.

- See the Keto Caramel Recipe Notes on page 359 for tips on substitutions and obtaining the best results for the caramel.

No-Bake Snickers Bars

These bars are really fun and extremely delicious. I will go as far to say that I think these bars are better than the Snickers bars you can buy in a store! The fresh ingredients send the flavors over the top.

Line an 8 x 4–inch (20 x 10–cm) loaf pan with parchment paper. Line a small baking sheet with another piece of parchment paper. Set both aside.

To make the nougat, place the macadamia nuts, coconut butter, coconut cream, maple syrup, 2 tablespoons (30 g) coconut oil and coconut flour in a blender. Blend, stopping to stir and scrape down the sides, to ensure a smooth texture. If your blender does not fully break down the macadamia nuts, that is okay—the bars will still be delicious. When the mixture is smooth, pour it into the prepared pan and top with the caramel. Sprinkle the caramel layer with the chopped peanuts. Place the pan in the freezer and allow the mixture to set for at least 1 hour.

Remove the pan from the freezer and pull the frozen bars out using the parchment paper. Slice into 8 bars and place the bars on the prepared baking sheet. Place the baking sheet in the freezer for 10 minutes. To make the chocolate coating, combine the chocolate chips and 2 teaspoons (10 g) coconut oil in a small microwave-safe bowl and microwave for 1 minute. Remove from the microwave and stir until the mixture is smooth and fully melted. (You can also use a double boiler for this step.) Pour the melted chocolate into a bowl wide enough to dip the bars into. Dip the bars, caramel-side down, into the chocolate and rotate side to side once so that the top and the sides are covered. Allow the excess chocolate to drip off, then place each bar back onto the parchment-lined baking sheet, chocolate-side up. Place the bars in the freezer for 1 hour to fully set the chocolate, then serve. Keep these bars in the refrigerator or freezer at all times, as the chocolate will melt at room temperature. Store them for up to 1 month in a sealed container.

Substitution Notes:

- To make this *dairy free*, use butter-flavored coconut oil in the caramel and dairy-free dark chocolate chips.

- To make this *Paleo*, use butter-flavored coconut oil in the caramel and dairy-free dark chocolate chips, and use real honey or maple syrup instead of sugar-free honey and sugar-free maple syrup.

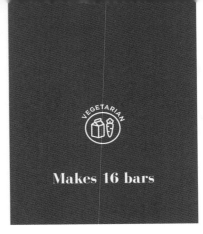

Makes 16 bars

Keto Twix Bars

Twix bars are my favorite candy, but these Keto Twix Bars are my new addiction. You get all of the great flavors of a Twix without all of the sugar. These bars need to stay cold, which makes them perfect to eat on those hot summer days when you want something cold and chocolatey.

½ cup (112 g) salted butter or vegan butter

⅓ cup (70 g) keto granulated sugar

2 oz (57 g) cream cheese (dairy or nondairy)

1 large egg

1 tsp vanilla extract

1 cup (116 g) blanched almond flour

¼ cup (42 g) coconut flour

1 recipe Keto Caramel (page 359)

12 oz (340 g) dark chocolate chips

3 tbsp (45 g) coconut oil

Preheat the oven to 350°F (175°C). Line a 9 x 5–inch (23 x 13–cm) loaf pan with parchment paper. Line a baking sheet with a piece of parchment paper. Set both aside.

In a mixer, cream the butter and sugar until fluffy. Add the cream cheese, egg and vanilla and mix until combined. Add the almond flour and coconut flour and mix until a thick dough forms. Place the dough in the refrigerator for 30 minutes to harden. Turn the dough onto the prepared pan and press it down evenly. Bake for 25 to 30 minutes, until golden brown. Remove the pan from the oven and allow the shortbread to cool completely in the pan.

When the shortbread is completely cool, pour the caramel over the shortbread (make sure the caramel is cool, not warm, for this step). Place the pan in the refrigerator for 2 hours.

To make the chocolate coating, in a microwave-safe bowl, melt the chocolate and coconut oil in 30-second intervals until fully melted. Pour the melted chocolate into a bowl wide enough to dip the bars into.

Cut the chilled shortbread into 16 pieces and dip each piece into the chocolate, coating the entire bar by turning until completely covered. Place the bars on the parchment-lined baking sheet and put the sheet in the refrigerator for 10 minutes, or until the chocolate is fully hardened. Serve or place in a sealed container and store in the refrigerator for up to 2 weeks or in the freezer for up to 1 month.

Substitution Notes:

- To make this *dairy free*, use dairy-free cream cheese and vegan butter.

- To make this *Paleo*, use brown sugar and regular maple syrup and omit the sukrin gold and sugar-free maple syrup when making the Keto Caramel.

Makes 12 brownies

No-Bake Hazelnut Fudge Brownies

I really wanted to include an egg-free brownie option in this book because eggs are a common allergy. Plus, this recipe is a really fun and easy way for you to get a brownie fix without having to spend much time in the kitchen. The texture is fudgy and absolutely wonderful and will remind you of Nutella, thanks to the addition of delicious toasted hazelnuts.

Brownies

¾ cup (100 g) toasted hazelnuts

¾ cup (75 g) raw unsalted walnuts

1½ cups (200 g) roasted and salted macadamia nuts

2 tsp (10 ml) vanilla extract

¼ cup (60 ml) sugar-free honey or sugar-free maple syrup

¼ cup (30 g) keto powdered sugar

¼ cup (20 g) cocoa powder

¼ tsp Himalayan salt

Chocolate Ganache

2 tbsp (30 ml) softened or melted coconut oil

2½ tbsp (23 g) cocoa powder

1 tsp vanilla extract

¼ cup (60 ml) sugar-free honey or sugar-free maple syrup

Small pinch of salt

Preheat the oven 350°F (175°C). Line an 8½ x 5-inch (22 x 13-cm) bread pan with parchment paper.

To make the brownies, place the hazelnuts on a rimmed baking sheet and toast for 10 to 15 minutes. Remove the sheet from the oven and allow the nuts to cool. Rub the hazelnuts in a kitchen towel to remove all the skins.

Place the cooled, skinless hazelnuts, walnuts, macadamia nuts, vanilla, honey, powdered sugar, cocoa powder and salt in a food processor. Process for about 15 seconds, stop and wipe the sides down, then process again just until the mixture is smooth and shiny. Do not overprocess or the oils will begin to separate. (If this happens, just wipe the excess oil off the bars with paper towels. They will be slightly more fragile but still delicious.)

Pour the mixture in the prepared pan and press it down to create an even surface. Cover the pan and place it in the refrigerator for several hours, or overnight.

To make the chocolate ganache, whisk the coconut oil, cocoa powder, vanilla, honey and salt together until it is smooth and fluffy. The ganache can be spread on the brownies right after they are made or after they have chilled.

For the best results, store the brownies in the refrigerator for up to 2 weeks.

Substitution Notes:

- To make this **nut free**, swap the nuts out for raw pumpkin seeds and sunflower seeds.

- To make this **Paleo**, use real honey or real maple syrup. Omit the keto powdered sugar, or add 1 to 2 tablespoons (25 to 50 g) of palm sugar for a sweeter brownie.

NUT FREE **VEGETARIAN**

Makes 12 to 16 brownies (see Recipe Notes)

Perfect Low-Carb Brownies

Coming up with this brownie recipe was quite an adventure and one I would be fine not reliving. I tested this recipe 23 times, using different types of flour, different amounts of egg and various keto sugars. I was determined to figure out the best way to make low-carb brownies and my destination ended with these delicious gooey and fudgy brownies.

10 oz (283 g) dark chocolate chips (see Recipe Notes)

½ cup (112 g) salted butter

¾ cup (150 g) keto granulated sugar

1 to 2 tbsp (5 to 10 g) ground coffee (optional)

¼ tsp Himalayan salt

½ cup (50 g) lupin flour

¼ tsp double-acting baking powder

2 large eggs (room temperature; see Recipe Notes)

1 egg yolk (room temperature; see Recipe Notes)

2 tsp (10 ml) vanilla extract (or other extract of choice such as cherry, raspberry, peppermint, almond or hazelnut)

Preheat the oven to 350°F (175°C). Line a 7 x 7-inch (18 x 18-cm) or an 8 x 8-inch (20 x 20-cm) baking pan with parchment paper.

Place the chocolate and butter in a microwave-safe bowl and microwave for 1 minute. Mix until the mixture is smooth and the chocolate is melted. Stir in the sugar, coffee (if using), salt, lupin flour and baking powder. Add the eggs, egg yolk and vanilla. Stir together until the batter is fully mixed and smooth. Pour the batter into the prepared pan and bake for 25 to 26 minutes, until the brownies are still soft in the center but do not jiggle when moved.

Allow the brownies to fully cool for several hours before slicing. (They will finish baking while they cool.)

Recipe Notes:

- If you wish to drop the carbs in the recipe, you can use as little as 8 ounces (227 g) of chocolate chips.

- If you use Lily's chocolate chips, cut down the sugar to ½ cup (100 g) or your brownies will have a weird aftertaste.

- It is very important to allow the eggs to come to room temperature. Cold eggs will cause the chocolate to seize up.

- The fun part about this recipe is the adaptability. If keto sugars are not your preference and you aren't concerned about carbs, you can use coconut palm sugar or even organic cane sugar. The baking time will need to be increased, potentially up to 30 minutes, if using these sugars.

Substitution Note:

To make this ***dairy free***, use Enjoy Life's dark chocolate morsels and ghee or Nutiva brand flavored coconut oil for the butter.

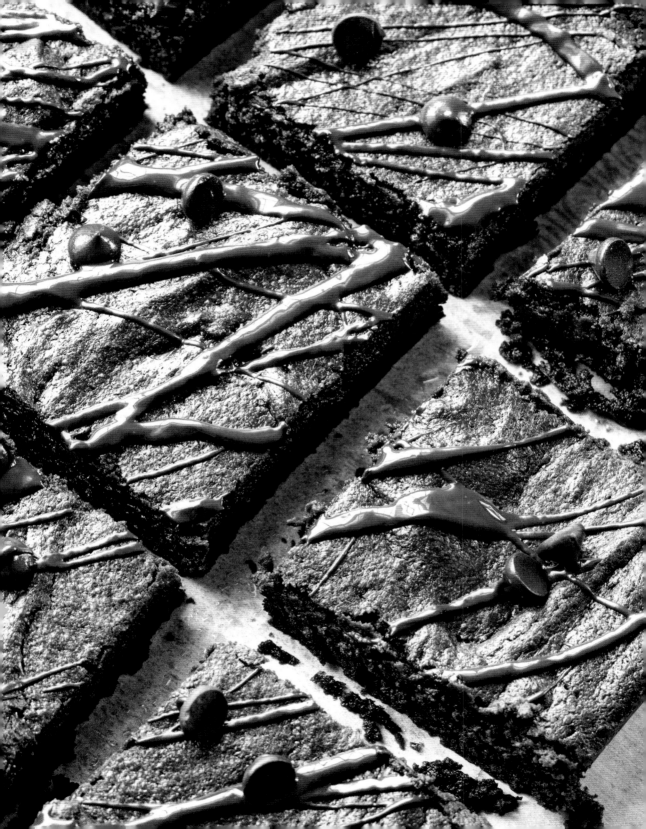

NUT FREE · VEGETARIAN

Makes 12 to 16 brownies

3 oz (85 g) cream cheese

1 egg white

¼ tsp vanilla extract

2 tsp (10 ml) sugar-free honey or keto powdered sugar

Small pinch of salt

1 recipe Perfect Low-Carb Brownies (page 352), unbaked

Cream Cheese Swirl Brownies

Using the Perfect Low-Carb Brownies (page 352) as a base, you can spin off so many fun brownie flavors. Adding a cream cheese swirl variation felt like the sensible thing to do! This recipe is absolutely decadent and delicious. I promise you can bring them to any gathering and no one will guess they are gluten free or keto.

Preheat the oven to 350°F (175°C). Line a 7 x 7-inch (18 x 18-cm) or an 8 x 8-inch (20 x 20-cm) baking pan with parchment paper.

To make the topping, in a small bowl, combine the cream cheese, egg white, vanilla, honey and salt and mix by hand until smooth. Set aside.

Pour the brownie batter into the prepared pan, then place dollops of the prepared cream cheese topping on the top of the brownies, leaving space between the dollops. Using a table knife, carefully swirl the cream cheese into the brownie batter. For the best results, clean off the knife a few times during this process. Promptly place the pan in the oven and bake for 25 to 26 minutes, until the brownies are still soft in the center but do not jiggle when moved.

Allow the brownies to fully cool for several hours before slicing. (They will finish baking while they cool.)

Recipe Note:

If you would like extra cream cheese, you can double this recipe and layer it into the bars. Do this by putting half of the brownie batter into the prepared pan, and dolloping with half of the cream cheese mixture. Swirl and spread the cream cheese, then top with the second half of the brownie batter and the remaining cream cheese. Repeat the swirling process.

Substitution Note:

To make this **dairy free**, use Enjoy Life's dark chocolate morsels, ghee or Nutiva brand flavored coconut oil in place of the butter and Kite Hill brand cream cheese for the topping.

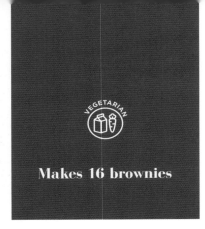

Makes 16 brownies

1 recipe Perfect Low-Carb Brownies (page 352)

1 recipe Keto Caramel (page 359)

½ recipe Chocolate Peanut Butter Cups (page 358), chopped

PMS Brownies

Back in 2015, I created the original PMS brownie recipe and it took the internet by storm. It quickly became one of the most popular recipes I have created in my 10-year career. It was an extremely indulgent Paleo brownie that was loaded with carbs and sugar. When I began the process of writing this book, it was my #1 goal to re-create that recipe in a much healthier way, which was not an easy process.

After many trial runs on the brownie base, figuring out a delicious caramel recipe and perfecting keto peanut butter cups, I was able to put together this glorious be-all, end-all brownie recipe. You start with a fudgy brownie, then dump on some caramel and top with peanut butter cups. The original recipe called for a layer of chocolate ganache and extra chocolate chips on top, but for the sake of carbs I opted to leave those out this round. Truth be told, while I used keto ingredients exclusively, these brownies have a lot of dark chocolate, which raised the carb count quite a bit. So, these brownies are still a special-occasion kind of treat. Although they come with all the indulgence that comes with the PMS brownie name, they have far less sugar.

Pour the caramel sauce over the top of the (cooled) pan of brownies and top with chopped peanut butter cups.

Substitution Notes:

* To make this **nut free**, use almond or SunButter in the peanut butter cups.

* To make this **dairy free**, use coconut oil and coconut cream instead of heavy cream and butter in the caramel. And use the dairy-free option in the brownies too.

(continued)

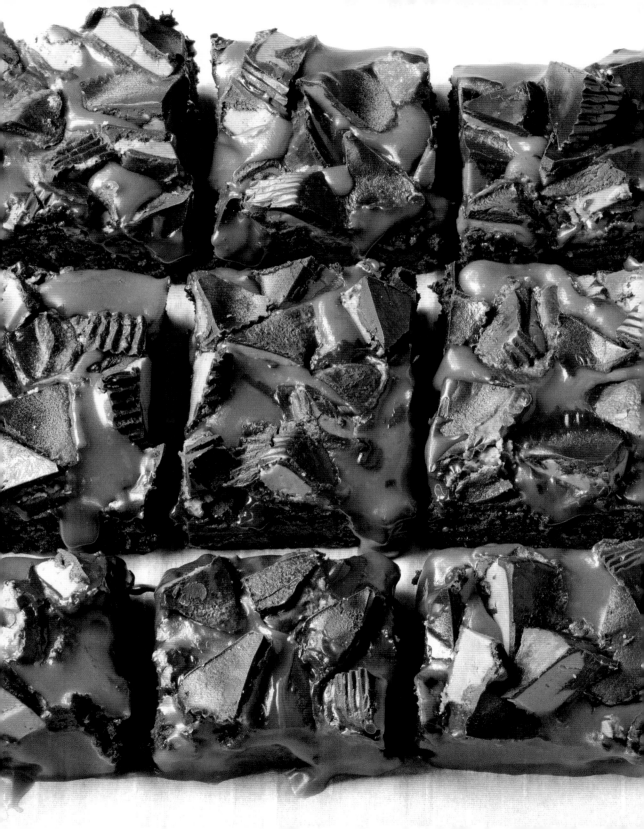

EGG FREE · DAIRY FREE · VEGETARIAN

Makes 32 chocolate peanut butter cups

2½ cups (420 g) dark chocolate chips

2½ tbsp (38 g) coconut oil

1 cup (256 g) peanut butter

2 tbsp (18 g) keto powdered sugar

1 tbsp (15 ml) sugar-free honey or sugar-free maple syrup

¼ tsp vanilla extract

⅛ tsp Himalayan salt

Chocolate Peanut Butter Cups

What combination is better than chocolate and peanut butter? Chocolate peanut butter cups with no sugar (and no one can tell the difference). These peanut butter cups are quick, easy and fun to make. For the best results, use regular dark chocolate chips—they have only one more carb per serving than low-carb brands of chocolate chips and taste much better. You can also use Enjoy Life brand dark chocolate morsels.

Put 32 aluminum cupcake liners on a baking tray. Set aside.

Combine the dark chocolate and coconut oil in a microwave-safe bowl. Melt the chocolate and coconut oil in the microwave, heating in 30-second intervals until fully melted. Using a teaspoon, drizzle the chocolate into the bottom of each of the cupcake liners. Refrigerate the cupcake liners for 10 minutes, until the chocolate is hard.

In a medium bowl, mix the peanut butter, powdered sugar, honey, vanilla and salt until smooth. Using a piping bag, fill the middle of the chocolate liners halfway with the peanut butter mixture. With the leftover chocolate, cover the peanut butter layer, using about 1½ teaspoons (19 g) of the chocolate mixture for each one.

Refrigerate for 15 minutes to set, then enjoy. Keep cold until ready to eat. Store in an airtight container in the refrigerator or freezer for up to 1 month.

Recipe Note:

For the best tasting PB cups, use regular dark chocolate chips rather than stevia-sweetened chips such as Lily's.

Substitution Notes:

- To make this **dairy free**, use Enjoy Life dark chocolate chips.

- To make this **Paleo**, use powdered honey or powdered maple sugar instead of powdered sugar and sugar-free honey, and use dairy-free dark chocolate chips.

EGG FREE · NUT FREE · VEGETARIAN

Makes 1½ cups (340 g)

¾ cup (180 ml) heavy cream or coconut cream skimmed off a can of unsweetened full-fat coconut milk

¼ cup (50 g) keto brown sugar (I recommend using Sukrin Gold brand for this recipe)

¼ cup (60 ml) sugar-free maple syrup or sugar-free honey

4 tbsp (56 g) salted butter (dairy or nondairy) or coconut oil

1 tbsp (15 ml) molasses (see Recipe Notes)

¼ tsp Himalayan salt

Keto Caramel

Get ready to be blown away. This caramel is the real deal! It doesn't taste like it's low in sugar—you could trick anyone with it. The flavor is incredible—I put it on everything.

Add the heavy cream, brown sugar, maple syrup, butter, molasses and salt to a saucepan over medium heat. Stir to combine the ingredients and allow the mixture to gently boil for 20 to 30 minutes until it reaches your desired thickness. Store the caramel in the refrigerator in a sealed container for up to 1 week.

Recipe Notes:

- If you use Sukrin Gold brand brown sugar and sugar-free honey, your caramel will remain a thick sauce that doesn't fully solidify unless frozen. This would be helpful in recipes where you want a looser, more pourable sauce. If you use another brand of keto brown sugar + sugar-free maple syrup, your caramel will solidify as it sits at room temperature. This can be useful in recipes that call for dipping the caramel in chocolate.

- If the caramel starts to separate while it is cooking, add more cream, 1 teaspoon at a time, and whisk well.

- If you want to make this dairy free, I recommend using butter-flavored coconut oil. Regular coconut oil will also work, but the flavor is best if you stick with a butter-flavored product.

- Molasses does have carbs and sugar. Using a little does wonders for the flavor. The recommended amount for this recipe is 1 tablespoon (15 ml) but you can use as little as 1 teaspoon.

Substitution Notes:

- To make this **dairy free**, use coconut cream and butter-flavored coconut oil.

- To make this **Paleo**, use palm sugar and real honey or maple syrup.

Makes 16 brownies

Blackberry Swirl Cheesecake Brownies

This is another super-indulgent brownie recipe that you won't be able to tell are substantially healthier than regular brownies. Make them as a special-occasion treat—the carbs are a bit higher than most keto desserts, but I promise they are worth the splurge.

Preheat the oven to 350°F (175°C). Line an 8 x 8–inch (20 x 20–cm) baking pan with parchment paper; set aside.

To make the brownie batter, add the dark chocolate and butter to a microwave-safe bowl. Melt the chocolate and butter in the microwave, heating in 30-second intervals until fully melted and smooth. Mix in the sugar, salt, flour, baking powder, eggs, yolk and vanilla. Stir well to combine. Pour the batter into the prepared pan and bake for 20 to 25 minutes. (Use a knife or toothpick to poke through the middle to make sure it is baked through. If the knife does not come out clean, bake for a few minutes longer.) Set aside to cool.

To make the cheesecake, using a hand mixer, mix the cream cheese in a medium bowl until smooth. When the cream cheese is smooth, add the heavy cream, vanilla and stevia extract. Use a spatula to smooth the cheesecake mixture onto the cooled brownies.

To make the blackberry sauce, place the blackberries, honey, vanilla, salt and 1 teaspoon of water in a small saucepan and bring to a simmer for 10 to 15 minutes over medium heat. Mash the blackberries occasionally to help them break down. The sauce is done when it is thick and the blackberries are completely broken down. (Note: You can also use an immersion blender to make the sauce smooth.) Let the sauce cool for a few minutes. Spoon the blackberry syrup on top of the cheesecake layer. Use a knife to lightly swirl the syrup into the cheesecake.

Brownie Batter

10 oz (283 g) dark chocolate chips

½ cup (112 g) salted butter

¾ cup (150 g) keto granulated sugar

¼ tsp Himalayan salt

½ cup (50 g) lupin flour

¼ tsp double-acting baking powder

2 large eggs (room temperature)

1 yolk (room temperature)

2 tsp (10 ml) vanilla extract

No-Bake Cheesecake

8 oz (227 g) cream cheese

½ cup (120 ml) heavy whipping cream or coconut cream

1 tsp vanilla extract

¼ tsp stevia extract or monk fruit extract

Blackberry Syrup

¾ cup (115 g) fresh or frozen blackberries

1½ tbsp (22 ml) sugar-free honey or sugar-free maple syrup

1 tsp vanilla extract

Pinch of Himalayan salt

Fresh sliced blackberries, for topping (optional)

Recipe Note:

See the Recipe Notes on page 352 for tips on substitutions and other brownie tips.

Substitution Note:

To make this ***dairy free***, use coconut cream instead of heavy whipping cream. Instead of cream cheese, use a dairy-free cream cheese. Use vegan butter and dairy-free dark chocolate chips.

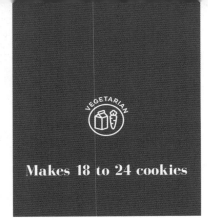

VEGETARIAN

Makes 18 to 24 cookies

Traditional Cut-Out Sugar Cookies

These cookies are really fun to make, as the dough will feel similar to classic sugar cookie dough. This is a great recipe to use with your favorite cookie cutters. For the best results, please use a kitchen scale to weigh the ingredients, using the gram measurements.

5 tbsp (70 g) salted butter slightly softened (or vegan buttery sticks)

2 tsp (10 ml) vanilla extract

1 large egg

½ cup (100 g) keto granulated sugar

1¼ cups (145 g) blanched almond flour

2 tbsp (10 g) oat fiber, plus more for rolling

¾ tsp xanthan or guar gum

1 tsp double-acting baking powder

¼ tsp Himalayan salt

Buttercream Frosting (page 388, optional)

Unsweetened coconut flakes, for topping (optional)

Using a hand mixer or in the bowl of a stand mixer, whip the butter, vanilla, egg and sugar. Add the almond flour, oat fiber, xanthan gum, baking powder and salt and mix until a smooth dough forms. Cover the bowl and place the dough in the refrigerator to chill for 1 hour.

After the dough has chilled, preheat the oven to 350°F (175°C). Line two baking sheets with parchment paper.

Place a sheet of parchment down on your work surface and sprinkle with some oat fiber. Place the dough on the parchment and sprinkle it with some additional oat fiber. Roll out the dough to about ¼ to ½ inch (6 to 13 mm) thick. If your dough is sticky, sprinkle more oat fiber on top, or place another sheet of parchment over the dough when rolling. Use the cookie cutters of your choice, and place the cookies on the prepared baking pans. Bake one pan at a time for 9 to 11 minutes (depending on the size of the cookie cutters you use), until they are lightly golden on the bottom.

Remove from the oven and cool fully before eating. Frost, if you wish, with the Buttercream Frosting and garnish with coconut flakes (if using). Store at room temperature, in the refrigerator or the freezer. Eat within 1 week for the best flavor.

Substitution Note:

To make this ***dairy free***, use dairy-free butter or Spectrum shortening in place of the butter.

Makes 16 cookies

½ cup (84 g) coconut flour

¾ cup + 2 tbsp (87 g) lupin flour, divided

1 cup (192 g) palm shortening or lard

½ cup (106 g) keto granulated sugar

1 tsp xanthan or guar gum

2 tsp (10 ml) vanilla extract

1 tsp almond extract (optional)

1 tsp double-acting baking powder

1 large egg

½ tsp Himalayan salt

Buttercream Frosting (page 388, optional)

Unsweetened coconut flakes, for topping (optional)

Shortbread Sugar Cookies

This recipe is a keto variation of the popular grain-free loft house–style sugar cookie recipe on my website. The texture is a bit different, as these are more of a shortbread cookie—different, but still delicious. The dough is a little bit fragile, but still workable. If making cookies with kids, my Traditional Cut-Out Sugar Cookie recipe (page 362) is better suited for all cookie cutters. For these shortbread cookies, I use a 2½-inch (6-cm) round cookie cutter and make these cookies thick. For the best results, please use a kitchen scale to weigh the ingredients, using the gram measurements.

Combine the coconut flour, ¾ cup (75 g) lupin flour, shortening, sugar, xanthan gum, vanilla, almond extract (if using), baking powder, egg and salt in the bowl of a stand mixer (or large bowl if mixing by hand). Mix until a smooth dough comes together. Place in the refrigerator for 30 to 60 minutes to chill.

Preheat the oven to 325°F (165°C). Line one to two baking sheets with parchment paper.

Line your work space with parchment, and dust a little lupin flour, about 2 tablespoons (12 g), on it. Place the cookie dough on the parchment, and place another piece of parchment on top of the dough, dusting with a little more lupin flour if needed to prevent sticking. Roll out the dough so it is ½ to ¾ inch (6 to 13 mm) thick. Use a 2½-inch (6-cm), or similar size, round cookie or biscuit cutter to cut out the cookies. Carefully remove the cookies from the parchment, lifting the parchment as needed to remove without breaking. Place all the cookies on the prepared pans. Bake for 10 to 13 minutes, until the bottoms are golden brown. Allow the cookies to cool fully, otherwise the cookies will crumble.

When fully cooled, you can frost the cookies using the Buttercream Frosting recipe, if desired, and garnish with coconut flakes (if using). Store in the refrigerator or freezer for up to 1 month.

Substitution Note:

To make this *Paleo*, use granulated palm sugar, granulated honey or granulated maple sugar.

Makes 18 cookies

Keto Samoa Cookies

Now you don't have to wait for that time of the year to get Girl Scout cookies; you can make them any time you like. These samoas are my favorite cookies and they are fun to make. If you can't find a donut cutter, I recommend a 2-inch (5-cm)-wide biscuit cutter and using an apple core tool to cut out the center piece!

2 cups (232 g) blanched almond flour

1 tbsp (10 g) tapioca starch

3 tbsp (42 g) salted butter

⅓ cup (65 g) keto granulated sugar

⅛ tsp Himalayan salt

¼ tsp double-acting baking powder

1 tbsp (15 ml) vanilla extract

1 tbsp (15 g) cream cheese (dairy or nondairy)

1 cup (168 g) dark chocolate chips

1 tbsp (15 g) coconut oil

1 cup (75 g) unsweetened coconut flakes

1 recipe Keto Caramel (page 359)

Preheat the oven to 350°F (175°C). Line two cookie sheets with parchment paper; set aside.

To make the cookies, in a food processor or by hand, mix the almond flour, tapioca starch, butter, sugar, salt, baking powder, vanilla and cream cheese together until a dough forms. Between two sheets of parchment paper roll out the dough to about ¼ inch (6 mm) thick, then use a donut cutter or a circle cookie cutter to create rings. Place the rings on the prepared baking sheet and bake the cookies for 10 to 12 minutes, until the edges of the cookies are golden. They will come out soft and chewy but as they cool the cookies will harden. Cool the cookies completely. Set the parchment-lined cookie sheets aside.

To make the topping, in a microwave-safe bowl, combine the chocolate chips and coconut oil and microwave in 30-second intervals until both are completely melted; stir to mix well. To toast the coconut flakes, add them to a small dry pan and cook over medium heat until golden brown, tossing often. Pour in a bowl so they don't continue toasting.

Dunk the bottom of each cookie in the chocolate, swirl to coat, then lightly shake off the excess chocolate. Place the cookies, chocolate-side up, back on the parchment-lined cookie sheets and place in the refrigerator to harden for 10 to 15 minutes.

When the chocolate is hard, flip the cookies and dunk the sides not covered in chocolate in the caramel, then sprinkle on the toasted coconut flakes. Place the cookies back in the refrigerator to harden again for a few minutes and then drizzle the leftover chocolate over the caramel and coconut flakes. Allow the chocolate to harden before serving. Store in a sealed container in the refrigerator for up to 1 week or in the freezer for up to 1 month.

Substitution Notes:

- To make this **_dairy free_**, use applesauce instead of the cream cheese. Swap the butter for palm shortening.

- To make this **_Paleo_**, use palm sugar and real honey.

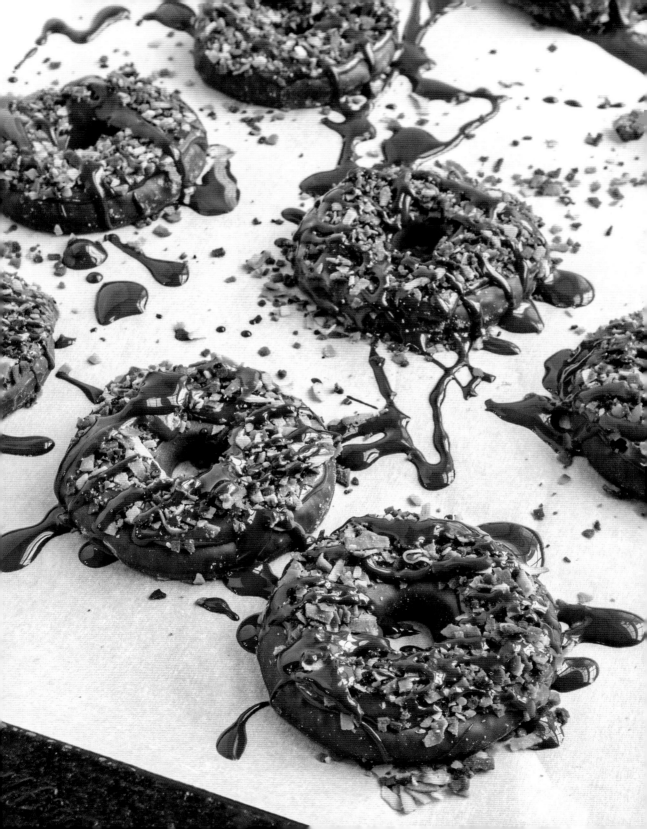

Makes 10 cookies

Quick Peanut Butter Chocolate Chip Cookies

This recipe could not be easier. Throw these cookies together in 5 minutes and eat them within 30. They taste like classic peanut butter cookies with real sugar.

1 cup (256 g) creamy peanut butter

⅓ cup (65 g) keto granulated sugar

1 large egg

1 tsp vanilla extract

¼ tsp Himalayan salt

¼ cup (42 g) dark chocolate chips (dairy or nondairy)

Preheat the oven to 350°F (175°C). Line a baking sheet with parchment.

In a large bowl, mix together the peanut butter, sugar, egg, vanilla, salt and chocolate chips. Stir until a smooth dough forms.

Scoop out about 1½ tablespoons (30 g) of dough per cookie and roll them into balls. Place them on the baking sheet 1 inch (3 cm) apart. Press each cookie with a fork twice to flatten and make a cross-hatch pattern. Bake for 10 to 13 minutes, until the edges are golden. Let cool and eat. Store in a container at room temperature for 1 week or in the freezer for up to 1 month.

Substitution Notes:

- To make this ***dairy free***, use dairy-free chocolate chips.

- To make this ***Paleo***, use coconut palm sugar.

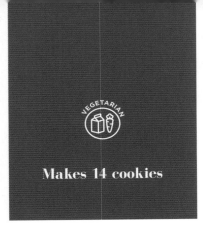

Makes 14 cookies

Classic Scoop-and-Bake Chocolate Chip Cookies

I went on a mission to create a chocolate chip cookie that could be scooped and baked. There is something so satisfying about a cookie melting down into the perfect shape. These cookies are crisp on the edges and soft on the inside. For the best results, please use a kitchen scale to weigh the ingredients, using the gram measurements.

1 stick (8 tbsp [112 g]) slightly softened salted butter (or nondairy buttery sticks)

½ cup (100 g) keto granulated sugar or pure erythritol

1 large egg

1½ cups (174 g) blanched almond flour

¼ tsp Himalayan salt

¼ tsp double-acting baking powder

½ to ¾ cup (84 to 126 g) dark chocolate chips (dairy or nondairy)

Preheat the oven to 350°F (175°C). Place a sheet of parchment paper on a large cookie sheet.

Using a hand mixer or stand mixer, beat the butter, sugar and egg together at high speed. Add the almond flour, salt and baking powder and beat until a smooth cookie dough forms. Stir in the chocolate chips. Using a medium cookie scoop, scoop out 14 cookies and place them on the baking sheet ½ inch (13 mm) or so apart. Bake for 12 to 14 minutes, until golden brown on the bottoms.

Allow the cookies to cool on the pan for 30 minutes before transferring to a storage container. Store in an airtight container at room temperature for up to 1 week or in the freezer for up to 1 month.

Substitution Notes:

- To make this **dairy free**, use dairy-free butter and dairy-free chocolate chips.

- To make this **Paleo**, use granulated palm sugar, granulated honey or granulated maple sugar.

Makes 12 cookies

2 cups (232 g) blanched almond flour

½ cup (100 g) keto granulated sugar

1 tsp double-acting baking powder

¼ tsp Himalayan salt

3 tbsp + 1 tsp (50 g) coconut oil

1 tbsp (15 ml) vanilla extract

2 tbsp (30 ml) unsweetened nondairy milk

½ cup (82 g) dairy-free dark chocolate chunks (I recommend Enjoy Life brand)

Dairy- and Egg-Free Chocolate Chunk Cookies

These cookies are a great option for those needing to avoid eggs and/or dairy. The dough may feel a little crumbly at first, but after about 30 seconds of mixing with your hands, it will start to become moist and will hold together well. Do not knead the dough much longer beyond when it comes together, or it will become oily and crumbly.

Preheat the oven to 350°F (175°C). Line a cookie sheet with parchment paper.

In the bowl of a stand mixer (or by hand), combine the almond flour, sugar, baking powder and salt, then add the coconut oil, vanilla and nondairy milk and mix until the dough is well combined. When the dough is incorporated, stir in the chocolate chunks. Divide the dough into 12 equal pieces and form each piece into patties about ¾ inch (2 cm) thick and about 3 inches (8 cm) wide. Place the cookies on the prepared cookie sheet.

Bake for 13 to 15 minutes, until the bottom and the edges start to turn golden brown. Let the cookies cool completely before removing from the pan. Store in a sealed bag in the refrigerator for up to 1 week or the freezer for up to 1 month.

Substitution Note:

To make this **Paleo**, use granulated sugar, granulated maple or granulated honey in place of the keto sugar.

Cakes, Pies and Ice Cream

This chapter doesn't have to be opened only when prepping for birthdays and celebrations as these recipes are healthy enough to enjoy any day of the year.

← See recipe on page 379.

Makes 8 to 10 servings

Citrus Rose Angel Food Cake

This elegant two-toned cake has a delicious light citrus flavor, and the texture of the cake is spot on when compared to a cake filled with sugar and starch. You have a few options when it comes to coloring this cake. I used the Pink Pitaya powder, which turns a light orange color when baked. If you wish for a bolder two-color effect you can use gel food coloring. Pink or orange would both be really beautiful options. You can use as little or as much of the gel food coloring as you would like. The same goes for the citrus glaze; I used a bit of Suncore's Sunglow Goji Berry powder to give the frosting a pastel color, but feel free to use food coloring here as well.

Cake

1 cup (125 g) keto powdered sugar

¼ cup (20 g) oat fiber

¾ cup (93 g) cassava flour

Zest of 2 lemons or 1 large orange

12 large egg whites, chilled

2 tsp (6 g) cream of tartar

1 tbsp (8 g) pink pitaya powder (or pink or orange gel food coloring; the amount used is up to you)

Preheat the oven to 350°F (175°C). Clean and dry a standard-sized angel food cake pan but *do not* grease it.

To make the cake, use a scale to weigh out the powdered sugar, oat fiber and cassava flour using the gram measurements, then add them to a mixing bowl. Stir them to combine and then sift them. Add the citrus zest to the dry ingredients.

Place the chilled egg whites in a large bowl. Using a hand mixer, mix on high for about 30 seconds, until the eggs are frothy. Add the cream of tartar, then turn the hand mixer back on high and mix until the eggs form soft peaks. Gently fold in one-third of the dry ingredients, using a spatula. Mix as little as possible, stirring only to incorporate. Repeat with another third of the dry ingredients, again mixing as little as possible. Fold in the last third of the dry ingredients.

To color, put half of the batter in a second bowl. Add the pink pitaya powder (or optional gel food coloring) to one of the bowls.

Pour the pink batter into the cake pan. Without smoothing out the pink batter first, add the plain batter to the top, then smooth the top of the plain batter. Carefully place the cake pan on the center rack in the preheated oven. Bake for 40 to 45 minutes, until a long toothpick comes out clean and the cake feels springy and firm to the touch. Note that you should *not* open the oven door for the first 30 minutes of baking.

(continued)

Citrus Rose Angel Food Cake (cont.)

Citrus Glaze

¾ cup (180 ml) full-fat coconut cream from a can

¼ cup (60 ml) coconut water (from the same can)

4 tbsp (35 g) keto powdered sugar

Zest of 1 lemon or orange

½ tsp vanilla extract

⅛ tsp Himalayan salt

1 tbsp (7 g) Suncore Foods Sunglow Goji Berry powder or food coloring

1½ thinly sliced lemons, for garnish

Dried edible rose petals from Suncore Foods, for garnish (optional)

Optional Toppings

Whipped cream or Dairy-Free Whipped Topping (page 484)

Fresh berries

When the cake is done, remove the pan from the oven and quickly flip it upside down on a baking rack. Allow the cake to cool in this position for 2 hours or more. If you are in a rush, after the first 30 minutes of cooling the cake can be placed upside down in the refrigerator for another 30 to 60 minutes.

While the cake is cooling, whisk the coconut cream, coconut water, powdered sugar, citrus zest, vanilla, salt and coloring in a small bowl until completely smooth.

When the cake is completely cool, using a small knife or small offset spatula, carefully cut the cake out of the pan. Drizzle the cake with the glaze, then add the lemon slices and rose petals or whipped cream and berries. Cover and store at room temperature (unless it has been glazed, in which case it will age best in the refrigerator, fully covered) for 3 to 4 days.

Recipe Notes:

- Don't skip the sifting step. It's very important and will ensure that your cake turns out smooth and fluffy.

- Be sure to have all your ingredients out and prepared before you start preparing the eggs, as you want to work fairly quickly once they reach soft peaks, to get the flour and sugar mixed in and to get the cake into the oven.

- Before you whip the egg whites you may want to watch a YouTube video on the difference between egg whites going from soft peaks to hard peaks. Knowing the difference is what will make or break this cake. Always cool upside down or your cake will sink.

- If you wish to further decrease the carb count in this cake, ¼ cup (31 g) of the cassava flour can be swapped for ¼ cup (24 g) of vanilla whey protein powder.

- If your house is cold, your coconut cream may be solid. If this is the case, warm it up briefly in a saucepan or microwave just until it's smooth when whisked.

Substitution Note:

To make this **Paleo**, swap the keto powdered sugar for powdered honey or powdered maple sugar. Omit the oat fiber and instead use 1 cup (122 g) of cassava flour.

NUT FREE **VEGETARIAN**

Makes 8 to 10 servings

Cake

1 cup (125 g) keto powdered sugar

¼ cup (20 g) oat fiber

½ cup (62 g) cassava flour

¼ cup (21 g) vanilla whey protein powder

12 large egg whites, chilled

2 tsp (6 g) cream of tartar

Seeds from 1 vanilla bean (optional)

Vanilla Angell Food Cake with Lavender Lime Glaze

Because I spent lots of time testing and coming up with this recipe, I think it's fair to give it my last name, as the spelling is only one letter different. You'll be blown away by how great this Angel(l) food cake is despite being completely sugar free and low carb. I suggest using only Otto's brand cassava flour in this recipe as other brands don't work the same. I used whey-based vanilla protein powder in this recipe to keep the carbs super low, but if you have a dairy sensitivity you can swap out the protein powder for an additional quarter cup (31 g) of cassava flour (making it a grand total of three-quarters of a cup [93 g]). This brings the carb count up just a tiny bit.

Preheat the oven to 350°F (175°C). Clean and dry a standard-sized angel food cake pan but *do not* grease it.

To make the cake, use a scale to weigh out the powdered sugar, oat fiber, cassava flour and whey protein using the gram measurements, then add them to a mixing bowl. Stir them to combine and then sift them.

Place the chilled egg whites in a large bowl. Using a hand mixer, mix on high for about 30 seconds, until the eggs are frothy. Add the cream of tartar, then turn the hand mixer back on high and mix until the eggs form soft peaks. Gently fold in the vanilla and one-third of the dry ingredients, using a spatula. Mix as little as possible, stirring only to incorporate. Repeat with another third of the dry ingredients, again mixing as little as possible. Fold in the last third of dry ingredients.

Add the batter to the cake pan and smooth the top with a spatula. Carefully place the cake pan on the center rack in the preheated oven. Bake for 40 to 45 minutes, until a long toothpick comes out clean and the cake feels springy and firm to the touch. Note that you should *not* open the oven door for the first 30 minutes of baking.

(continued)

Vanilla Angell Food Cake with Lavender Lime Glaze (cont.)

Lavender Lime Glaze

¾ cup (180 ml) coconut cream from a can

¼ cup (60 ml) coconut water (from the same can)

4 tbsp (35 g) keto powdered sugar

Zest of 1 lime

⅛ tsp Himalayan salt

½ tsp lavender oil (optional)

2 tsp (10 ml) lime juice

1 tsp pink pitaya powder (optional)

1¼ tsp (6 g) sapphire wolfberry powder or food coloring (optional)

Optional Toppings

Lime slices

Whipped cream or Dairy-Free Whipped Topping (page 484)

Fresh berries

When the cake is done, remove the pan from the oven and quickly flip it upside down on a baking rack. Allow the cake to cool in this position for 2 hours or more. If you are in a rush, after the first 30 minutes of cooling the cake can be placed upside down in the refrigerator for another 30 to 60 minutes.

While the cake is cooling, whisk the coconut cream, coconut water, powdered sugar, lime zest, salt, lavender oil (if using), lime juice, pitaya powder (if using) and sapphire wolfberry powder or food coloring (if using) in a small bowl until completely smooth.

When the cake is completely cool, using a small knife or small offset spatula, carefully cut the cake out of the pan. Top with the glaze and limes or whipped cream and berries. Cover and store at room temperature (unless it has been glazed, in which case it will age best in the refrigerator fully covered) for 3 to 4 days.

Recipe Note:

If your house is cold, your coconut cream may be solid. If this is the case, warm it up briefly in a saucepan or microwave just until it's smooth when whisked.

Substitution Notes:

- To make this **dairy free**, swap the whey protein powder for ¼ cup (31 g) more cassava flour.

- To make this **Paleo**, swap the keto powdered sugar for powdered honey or powdered maple sugar. Omit the oat fiber and whey powder and use 1 cup (122 g) cassava flour instead.

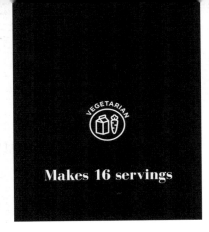

VEGETARIAN

Makes 16 servings

Pineapple Lime Coconut Cake

Cake is great for any occasion, but this pineapple lime coconut cake would make a great addition to a wedding shower or baby shower. If you are looking to reduce your carbs, halve the cake and frosting recipes and make a single layer.

Preheat the oven to 325°F (165°C). Line two 9-inch (23-cm) springform pans with parchment paper.

To make the cake, add the almond flour, lupin flour, oat fiber, baking powder, eggs, butter, sugar, pineapple extract, almond milk, lemon juice, lime zest and salt to a large mixing bowl. Mix until combined. Split the mixture between the two prepared pans. Place both springform pans in the oven and bake for 55 to 60 minutes, until the cake is golden brown and a toothpick inserted in the middle comes out clean.

To make the frosting, add the butter, powdered sugar, vanilla, shortening, water, pineapple extract, lime juice and lime zest to the bowl of a mixer (or use a large bowl and a hand mixer) and beat until fluffy and smooth. Remove from the mixing bowl and place in a container in the refrigerator to chill. Remove the frosting from the refrigerator 10 to 15 minutes prior to frosting the cake. Allow the cake to cool to room temperature and then frost and garnish with the coconut flakes. Store in an airtight container in the refrigerator for up to 7 to 10 days.

Cake

4 cups (464 g) blanched almond flour

1 cup (100 g) lupin flour

½ cup (40 g) oat fiber

1 tbsp (14 g) double-acting baking powder

8 large eggs

1 cup (224 g) softened butter

1⅓ cups (266 g) keto granulated sugar

6 tbsp (90 ml) pineapple extract

1½ cups (360 ml) unsweetened almond or coconut milk

2 tsp (10 ml) lemon juice

Zest of 1 lime

¼ tsp Himalayan salt

Frosting

28 tbsp (384 g) salted butter, softened

4 cups (500 g) keto powdered sugar

1 tsp vanilla extract

¾ cup (154 g) palm shortening

4 tbsp (60 ml) water or unsweetened almond milk

4 tbsp (60 ml) pineapple extract

6 tbsp (90 ml) lime juice

Zest of 1 lime

4 cups (300 g) unsweetened coconut flakes, for garnish

Recipe Notes:

- The coconut flakes pictured are large flakes, lightly toasted. However, any size coconut flakes can be used.

- If you are sensitive to the aftertaste of sugar alcohols, I recommend using the Cream Cheese Frosting recipe on page 234 instead of this one but with the following changes: instead of using the vanilla and cream in that recipe use 2 tablespoons (30 ml) of pineapple extract and 1 tablespoon (15 ml) of lemon juice plus the zest of half a lime.

Substitution Note:

To make this **dairy free**, use dairy-free butter.

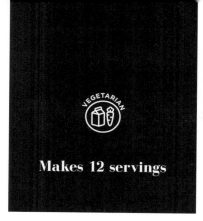

Low-Carb Marble Bundt Pound Cake

This is a special occasion cake fit for any gathering! You will need a 16-cup (3.8-L) Bundt pan, and at least two large mixing bowls. But I assure you this beautiful cake is a showstopper and well worth the effort (and added carbs). While it uses all low-carb ingredients, due to the fact that it is a very thick cake, the carb count does go up, so just be sure to watch your portions if keeping your net carbs low is important to you.

Vanilla Cake

Nonstick spray

2 cups (232 g) blanched almond flour

½ cup (113 g) salted butter or coconut oil, melted and cooled

8 oz (227 g) cream cheese

1¼ cups (265 g) keto granulated sugar

6 large eggs

1 tbsp (15 ml) vanilla extract

½ cup (40 g) oat fiber

¼ tsp Himalayan salt

1 tbsp (15 ml) water

2 tsp (9 g) double-acting baking powder

Chocolate Cake

2 cups (232 g) blanched almond flour

½ cup (40 g) cocoa powder

½ cup (113 g) salted butter or coconut oil, melted and cooled

8 oz (227 g) cream cheese

1¼ cups (265 g) keto granulated sugar

6 large eggs

1 tbsp (15 ml) vanilla extract

¼ cup (20 g) oat fiber

½ tsp Himalayan salt

1 tbsp (15 ml) water

2 tsp (9 g) double-acting baking powder

Preheat the oven to 350°F (175°C). Spray a 16-cup (3.8-L) Bundt pan with nonstick spray; set aside.

To make the vanilla cake, in a large bowl, using a hand mixer, beat the almond flour, melted butter, cream cheese, sugar and eggs until smooth. Stir in the vanilla, oat fiber, salt and water; set aside. Do not include the baking powder yet; you do not want it to activate too soon.

To make the chocolate cake, in a second clean large bowl, using a hand mixer, beat the almond flour, cocoa powder, melted butter, cream cheese, sugar and eggs until smooth. Stir in the vanilla, oat fiber, salt, water and baking powder; set aside.

Return to the vanilla cake and stir the baking powder into the batter.

Spoon two to three large spoonfuls of the vanilla cake batter into the prepared pan, then add two to three large spoonfuls of chocolate cake batter on top of the vanilla batter. Continue to alternate the batter until both flavors are gone. Stick a clean table knife into the cake and very carefully swirl around. For the best results, remove and clean off the knife, then repeat this process five to six times.

(continued)

Low-Carb Marble Bundt Pound Cake (cont.)

Icing

1 cup (125 g) keto powdered sugar or powdered erythritol

¼ cup (60 ml) heavy cream or coconut cream

½ tbsp (7 ml) vanilla

Pinch of Himalayan salt

Food coloring or about 2 tsp (1 g) Suncore Foods superfruit powders (I used sapphire wolfberry)

1 cup (150 g) sliced blackberries, for topping (optional)

Place the pan on the middle rack of the oven and set a timer for 30 minutes. After 30 minutes, gently tent the cake loosely with aluminum foil. Bake for an additional 30 minutes, until it's a deep golden brown and a cake tester or toothpick inserted in the middle comes out clean.

To make the glaze, in a small bowl, whisk together the powdered sugar, heavy cream, vanilla, salt and food coloring. Ice the cake after allowing it to fully cool. For added decoration, top with fresh blackberries (if using).

Substitution Note:

To make this **dairy free**, use the melted coconut oil option and dairy-free cream cheese. For the icing, use the coconut cream option.

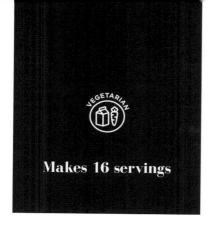

Makes 16 servings

Strawberry Lemonade Cake

This is the perfect kid's cake, particularly if you have a girly girl in your life who loves all things pink! The cake is delicious, soft and airy but definitely tastes like strawberry lemonade. If you are looking to reduce your carbs, halve the cake and frosting recipes and make a single layer.

Cake

4 cups (464 g) blanched almond flour

1 cup (100 g) lupin flour

½ cup (40 g) oat fiber

1 tbsp (14 g) double-acting baking powder

8 large eggs

1 cup (224 g) softened butter, melted coconut oil or mild-flavored oil

1⅓ cups (266 g) keto granulated sugar

5 tbsp (75 ml) strawberry extract

1½ cups (360 ml) unsweetened almond or coconut milk

2 tbsp + 2 tsp (40 ml) lemon juice

Zest of 1 large lemon

¼ tsp Himalayan salt

Preheat the oven to 325°F (165°C). Line two 9-inch (23-cm) springform pans with parchment paper.

To make the cake, add the almond flour, lupin flour, oat fiber, baking powder, eggs, butter, sugar, strawberry extract, almond milk, lemon juice, lemon zest and salt to a large mixing bowl. Mix until combined. Split the mixture between the two prepared pans. Place both springform pans in the oven and bake for 55 to 60 minutes, until the cake is golden and a toothpick inserted in the middle of the cake comes out clean.

(continued)

Strawberry Lemonade Cake (cont.)

Buttercream Frosting

28 tbsp (384 g) salted butter, dairy or nondairy, softened

4 cups (500 g) keto powdered sugar

1 tsp vanilla extract

¾ cup (154 g) shortening

4 tbsp (60 ml) water or unsweetened almond or coconut milk

2 to 4 tbsp (30 to 60 ml) strawberry extract, to taste (see Recipe Notes)

2 to 4 tbsp (30 to 60 ml) lemon juice, to taste (see Recipe Notes)

Zest of 2 lemons

2 tbsp (30 g) pink pitaya powder (optional for color) or pink or yellow food coloring

2 to 4 cups (200 to 400 g) sliced fresh strawberries, for topping (optional)

To make the frosting, add the butter, powdered sugar, vanilla, shortening, water, strawberry extract, lemon juice, lemon zest and pitaya powder (if using) to the bowl of a mixer (or use a large bowl and a hand mixer) and beat until fluffy and smooth. Remove from the mixing bowl and place in a container in the refrigerator to chill. Remove the frosting from the refrigerator 10 to 15 minutes prior to frosting the cake.

Allow the cake to cool to room temperature and then frost. Store in an airtight container in the refrigerator for up to 7 to 10 days. If desired, top with fresh sliced strawberries before serving.

Recipe Notes:

- The recipe has a range of amounts for the strawberry extract and lemon juice. Use the higher amounts for a more intense flavor.

- If you are sensitive to the aftertaste of sugar alcohols, I recommend using the Cream Cheese Frosting recipe on page 234 instead of this one, but with the following changes: instead of using the vanilla and cream in that recipe use 3 tablespoons (45 ml) of strawberry extract and the zest of half a lemon.

Substitution Note:

To make this *dairy free*, use dairy-free butter in the frosting recipe. And coconut oil or mild-flavored oil in the cake.

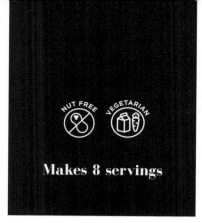

NUT FREE   VEGETARIAN

Makes 8 servings

Vanilla Bourbon Strawberry Shortcake with Mascarpone Whipped Cream

Strawberry shortcake is one of my all-time favorite desserts. This one takes it to another heavenly level. The vanilla and bourbon-soaked strawberries are so delicious all on their own. Then with the perfect keto biscuits, and mascarpone whipped cream you end up with an incredibly decadent summer dessert. For this recipe you will need to premake a batch of Fluffy and Flaky Biscuits from page 230.

Strawberries

¼ cup (60 ml) sugar-free honey or maple syrup

¼ cup (60 ml) bourbon

2 tsp (10 ml) vanilla extract

¼ tsp Himalayan salt

2½ cups (415 g) sliced strawberries, fresh or frozen (thawed if frozen)

Mascarpone Whipped Cream

1 cup (240 g) mascarpone

1 cup (240 ml) whipping cream

3 tbsp (45 ml) sugar-free honey or sugar-free maple syrup

¼ tsp nutmeg

1 tsp vanilla extract

Pinch of Himalayan salt

8 Fluffy and Flaky Biscuits (page 230)

To make the strawberries, mix the honey, bourbon, vanilla and salt in a microwave-safe bowl. Heat in the microwave for 1 minute, or transfer to a small saucepan and heat over medium heat just until the mixture reaches a gentle boil. Place in the refrigerator or freezer to cool.

Place the strawberries in a medium bowl. When the bourbon syrup is mostly cool, pour it over the strawberries. Set aside for 10 to 15 minutes.

To make the whipped cream, in another bowl, whip together the mascarpone, whipping cream, honey, nutmeg, vanilla extract and salt by hand or using a hand mixer until the ingredients are fully combined.

To assemble, cut each biscuit in half. On 8 of the halves, layer the strawberries and the mascarpone whipped cream, then place another biscuit half on top of each.

Substitution Note:

To make this ***dairy free***, mix 2 cups (160 g) of Dairy-Free Whipped Topping (page 484) with nutmeg, vanilla, sugar-free honey or sugar-free maple syrup to taste.

Makes 16 servings

Vanilla Nut-Free Cake Base

This recipe can be cut in half if you wish to only make a single-layer cake. For a single layer, use just one 6-inch (15-cm) pan. Frost or decorate this cake however you wish. I recommend serving it with your favorite type of fresh berries.

Nonstick spray

8 large eggs

½ cup (96 g) palm shortening

½ cup (84 g) coconut flour

½ cup (100 g) keto granulated sugar

1 tsp stevia extract or monk fruit extract

1 to 2 tbsp (15 to 30 ml) vanilla extract (or other extract of choice such as hazelnut, coconut, almond, cherry, raspberry, etc.)

¼ tsp salt

¼ tsp xanthan or guar gum

1 tsp double-acting baking powder

Zest of 1 lemon, lime or orange (optional)

Preheat the oven to 350°F (175°C). Grease a 9-inch (23-cm) cake pan or two 6-inch (15-cm) pans with cooking spray. (I highly recommend using springform pans for the easiest removal, as this cake tends to stick.)

Place the eggs in the bowl of a food processor or stand mixer. Blend on high until the eggs are fluffy. Add the shortening and blend again until smooth. Add the coconut flour, sugar, stevia extract, vanilla, salt, xanthan gum, baking powder and zest (if using) and blend until smooth. Pour the batter into the cake pan(s) and smooth the top(s) with a spatula.

Bake for 35 to 40 minutes, until a toothpick comes out clean. Let the cake(s) cool completely before removing from the pan(s) and decorating. Store at room temperature or in the refrigerator for up to 3 days or freeze for up to 1 month.

Substitution Note:

To make this **Paleo**, use coconut palm sugar in place of the keto granulated sugar and omit the stevia or monk fruit extract.

Nonstick spray

8 large eggs

½ cup (76 g) palm shortening

½ cup (84 g) coconut flour

½ cup (100 g) keto granulated sugar

1 tsp stevia extract or monk fruit extract

1 to 2 tbsp (15 to 30 ml) vanilla extract or other flavor extract of choice (hazelnut, coconut, almond, cherry, raspberry, etc.)

½ tsp Himalayan salt

1 tsp double-acting baking powder

⅓ cup (32 g) cocoa powder

Zest of 1 orange (optional)

Nut-Free Chocolate Cake Base

This recipe can be cut in half if you wish to only make a single-layer cake. For a single layer, use just one 6-inch (15-cm) pan. Frost or decorate this cake however you wish. The orange zest adds some good flavor but it's 100% optional.

Preheat the oven to 350°F (175°C) and grease two 7-inch (18-cm) springform pans or one 9-inch (23-cm) cake pan with cooking spray or oil. (I highly recommend using springform pans for the easiest removal, as this cake tends to stick.)

In a food processor, stand mixer or with a hand mixer, beat the eggs for about 2 minutes, until they are light and fluffy. Add the palm shortening, coconut flour, sugar, stevia extract, vanilla, salt, baking powder, cocoa powder and orange zest (if using) and mix until the ingredients are well combined.

Pour the batter into the cake pan(s) and smooth the top(s). Bake for 35 to 40 minutes, until a toothpick comes out clean. Let cool completely before removing from the pan(s) and decorating. Store at room temperature, in the refrigerator for up to 3 days or freeze for 1 month.

Substitution Note:

To make this *Paleo*, use coconut palm sugar in place of the granulated sugar and omit the stevia or monk fruit extract.

Makes 16 servings

Almond Flour Cake Base

This recipe makes a single 9-inch (23-cm) cake. It can be doubled with great success but may need to bake longer with two pans in the oven, up to 55 minutes.

Preheat the oven to 325°F (165°C). Line the bottom of a 9-inch (23-cm) springform pan with parchment.

Add the almond flour, lupin flour, oat fiber, baking powder, salt, butter, sugar, eggs, vanilla, heavy cream, lemon juice and zest (if using) to the bowl of a stand mixer or a large bowl if using a hand mixer. Beat until the batter is smooth.

Pour the batter into the prepared pan and tap the pan on the counter until the top is smooth. Bake for 45 to 50 minutes, until the cake is golden brown and a toothpick inserted in the center of the cake comes out clean. Let the cake cool fully before removing from the pan.

2 cups (232 g) blanched almond flour

½ cup (50 g) lupin flour

¼ cup (20 g) oat fiber

2 tsp (7 g) double-acting baking powder

½ tsp Himalayan salt

½ cup (120 ml) melted (salted) butter, melted coconut oil or mild-flavored oil

⅔ cup (140 g) keto granulated sugar

4 large eggs

1 to 3 tbsp (15 to 45 ml) vanilla or other flavor extract of choice

¾ cup (180 ml) heavy cream or unsweetened full-fat coconut milk

2 tsp (10 ml) lemon juice or apple cider vinegar

Zest of 1 lemon, lime or orange (optional)

Recipe Notes:

- The amount of extract you use depends on how strong you would like the flavor to be. If you only use 1 tablespoon (15 ml) of extract, use an extra 2 tablespoons (30 ml) of cream to make sure the batter is the correct consistency.

- If keto sugars aren't your cup of tea—organic cane sugar, granulated honey or granulated maple sugar can be used.

Substitution Note:

To make this ***dairy free***, shake a full-fat unsweetened can of coconut milk and use instead of heavy cream. Use melted coconut oil or mild-flavored oil option.

EGG FREE · **NUT FREE** · **VEGETARIAN**

Makes roughly 3 cups (680 g)

Frosting in Three Flavors

Making your own cake flavor is a blast, and with these frosting recipes you can really have fun and get creative mixing and matching your favorite flavors. Grab your favorite extract and choose whichever frosting works best for your diet. These frostings can be colored with food coloring, Suncore superfruit powders or you can make your own natural food dye from page 403.

Sugar-Free Buttercream

This recipe is the perfect amount for 1 batch of sugar cookies or can be used to frost a one-layer 9-inch (23-cm) cake. For a two-layer cake you will need 1½ to 2 batches of frosting.

14 tbsp (168 g) salted butter, softened (or vegan buttery sticks)

2 cups + 2 tbsp (270 g) keto powdered sugar

½ tsp vanilla extract

6 tbsp (84 g) palm shortening, room temperature

2 tbsp (30 ml) water or unsweetened dairy-free milk

1 tsp to 1 tbsp (5 to 15 ml) flavor extract such as almond, peppermint, coconut, maple, rum, coffee or orange (optional; see Recipe Notes)

Zest of 1 lemon, lime or orange (optional)

Add the butter, powdered sugar, vanilla, shortening, water, flavor extract (if using) and zest (if using) to the bowl of a stand mixer (or to a large bowl if using a hand mixer), and beat until fluffy and smooth.

Store the frosting in the refrigerator for a month or longer.

I recommend letting the frosting sit out at room temperature to soften for about 30 minutes before frosting a cake, as it will be easier to spread if warm.

Recipe Notes:

*   How much flavor extract you use will depend on your personal preference and the flavor strength you would like to achieve. Start with the lowest amount and add a bit more until you reach your desired flavor. To make chocolate buttercream, add ¼ cup (20 g) of cocoa powder to the frosting.

*   If you enjoy light and fluffy buttercream, whip the frosting in a stand mixer on high for 10 to 15 minutes.

*   If keto/low carb is not your goal, organic powdered sugar or powdered honey can be used instead.

Substitution Note:

To make this **dairy free**, use vegan butter.

(continued)

Peanut Butter or Sunbutter Frosting

This frosting is perfect for frosting a cake, cupcakes or cookies. It will frost one batch of cookies, a single-layer 9-inch (23-cm) cake or a two-layer 7-inch (18-cm) cake. If making a two-layer 8- or 9-inch (20- or 23-cm) cake, double this recipe.

½ cup (112 g) salted butter, softened (or shortening for dairy free)

1 cup (256 g) creamy peanut butter or creamy SunButter

1 to 2 cups (125 to 250 g) keto powdered sugar (to taste)

1 tbsp (15 ml) vanilla extract

2 tbsp (30 ml) unsweetened dairy-free milk

Blend the butter, peanut butter, powdered sugar, vanilla and milk in the bowl of a stand mixer (or in a large bowl if using a hand mixer) until smooth and fluffy. Store, covered, in the refrigerator for up to 1 month.

Recipe Notes:

- If keto/low carb is not your goal, organic powdered sugar or powdered honey can be used instead.

- Every brand of peanut butter is a little different so results might vary a little. If you find your frosting isn't fluffy and easy to spread, you can always increase the amount of unsweetened dairy-free milk a little at a time until you reach the desired consistency.

Substitution Notes:

- To make this **nut free**, use creamy SunButter or another creamy/smooth seed butter of your choice.

- To make this **dairy free**, use vegan butter or palm shortening. For the best flavor use vegan butter.

Cream Cheese Frosting

Cream cheese frosting is a staple when it comes to making many flavors of cake.

This recipe will cover a single-layer 9-inch (23-cm) cake or a two-layer 7-inch (18-cm) cake. If making a two-layer 8- or 9-inch (20- or 23-cm) cake, double this recipe. To make this frosting dairy free, I recommend Kite Hill cream cheese and Earth Balance buttery sticks.

---

2 (8-oz [227-g]) packages cream cheese or dairy-free cream cheese, room temperature

½ cup (112 g) salted butter or dairy-free butter, room temperature

⅓ cup (42 g) keto powdered sugar

1 to 2 tbsp (15 to 30 ml) vanilla extract or other flavor extract of choice

2 tbsp (30 ml) cream or unsweetened full-fat coconut milk

Zest of 1 lemon, lime or orange (optional)

Whip the cream cheese, butter, powdered sugar, vanilla, cream and zest (if using) in the bowl of a stand mixer (or in a large bowl if using a hand mixer) until smooth and fluffy. Store, covered, in the refrigerator for up to 1 month.

Recipe Notes:

- If keto/low carb is not your goal, organic powdered sugar or powdered honey can be used instead.

- The coconut milk should be room temperature and shaken (if using).

Substitution Note:

To make this **dairy free**, use vegan butter and dairy-free cream cheese.

Homemade Vibrant Natural Food Coloring

I pulled out all the stops with this natural food coloring project! I bought so many fruits and vegetables and various products and tried it all—I think we boiled 30 different combinations of things to find the best of the best combinations to make the most beautiful colors possible and we nailed it!

Important Tips

Don't let your fruit/veggies boil for too long or all the concentrated water will evaporate (very quickly). If this happens, just add more water and boil again. Keep in mind that the more you boil, the more intense the color will be. Keep an eye on the water and find a happy medium.

The end result of these recipes is a colored water that isn't quite as concentrated as the food coloring you buy from the store. Therefore, instead of using these colors in *addition* to the liquid in a recipe as you would with food coloring, you'll use this as a replacement of the liquid in the frosting recipe (milk or water, for example).

You may wonder if these natural food colors add any unusual flavors to your sweet frosting but in general, they do *not*. You can ever-so-slightly taste a little flavor with a few but the taste is not overpowering. However, feel free to add a little extra flavor to your frosting using vanilla beans or extracts to counteract the taste. The only exception to this is if you are using turmeric, which can flavor your frostings. I would recommend experimenting with turmeric ahead of time if you plan to use it as your coloring.

These natural food colors can be made ahead of time and frozen in ice-cube trays and thawed when you're ready to make frosting. Because they are all natural they will not stay fresh in the refrigerator or at room temperature for long.

These recipes have not been tested in baked goods. If you're using beet water in baking (such as for red velvet cake), make sure to add a little lemon juice to the beet water so it does not react with the baking soda in the cake recipe.

Orange

Add 1 cup (38 g) of chopped red beet stems, leaves removed (from 1 bunch of beets), 2 tablespoons (28 g) of peeled and finely chopped or grated red beets and 1 teaspoon of turmeric powder to a small pot and add enough water to cover the ingredients. Stir together, boil for about 30 minutes, then strain. The water will be a concentrated orange color. To use in frosting, add 2 teaspoons (10 ml) of concentrated orange color to ¾ cup (170 g) frosting and 2 teaspoons (4 g) of turmeric powder, the zest of 1 orange or ¼ teaspoon of orange extract for a subtle orange flavor; mix.

(continued)

Purple

Add 4 to 8 finely chopped or grated purple cabbage leaves (4 leaves for a pastel purple, 8 for a darker purple), and ¼ cup (25 g) of fresh or frozen cranberries to a medium pot and add enough water to cover the ingredients. Boil for about 40 minutes, then mash the cranberries as they start to "pop." Strain through a fine-mesh strainer or cheesecloth to remove the cranberry seeds and solids. Use 2 teaspoons (10 ml) of the purple water per ¾ cup (170 g) of frosting; mix.

Green

Add about 1 cup (136 g) of finely chopped or grated yellow/golden beets (skins on) to a medium pot, along with enough water to cover the beets, and boil for about 30 minutes. Strain. To use in frosting, add 1½ tablespoons (22 ml) of the yellow beet juice, ¼ teaspoon of ceremonial-grade matcha and ¼ teaspoon turmeric powder to ¾ cup (170 g) of frosting; mix.

Note:

It is important to use ceremonial-grade matcha for the best green color.

Yellow

Add about 1 cup (136 g) of finely chopped or grated yellow/golden beets (skins on) to a medium pot, along with enough water to cover the beets, and boil for about 30 minutes. Strain. To use in frosting, add 2 tablespoons (30 ml) of the yellow beet juice, 1 teaspoon of turmeric powder and the zest of 1 lemon or ¼ teaspoon of lemon extract for a subtle lemon flavor to ¾ cup (170 g) of frosting; mix.

Pink

For a pastel pink, add about 1 cup (136 g) of finely chopped or grated and peeled red beets to a small pot, add enough water to cover the beets, and boil for about 30 minutes. Strain. To use in frosting, to ¾ cup (170 g) of frosting add as much beet water as needed for your desired color, starting with 1 teaspoon and adding more in 1-teaspoon increments. Keep in mind that the more liquid you add, the thinner your frosting will become. Add more powdered sugar or powdered xylitol to your frosting if it becomes too thin.

For hot pink, add about 1 cup (100 g) of fresh or frozen cranberries to a small pot, add enough water to cover the cranberries, and boil for about 30 minutes. Mash the cranberries as they start to "pop." To use in frosting, to ¾ cup (170 g) frosting add as much cranberry water as needed for your desired color, starting with 1 teaspoon and adding more in 1-teaspoon increments. Add more powdered sugar or powdered xylitol to your frosting if it becomes too thin.

Red

Add about 1 cup (100 g) of fresh or frozen cranberries and about 1 cup (136 g) of finely chopped or grated and peeled red beets to a medium pot, add enough water to cover the ingredients and boil for about 30 minutes. Strain through a fine-mesh strainer or cheesecloth to remove the cranberry seeds and solids. To use in frosting, to ¾ cup (170 g) of frosting add 2½ tablespoons (37 ml) of beet/cranberry water and mix.

Note:

This recipe makes a gorgeous raspberry-red color (you will never get a true red color). To achieve a substantial color, you will need to add a fair amount of beet/cranberry water to your frosting. Add extra powdered sugar or xylitol to balance the liquid if necessary.

Sky Blue

Add 4 finely chopped or grated red cabbage leaves to a small pot and cover with water. Boil for about 30 minutes and strain. Add baking soda to the red cabbage water in ¼-teaspoon increments until you achieve a blue hue. To use in frosting, to ¾ cup (170 g) of frosting add 1 tablespoon (15 ml) plus 1 teaspoon of the cabbage/baking soda water and mix.

Color Variations

Blue Green: Add ¼ teaspoon of ceremonial-grade matcha to the Sky Blue base.

Sea Green: Add ¼ teaspoon of turmeric to the Sky Blue base.

Pastel Concord Grape: Mix equal parts Purple base with Sky Blue base.

Sunset Orange: Mix equal parts Red base with Orange base.

Makes 16 servings

Caramel Pumpkin Cheesecake with Chocolate Crust

This cheesecake makes for the perfect fall dessert: pumpkin, chocolate, caramel—yum!

Crust

1½ cups (174 g) blanched almond flour

3 tbsp (15 g) cocoa powder

¼ cup + 2 tbsp (75 g) keto granulated sugar

1½ tsp (7 ml) vanilla extract

¼ tsp Himalayan salt

⅓ cup (80 ml) melted butter

Cheesecake

32 oz (907 g) cream cheese, room temperature

3 large eggs

1½ tsp (7 ml) vanilla extract

¼ tsp Himalayan salt

1 cup (125 g) keto powdered sugar

¼ to ½ tsp stevia extract or monk fruit extract

½ cup (123 g) pumpkin purée

1½ tbsp (12 g) pumpkin pie spice

Topping

1 recipe Keto Caramel (page 359)

Shaved dark chocolate or dark chocolate chips

Preheat the oven to 350°F (175°C). Line an 8-inch (20-cm) springform pan or an 8-inch (20-cm) square pan with parchment paper.

To make the crust, combine the almond flour, cocoa powder, sugar, vanilla, salt and butter in a medium bowl and mix until a crumbly dough forms. Press the dough into the lined pan. Bake for 10 to 15 minutes, until the crust looks dry. Let cool.

To make the cheesecake, using a hand mixer in a large bowl, slowly whip together the cream cheese and eggs until smooth. Add the vanilla, salt, powdered sugar and stevia extract and mix until blended. Pour half of the cheesecake batter on top of the cooled crust.

To the remaining batter, add the pumpkin purée and pumpkin pie spice. Mix together to blend, then pour on top of the plain cheesecake batter. Bake for 45 to 50 minutes, until the cheesecake has set in the middle and is golden brown around the edges. Allow the cheesecake to cool for at least 1 hour before decorating. Top with the caramel and decorate with the shaved chocolate.

Let cool for 4 to 6 hours or overnight in the refrigerator before slicing. Store refrigerated, for up to 1 week.

EGG FREE   NUT FREE   DAIRY FREE

Makes 12 servings

1 (15-oz [444-ml]) can unsweetened full-fat coconut milk

2 tbsp (30 ml) brewed espresso or strong coffee

1 tsp vanilla extract

2 tsp (4 g) cocoa powder

3 tbsp (45 ml) sugar-free maple syrup (add more if extra sweetness is desired)

¼ tsp stevia extract or monk fruit extract (add more if extra sweetness is desired)

¼ tsp Himalayan salt

1 cup (240 ml) Irish whiskey

1 tbsp (9 g) organic gelatin

1 recipe Perfectly Flaky Piecrust (page 410), prebaked

Dairy-Free Whipped Topping (page 484), for garnish

Coffee beans, for garnish

Dairy-Free Irish Cream Pie

This keto Irish Cream Pie has all of the flavor without any of the traditional fillers. Using full-fat coconut milk helps to replace the traditional cream and the gelatin keeps it all together.

In a medium saucepan, combine the coconut milk, espresso, vanilla, cocoa powder, maple syrup, stevia extract, salt and Irish whisky. Sprinkle the gelatin over the mixture to avoid clumping. Stir to combine. If it clumps, smooth out with an immersion blender.

Place the saucepan over medium heat and bring the mixture to a low simmer, then remove from the heat. If you want a less boozy flavor, simmer the filling for a few minutes.

Pour the liquid into the prepared pie shell. Refrigerate for 1 to 2 hours. Garnish with whipped topping and coffee beans. Store, covered, in the refrigerator for up to 2 weeks.

Substitution Note:

To make this *Paleo*, substitute maple syrup for sugar-free maple syrup and omit the stevia extract. Use the Paleo copycat "Pillsbury" piecrust on BrittanyAngell.com.

Makes one 8-inch (20-cm) crust

Perfectly Flaky Piecrust

When I posted my Pillsbury copycat piecrust on my website, it took the Internet by storm and quickly became one of the most-made recipes on my site. I used that crust as my inspiration for this one and made just a few changes to make it low carb. It is extremely flaky and the flavor is wonderful. No one will ever guess that it is low carb. The only downside to low-carb dough is that it is slightly less sturdy to work with than I prefer, but it patches up really easily. This recipe makes one full-sized crust, so if you wish to have a top crust on your pie be sure to double the recipe.

1½ cups (174 g) blanched almond flour

½ cup (40 g) oat fiber, plus more for dusting

1 tsp xanthan or guar gum

4 tbsp (56 g) chilled salted butter or shortening

3½ oz (100 g) cream cheese (regular or Kite Hill dairy free)

½ tsp Himalayan salt

To the bowl of a food processor, add the almond flour, oat fiber and xanthan gum. Process for a few seconds to mix. Cut the butter and cream cheese into tablespoon-sized pieces, then add to the dry ingredients along with the salt. Process again just until a dough forms. Be careful not to overmix or too much oil will be released from the almond flour, which will make the dough less sturdy.

Use the dough immediately or keep chilled in the refrigerator for up to 1 week. The dough can also be frozen for up to 1 month.

To roll out the dough, place it between two sheets of parchment paper, dusting the top and bottom with a little oat fiber. Be careful not to use too much of the fiber or the texture of the dough will change.

Bake the crust at 350°F (175°C) for 14 to 15 minutes when being used for a no-bake filling. If baking longer than 15 minutes (with a filling), be sure to cover the edges with a pie cover or aluminum foil.

Recipe Note:

Due to the fact that this dough is low carb/high fat you may notice that it browns faster in the oven. As a general rule do not bake the crust for more than 25 to 30 minutes even with a filling. If using this for a fruit filling or pot pie, I would recommend precooking the filling on the stovetop so that you can limit how long this crust has to be in the oven.

Substitution Notes:

- To make this **dairy free,** use Kite Hill cream cheese and shortening instead of butter. Or use vegan butter for the best flavor.

- To make this **Paleo,** use the Paleo Copycat "Pillsbury" piecrust recipe on BrittanyAngell.com.

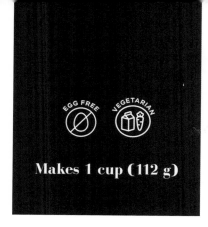

EGG FREE · VEGETARIAN

Makes 1 cup (112 g)

1 cup (110 g) raw unsalted pecans (left whole or chopped)

1 tsp ground cinnamon

4 tbsp (56 g) butter, ghee or butter-flavored coconut oil

¼ cup (50 g) keto brown sugar

2 tsp (10 ml) vanilla extract

¼ tsp Himalayan salt

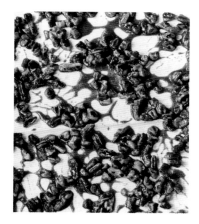

Candied Pecans

This recipe could not be simpler and the results are heavenly. Use these pecans to top salads or ice cream or eat them on their own.

Line a baking sheet with parchment paper.

Add the pecans, cinnamon, butter, brown sugar, vanilla and salt to a frying pan and toss well to combine. Heat the nut mixture over medium heat for 2 to 5 minutes, until the pecans are toasted and the sauce is thick.

Pour the nut mixture onto the prepared baking sheet, and refrigerate or freeze until hard, 10 to 15 minutes in the refrigerator and 5 to 10 minutes in the freezer. Store in a sealed container in the refrigerator for up to 2 months.

Substitution Notes:

* To make this **dairy free**, use the coconut oil.

* To make this **Paleo**, use coconut palm sugar and the coconut oil.

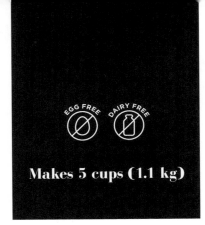

Makes 5 cups (1.1 kg)

Caramel Candied Pecan Ice Cream

This ice cream is what dreams are made of—the flavors are spectacular! You could serve this to anyone and they would never suspect it was sugar free. If alcohol is something that you prefer to avoid, it can be left out of the recipe entirely. Just use two full cans of coconut milk if omitting the rum. For the lowest carb option, use the macadamia nuts.

1¾ (13.5-oz [400-ml]) cans of full-fat coconut cream

½ cup (120 ml) sugar-free maple syrup

½ tsp stevia extract or monk fruit extract

½ cup (120 ml) spiced rum or whiskey

¼ tsp Himalayan salt

2 tsp (6 g) gelatin (if using)

¾ cup (100 g) unsalted roasted macadamia nuts or unsalted roasted cashews

1 recipe Candied Pecans (page 411; make the dairy-free option if you want to keep this recipe dairy free)

¼ cup (45 g) shaved dairy-free dark chocolate (optional)

1 recipe Keto Caramel (page 359; make the dairy-free option if you want to keep this recipe dairy free)

To make the ice cream, pour the coconut milk, maple syrup, stevia extract, rum, salt and gelatin into a blender. Blend on high for 1 minute. Pour the nuts into the blender, and let them soak in the milk mixture for 15 to 20 minutes. After soaking, turn the blender on high and process until the mixture is extremely smooth. If using macadamia nuts, this may take a few minutes.

To heat the mixture to activate the gelatin (if using), you can use a high-speed blender or the stovetop. In a high-speed blender use the soup setting, and it will heat the mixture until steaming hot. If using the stovetop option, pour the mixture into a saucepan and bring to a simmer over medium heat. Remove the pot from the heat.

Place the heated mixture in a sealed container and add about three-quarters of the candied pecans (reserving the rest for a topping), then freeze for 1 to 2 hours until it is cold, but not yet frozen. Pour the cold mixture into an ice cream maker and mix in the shaved chocolate (if using). Follow the manufacturer's instructions. After your ice cream is made, add it to a sealable container in layers, adding some caramel in between each layer. You may not want to use all of the caramel in this recipe; I used about half of the batch and stored the remaining amount in the refrigerator in a sealed jar. Store the ice cream in the freezer, and for the best flavor and texture eat within a few days.

Substitution Notes:

- To make this **Paleo**, use real honey or maple syrup in both the ice cream and caramel recipes.

- To make this **vegetarian**, omit the gelatin and skip the heating process.

- To make this **nut free**, omit the pecans.

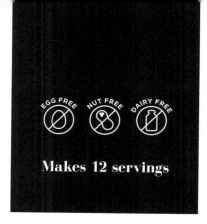

Makes 12 servings

Coconut, Rum and Pineapple Cream Pie

Cream pies are the best! Add a little rum, coconut and pineapple and you have yourself a delicious taste of summer. This pie can be made strong or not. A strong coconut rum cream pie would be great for an adults-only block party. But if kiddos are around, simply make the filling less strong by heating it before baking. However you choose to make it, you will certainly enjoy it.

1 (15-oz [444-ml]) can unsweetened full-fat coconut milk

1 tsp vanilla extract

1 tbsp (15 ml) pineapple extract

3 tbsp (45 ml) sugar-free maple syrup (add more if extra sweetness is desired)

¼ tsp stevia extract (add more if extra sweetness is desired)

¼ tsp Himalayan salt

1 tbsp (9 g) gelatin (organic)

½ tsp turmeric (optional, for color)

1 cup (240 ml) coconut rum

1 recipe Perfectly Flaky Piecrust (page 410), prebaked

¼ cup (19 g) toasted unsweetened coconut flakes, as garnish (optional)

Dairy-Free Whipped Topping (page 484, optional)

For a strong rum cream pie:

In a medium saucepan, combine the coconut milk, vanilla, pineapple extract, maple syrup, stevia extract, salt, gelatin and turmeric (if using) over medium heat. Bring the mixture to a boil, then immediately reduce to a simmer and cook for 2 to 3 minutes, whisking to combine. Remove the pan from the heat and allow the mixture to cool for 10 minutes. When cooled, add the coconut rum. Pour the filling into the prepared prebaked pie shell. Cover the pie with plastic wrap and refrigerate for 1 to 2 hours.

For a less strong cream pie:

In a medium saucepan, combine the coconut milk, vanilla, pineapple extract, maple syrup, stevia extract, salt, coconut rum, gelatin and turmeric (if using) over medium heat. Bring to a boil and allow the liquid to reduce by one-third, about 10 minutes. Remove the pan from the heat and allow the mixture to cool for 10 minutes. Pour the filling into the prepared prebaked pie shell. Refrigerate for 1 to 2 hours.

Top with the toasted unsweetened coconut flakes and whipped topping (if using). Store covered in the refrigerator for up to 2 weeks.

Substitution Note:

To make this **Paleo**, substitute maple syrup for sugar-free maple syrup and omit the stevia extract. Use the Paleo copycat "Pillsbury" piecrust recipe on BrittanyAngell.com.

Makes 12 mini pie tart tins (about 1½-inch [4-cm] diameter)

Crust

½ cup (66 g) salted and roasted macadamia nuts

1½ cups (144 g) unsweetened shredded coconut, toasted

3 tbsp (45 ml) tahini

3 tbsp (45 ml) sugar-free honey or sugar-free maple syrup

¼ tsp stevia extract or monk fruit extract

Filling

½ cup (120 g) coconut oil

2 avocados

½ cup (120 ml) coconut cream from a can (skimmed off the top)

¼ cup (60 ml) lime juice

⅓ cup (80 ml) sugar-free honey

¼ tsp stevia extract or monk fruit extract

Optional Toppings

Dairy-free Whipped Topping (page 484)

Lime peel slices

No-Bake Key Lime Tarts

These fresh, healthy little tarts will fill your dessert cravings but they're not just for dessert—you can eat them for breakfast, too. Keep them in the refrigerator in a sealed container for 1 to 2 weeks and eat one whenever you want a quick treat.

To make the crust, add the macadamia nuts to a food processor and pulse until finely chopped. Add the shredded coconut, tahini, honey and stevia extract. Blend until combined, 1 to 2 minutes. Put the mixture in a bowl and refrigerate for 5 to 10 minutes. Remove from the refrigerator and press into mini pie tart tins. Place the filled tart tins on a baking sheet.

To make the filling, add the coconut oil, avocados, coconut cream, lime juice, honey and stevia extract to a food processor or high-speed blender and blend until smooth. Pour the filling into the prepared tart tins, then refrigerate for 2 hours or until firm. Top with Dairy-Free Whipped Topping and lime peel slices (if using).

Recipe Note:

You can buy already-toasted coconut or toast it yourself. To toast it at home, heat a small skillet over high heat for 2 minutes. Reduce the heat to medium–low and add the shredded coconut to the skillet. Stir constantly until golden brown (2 to 4 minutes). As soon as the coconut turns golden brown, remove from the heat and set aside in a mixing bowl to cool.

Substitution Notes:

- To make this **nut free,** use sunflower seeds instead of macadamia nuts.

- To make this **Paleo**, use real honey or maple syrup and omit the stevia.

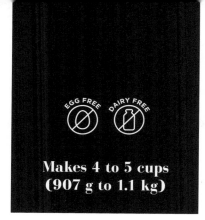

**Makes 4 to 5 cups
(907 g to 1.1 kg)**

2 (13.5-oz [400-ml]) cans unsweetened full-fat coconut milk

½ cup (120 ml) sugar-free honey or sugar-free maple syrup

½ tsp stevia extract or monk fruit extract

¼ tsp Himalayan salt

1 tbsp (15 ml) vanilla extract

2 tsp (6 g) gelatin (optional)

¾ cup (100 g) raw, unsalted macadamia nuts or cashews

Perfect Keto Vanilla Ice Cream

I spent many days testing dairy-free ice cream, and I have come to the conclusion that combining coconut milk and a nut such as macadamias or cashews is the way to go. Blending the two together creates an incredible flavor and texture, without either of the flavors dominating too much. In this recipe, you will see that I have given the option to use macadamia nuts or cashews. Macadamias are the lower carb option. If you are less concerned with carbs, then cashews work just as well and are a cheaper option. One important thing to keep in mind is that sugar is the ingredient that keeps ice cream from freezing super hard. So, this ice cream tastes best eaten within a few days. Allow for a few extra minutes of time for the ice cream to thaw before serving.

Pour the coconut milk, honey, stevia extract, salt, vanilla and gelatin (if using) into a blender. Blend on high for 1 minute. Add the nuts to the blender, and let the nuts soak in the milk mixture for 15 to 20 minutes. After soaking, turn the blender on high and process until the mixture is extremely smooth. If using macadamia nuts, this may take a few minutes.

To heat the mixture to activate the gelatin (if using), you can use a high-speed blender or the stovetop. In a high-speed blender, use the soup setting, and it will heat the mixture until steaming hot. If using the stovetop option, pour the mixture into a saucepan and bring to a simmer over medium heat. Remove the pot from the heat.

Place the heated mixture in a sealed container and freeze for 1 to 2 hours until it is cold, but not yet frozen. Pour the cold mixture into an ice cream maker and follow the manufacturer's instructions. Place the finished ice cream in a sealed container and store in the freezer or eat immediately.

Top with any of your favorite ice cream accompaniments, such as a sugar-free chocolate syrup and my Keto Caramel from page 359.

Substitution Notes:

- To make this **Paleo**, use real honey or maple syrup and omit the stevia.

- To make this **vegetarian**, omit the gelatin and skip the heating process.

**Makes 4 to 5 cups
(907 g to 1.1 kg)**

2 (13.5-oz [400-ml]) cans unsweetened full-fat coconut milk

½ cup (120 ml) sugar-free honey or sugar-free maple syrup

½ tsp stevia extract or monk fruit extract

¼ tsp Himalayan salt

2 tsp (6 g) gelatin (optional)

1 tbsp (15 ml) vanilla extract

1 tsp ube extract, to taste

¾ cup (100 g) raw, unsalted macadamia nuts or cashews

½ recipe Sugar-Free Marshmallows (page 335), cut into ½-inch (13-mm) cubes

Dairy-Free Marshmallow Ube Ice Cream

Ube perfectly captures the earthy sweetness of a sweet potato. It's a delicate and sweet flavor that makes the perfect violet ice cream. Combined with keto marshmallows, this ice cream becomes the perfect summer comfort food. Please note that ube extract is colored with purple food dye. If you prefer to not use any artificial color in recipes, choose one of the other delicious ice cream flavors in this book.

Pour the coconut milk, honey, stevia extract, salt, gelatin (if using), vanilla and ube extract into a blender. Blend on high for 1 minute. Pour the nuts into the blender, and let them soak in the milk mixture for 15 to 20 minutes. After soaking, turn the blender on high and process until the mixture is extremely smooth. If using macadamia nuts, this may take a few minutes.

To heat the mixture to activate the gelatin (if using), you can use a high-speed blender or the stovetop. In a high-speed blender, use the soup setting, and it will heat the mixture until steaming hot. If using the stovetop option, pour the mixture into a saucepan and bring to a simmer over medium heat. Remove the pot from the heat.

Place the heated mixture in a sealed container and freeze for 1 to 2 hours until it is cold, but not yet frozen. Pour the cold mixture into an ice cream maker. Follow the manufacturer's instructions to churn. After churning the ice cream, transfer to a freezer-safe container, layering in the marshmallows. Store in the freezer or eat immediately.

Substitution Notes:

- To make this **Paleo**, use real honey or maple syrup and omit the stevia.

- To make this **vegetarian**, omit the gelatin and skip the heating process. Omit the marshmallows or use vegan marshmallows.

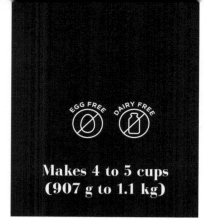

**Makes 4 to 5 cups
(907 g to 1.1 kg)**

Dairy-Free Pistachio Chip Ice Cream

Pistachios have a higher carb count than some other nuts, so I have opted to use pistachio extract for the base of the ice cream, which provides all the awesome pistachio flavor. The shaved chocolate and pistachios take this ice cream to the next level but if you are trying to keep your carbs super low, feel free to omit one or both.

---

2 (13.5-oz [400-ml]) cans unsweetened full-fat coconut milk

½ cup (120 ml) sugar-free honey or sugar-free maple syrup

½ tsp stevia extract or monk fruit extract

¼ tsp Himalayan salt

2 tsp (6 g) gelatin (optional)

1 tsp vanilla extract

1 tbsp (15 ml) pistachio extract

¾ cup (100 g) raw, unsalted macadamia nuts or cashews

¼ to ½ cup (31 to 62 g) chopped pistachios

¼ to ½ cup (50 to 100 g) dairy-free chocolate shavings

Pour the coconut milk, honey, stevia extract, salt, gelatin (if using), vanilla and pistachio extract into a blender. Blend on high for 1 minute. Pour the nuts into the blender, and let them soak in the milk mixture for 15 to 20 minutes. After soaking, turn the blender on high and process until the mixture is extremely smooth. If using macadamia nuts, this may take a few minutes.

To heat the mixture to activate the gelatin (if using), you can use a high-speed blender or the stovetop. In a high-speed blender, use the soup setting, and it will heat the mixture until steaming hot. If using the stovetop option, pour the mixture into a saucepan and bring to a simmer over medium heat. Remove the pot from the heat.

Place the heated mixture in a sealed container and add the chopped pistachios, then freeze for 1 to 2 hours until it is cold, but not yet frozen. Pour the cold mixture into an ice cream maker and mix in the shaved chocolate. Follow the manufacturer's instructions. Place the finished ice cream in a sealed container and store in the freezer or eat immediately.

Substitution Notes:

*   To make this **Paleo**, use real honey or maple syrup and omit the stevia extract.

*   To make this **vegetarian**, omit the gelatin and skip the heating process.

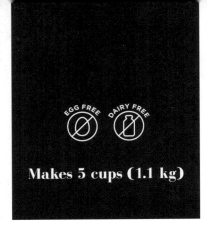

Makes 5 cups (1.1 kg)

2 (13.5-oz [400-ml]) cans unsweetened full-fat coconut milk

½ cup (120 ml) sugar-free honey or sugar-free maple syrup

½ tsp stevia extract or monk fruit extract

½ tsp Himalayan salt

2 tsp (6 g) gelatin (optional)

2 tbsp (30 ml) cotton candy extract

1 tsp vanilla extract

¾ cup (100 g) raw, unsalted macadamia nuts or cashews

1½ tsp (4 g) pink pitaya powder or a few drops of pink food coloring

1½ tsp (4 g) blue spirulina powder or a few drops of blue food coloring

Dairy-Free Cotton Candy Ice Cream

Cotton candy extract will really make you think you are eating real cotton candy. The extract captures the flavor without making the ice cream taste too sweet. You'll feel like a kid again with every pink and blue bite.

Pour the coconut milk, honey, stevia extract, salt, gelatin (if using), cotton candy extract and vanilla into a blender. Blend on high for 1 minute. Pour the nuts into the blender, and let them soak in the milk mixture for 15 to 20 minutes. After soaking, turn the blender on high and process until the mixture is extremely smooth. If using macadamia nuts, this may take a few minutes.

To heat the mixture to activate the gelatin (if using), you can use a high-speed blender or the stovetop. In a high-speed blender, use the soup setting, and it will heat the mixture until steaming hot. If using the stovetop option, pour the mixture into a saucepan and bring to a simmer over medium heat. Remove the pot from the heat.

Place the heated mixture in a sealed container and freeze for 1 to 2 hours until it is cold, but not yet frozen. Divide the semi-frozen mixture in half and put in two bowls, about 2½ cups (600 ml) each. Add the pink superfruit powder or food coloring to one, and the blue spirulina powder or food coloring to the other. Pour the pink mixture into the ice cream maker and churn for about 15 minutes, until thick. Remove the pink mixture and pour it into a sealed container. Quickly rinse the ice cream bowl and maker with cold water. Then add the blue ice cream mix. Churn until frozen, then add the blue ice cream into the container with the pink. Store in the freezer or eat immediately.

Substitution Notes:

- To make this **Paleo**, use real honey or maple syrup and omit the stevia extract.

- To make this **vegetarian**, omit the gelatin and skip the heating process.

Recipe Note:

I have noticed that these freezer bowls have about 45 minutes of being cold enough to freeze ice cream. If you wait too long before adding the second color of ice cream, your bowl will melt too much to freeze the second batch of ice cream. If you have a second bowl on hand, use that or you can put the ice cream bowl back in the freezer for a day and then churn the second batch of ice cream the next day.

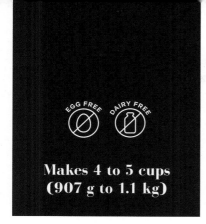

EGG FREE **DAIRY FREE**

Makes 4 to 5 cups (907 g to 1.1 kg)

Dairy-Free Tangerine Creamsicle Ice Cream

Tangerine Creamsicle Ice Cream is such a dream. This is very reminiscent of childhood push pops. One word of caution with the tangerine extract: adding more than recommended can turn the flavor a bit sour. The orange food coloring is optional but it gives the ice cream a super fun color.

2 (13.5-oz [400-ml]) cans unsweetened full-fat coconut milk

½ cup (120 ml) sugar-free honey

½ tsp stevia extract or monk fruit extract

¼ tsp Himalayan salt

2 tsp (6 g) gelatin (optional)

Zest of 1 large orange

1 tbsp + 1 tsp (20 ml) tangerine extract

¾ cup (100 g) raw, unsalted macadamia nuts or cashews

10 drops orange food coloring (optional, for color)

Pour the coconut milk, honey, stevia extract, salt, gelatin (if using), orange zest and tangerine extract into a blender. Blend on high for 1 minute. Pour the nuts into the blender, and let them soak in the milk mixture for 15 to 20 minutes. After soaking, turn the blender on high and process until the mixture is extremely smooth. If using macadamia nuts, this may take a few minutes.

To heat the mixture to activate the gelatin (if using), you can use a high-speed blender or the stovetop. In a high-speed blender, use the soup setting, and it will heat the mixture until steaming hot. If using the stovetop option, pour the mixture into a saucepan and bring to a simmer over medium heat. Remove the pot from the heat.

Place the heated mixture in a sealed container and transfer to the freezer for 1 to 2 hours until it is cold, but not yet frozen. Pour the cold ice cream mixture into your ice cream maker and follow the manufacturer's instructions. While the ice cream is churning, add the food coloring.

After your ice cream is made, place it in a sealed container and store in the freezer or eat immediately.

Substitution Notes:

- To make this **Paleo**, use real honey and omit the stevia extract.

- To make this **vegetarian**, omit the gelatin and skip the heating process.

**Makes 4 to 5 cups
(784 to 980 g)**

½ cup (120 ml) lime juice

1 (15-oz [444-ml]) can unsweetened full-fat coconut milk

½ cup (120 ml) water

½ cup (120 ml) sugar-free honey

½ tsp stevia extract or monk fruit extract

⅛ tsp Himalayan salt

Green food coloring or 2 tsp (2 g) matcha powder

Lime Sherbet

This zingy sherbet is perfect for a hot day. It has just the right amount of sweetness. As with keto ice cream, it is best to eat this within a few days of making it as it will eventually freeze rock solid because it is sugar free.

Mix the lime juice, coconut milk, water, honey, stevia extract, salt and food coloring in a medium bowl. (If adding matcha powder, mix in a blender instead.) Place the mixture in the refrigerator to chill for 1 hour.

Place the chilled mixture in an ice cream maker and follow the manufacturer's instructions. When frozen, place in an airtight container and store in the freezer.

Recipe Note:

If you are not following a keto diet and do not want to use coconut milk, you can use 1¾ cups (420 ml) of whole milk instead.

Substitution Note:

To make this *Paleo*, use ¾ cup (180 ml) of real honey and omit the sugar-free honey and stevia extract.

Homemade Liqueurs and Cocktails

These homemade liqueurs, and the cocktails made with them, are something special. You'll be amazed by how wonderful they taste without any of the funky aftertastes often associated with sugar-free sweeteners.
Be sure to try all of the margarita recipes.

← See recipe on page 452.

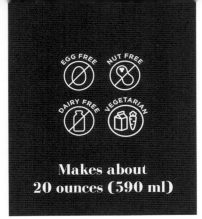

**Makes about
20 ounces (590 ml)**

Liqueur

1½ whole vanilla beans

2 cups (480 ml) vodka

½ cup (120 ml) water

½ cup (100 g) dark-roast coffee beans

½ cup (120 ml) sugar-free honey or sugar-free maple syrup

¼ tsp stevia extract or monk fruit extract

⅛ tsp Himalayan salt

Finishing

¼ tsp Himalayan salt

1 tbsp (15 ml) sugar-free honey or sugar-free maple syrup

¼ tsp stevia extract or monk fruit extract

Homemade Kahlua

Homemade kahlua is surprisingly simple to make. Combine all the ingredients, wait a few weeks and then you have a delicious coffee-flavored liqueur that you can drink straight or mix into your favorite cocktail. This is used in my Dairy-Free White Russian (page 464) and Dairy-Free Mudslide (page 472) recipes. It can be used in any cocktail you love, cup-for-cup, as store-bought kahlua would be used.

To make the liqueur, place the vanilla beans on a cutting board. Split the beans with a sharp paring knife. Take a small spoon and remove the seeds from the pods and add them to a 28-ounce (828-ml) or 32-ounce (946-ml) glass jar. Add the vodka, water, dark-roast coffee beans, honey, stevia extract and salt. Mix to combine. Allow the mixture to steep in a cool dark place, covered, for 2 to 3 weeks.

After steeping, strain the mixture into a clean glass jar. Add the salt, honey and stevia extract. Mix to combine. Store in the refrigerator. Use within 6 months.

Recipe Note:

Aging this kahlua in a Mason jar with a lid works really well.

**Makes about
24 ounces (710 ml)**

Homemade Blue Curaçao

Blue Curaçao is a citrus liqueur that looks as tropical as it tastes. Historically, Curaçao is made from the dried peels of the laraha, a bitter orange native to the island of Curaçao. This version makes it a bit more accessible by using oranges you can find in any grocery store. These flavors remind me of summer and sunshine. Add a mixer to make your favorite cocktail or try this in The Blue Hawaiian (page 467). For food coloring, I recommend blue spirulina powder from Toogood Botanics or Suncore Foods.

Liqueur

1 cup (240 ml) vodka

1 cup (240 ml) gin

½ cup (120 ml) water

Zest of 2 large oranges or 4 small oranges

1 tsp dried orange peel

5 whole cloves

½ cup (120 ml) sugar-free honey

¼ tsp stevia extract or monk fruit extract

¼ tsp Himalayan salt

¾ to 1 tsp blue spirulina powder or blue food coloring (add more or less depending on desired color)

Finishing

¼ tsp Himalayan salt

1 tbsp (15 ml) sugar-free honey

¼ tsp stevia extract or monk fruit extract

To make the liqueur, combine the vodka, gin, water, orange zest, orange peel, cloves, honey, stevia extract, salt and spirulina powder or food coloring in a 28-ounce (828-ml) or 32-ounce (946-ml) glass jar. Mix well, seal tightly and allow to steep in a cool dark place for 2 weeks.

After steeping, strain the mixture into a clean glass jar. Add the salt, honey and stevia extract. Mix to combine. Store in the refrigerator. Use within 6 months.

Recipe Note:

Aging this Blue Curaçao in a Mason jar with a lid works really well.

**Makes about
24 ounces (710 ml)**

Liqueur

2 cups (340 g) raw hazelnuts

1 cup (240 ml) vodka

½ cup (120 ml) brandy

½ cup (120 ml) water

½ cup (120 ml) sugar-free maple syrup

¼ tsp stevia extract or monk fruit extract

¼ tsp Himalayan salt

½ vanilla bean, split

Finishing

¼ tsp Himalayan salt

1 tbsp (15 ml) sugar-free honey

¼ tsp stevia extract or monk fruit extract

Homemade Frangelico

This is a warm, nutty liqueur that is great for many cocktails.

Combine the hazelnuts, vodka, brandy, water, maple syrup, stevia extract, salt and vanilla bean in a 28-ounce (828-ml) or 32-ounce (946-ml) glass jar. Stir well and allow to steep for 2 to 3 weeks covered in a cool dark place.

After steeping, pour through a fine-mesh strainer into a clean jar. Add the salt, honey and stevia extract. Stir to combine. Store in the refrigerator. Use within 6 months.

Recipe Note:

I like to use Mason jars to age and store all my homemade liqueurs.

Substitution Note:

To make this **Paleo**, use regular maple syrup, real honey and omit the stevia extract.

**Makes about
24 ounces (710 ml)**

Homemade Limoncello

Limoncello is a summertime favorite. Zesting the lemons does take a little effort but it is so worth it in the end.

Combine the vodka, water and lemon zest in a 28-ounce (828-ml) or 32-ounce (946-ml) glass jar. Stir well and allow to steep for 2 to 3 weeks covered in a cool dark place.

After steeping, pour through a fine-mesh strainer into a clean jar. Add the salt, honey, stevia extract and turmeric (if using). Stir to combine. Store in the refrigerator. Use within 6 months.

Liqueur

2 cups (480 ml) vodka

½ cup (120 ml) water

Zest of 4 large lemons or 6 small lemons

Finishing

¼ tsp Himalayan salt

½ cup (120 ml) sugar-free honey

½ tsp stevia extract or monk fruit extract

Pinch of turmeric (optional, for color)

Recipe Note:

Be sure to only zest the skin and do not get any of the white part (pith) as it is bitter and will ruin the limoncello.

Substitution Note:

To make this **Paleo**, use regular honey instead of the sugar-free version and omit the stevia extract.

EGG FREE · DAIRY FREE · VEGETARIAN

**Makes about
24 ounces (710 ml)**

Harvest Spice Liqueur

This liqueur is a total original. It's the perfect drink for those crisp fall days or to have in front of a roaring fire. I especially enjoy using this recipe as part of a mixed drink. I created a brand-new cocktail featuring this delicious liqueur—the Harvest Spice Cocktail on page 475.

Combine the vodka, water, rum, orange zest, cloves, ginger, nutmeg, cinnamon, maple syrup, stevia extract and almond extract in a 28-ounce (828-ml) or 32-ounce (946-ml) glass jar. Mix well and allow to steep for 2 to 3 weeks covered in a cool dark place.

After steeping, pour through a fine-mesh strainer into a clean jar. Add the salt, honey and stevia extract. Stir to combine. Store in the refrigerator. Use within 6 months.

Substitution Note:

To make this ***Paleo***, use regular maple syrup or regular honey instead of the sugar-free version and omit the stevia extract.

Liqueur

2 cups (480 ml) vodka

½ cup (120 ml) water

¼ cup (60 ml) rum or coconut rum

Zest of 1 large orange or 2 small oranges

20 whole cloves

1 tsp grated ginger

¾ tsp ground nutmeg

½ tsp ground cinnamon

½ cup (120 ml) sugar-free maple syrup or sugar-free honey

½ tsp stevia extract or monk fruit extract

¼ tsp almond extract

Finishing

¼ tsp Himalayan salt

1 tbsp (15 ml) sugar-free honey or sugar-free maple syrup

¼ tsp stevia extract or monk fruit extract

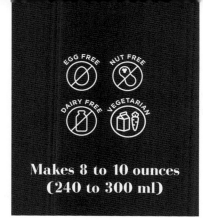

**Makes 8 to 10 ounces
(240 to 300 ml)**

Healthier Grenadine

Grenadine is typically made from pomegranate juice. However, this recipe calls for a mix of cranberries and raspberries, which I think tastes better than the original version. It mimics the flavor so closely but the amount of sugar drops substantially. Use this as a mixer in your favorite cocktail or with fizzy water. The color is rich and beautiful and would work fabulously with sugar-free lemon-lime soda to make a Shirley Temple for any kids in your life.

2 cups (200 g) frozen or fresh cranberries

1 cup (140 g) frozen raspberries

6 cups (1.5 L) water

½ cup (120 ml) sugar-free honey or sugar-free maple syrup

¼ tsp stevia extract or monk fruit extract

½ tsp orange extract

¼ tsp Himalayan salt

Place the cranberries, frozen raspberries and water in a large saucepan. Bring to a boil over medium heat and allow to reduce down to about 2½ cups (600 ml), stirring occasionally; this will take 20 to 30 minutes. Remove the mixture from the heat and allow it to cool to room temperature.

Pour the mixture through a fine-mesh strainer into a 28-ounce (828-ml) or 32-ounce (946-ml) glass jar. Add the honey, stevia extract, orange extract and salt. Mix to combine. Store in a tightly sealed container in the refrigerator. Use within 2 to 3 weeks.

Substitution Note:

To make this **Paleo**, use regular maple syrup or regular honey instead of the sugar-free version and omit the stevia extract.

**Makes about
2 cups (480 ml)**

1 (15-oz [444-ml]) can unsweetened full-fat coconut milk

2 tbsp (30 ml) brewed espresso or strong coffee

1 tsp vanilla extract

2 tsp (4 g) cocoa powder

3 tbsp (45 ml) sugar-free maple syrup (or to taste)

¼ tsp stevia extract or monk fruit extract (or to taste)

¼ tsp Himalayan salt

1 cup (240 ml) Irish whiskey

Dairy-Free Irish Crème

To say that this is a crowd-pleaser would be an understatement. This is one keto recipe that will totally fool your friends and make you the hit of any party.

In a medium saucepan, combine the coconut milk, espresso, vanilla, cocoa powder, maple syrup, stevia extract and salt. Bring to a boil over high heat. Stirring constantly, allow the mixture to boil until it begins to thicken, 2 to 3 minutes. Decrease the heat to medium. Keep stirring and allow it to boil until the liquid has reduced by half, 5 to 10 minutes.

Remove from the heat and allow it to cool 5 minutes, then stir in the whiskey. Pour into a jar and chill in the refrigerator for 1 hour. Store, covered, in a sealed container in the refrigerator for up to 2 weeks.

Recipe Notes:

- This Irish crème may thicken a bit as it chills. If you prefer it thinner, a little bit of water can be added.

- Some brands of coconut milk may separate a little or get chunks of fat as it chills. If this happens, just throw it in the blender until it's smooth and creamy again.

Substitution Note:

To make this **Paleo**, use regular maple syrup instead of the sugar-free version and omit the stevia.

EGG FREE   NUT FREE

DAIRY FREE   VEGETARIAN

Makes 12 servings

Pineapple and Lime Coconut Rum White Sangria

This tropical sangria is refreshing and delicious. You'll be amazed by how much pineapple flavor comes from the extract.

1 (25.4-oz [750-ml]) bottle white wine (such as pinot grigio)

¾ cup (180 ml) coconut rum

2 (7.5-oz [222-ml]) cans zero-sugar ginger ale (such as Zevia brand)

¼ cup (60 ml) sugar-free honey

2½ tbsp (37 ml) pineapple extract

¼ tsp Himalayan salt

1 lemon, sliced (seeds removed; see Recipe Note)

2 limes, sliced (seeds removed; see Recipe Note)

Optional garnishes: fresh mint, raspberries, blackberries, 1 green apple (cut into bite-size chunks), unsweetened coconut flesh

Combine the white wine, coconut rum, ginger ale, honey, pineapple extract, salt and lemon and lime slices in a large jar or container. Add any of the optional garnishes. Place the mixture in the refrigerator to chill for several hours before serving.

Recipe Note:

Some sangrias can sit for days and get more and more delicious. That is not the case with this recipe. As it sits the alcohol will begin to pull out the bitterness from the lemon and lime peels. So, I would recommend only leaving them in the sangria for a few hours. If you want to keep leftovers, remove the lemon and lime slices, and the sangria will be delicious for the next several days kept in the refrigerator. The other fruits can stay in the sangria for several days. Skip adding the lemons and limes if you don't want to be bothered with having to remove them, in which case I would suggest adding 1 tablespoon (15 ml) of lime juice instead for the perfect citrus flavor.

Substitution Note:

To make this *Paleo*, replace the sugar-free honey with 3 tablespoons (45 ml) of organic honey or agave.

EGG FREE · NUT FREE · DAIRY FREE · VEGETARIAN

Makes 6 to 8 servings

Mulled Wine Cranberry Sangria

This mulled wine sangria is a drink that can be served year-round. For warmer months, serve chilled or over ice. For colder months, serve warm. This recipe will definitely make your kitchen smell like Christmas. So whether you are celebrating Christmas in July or in December, this is one drink you shouldn't miss.

1 (25.4-oz [750-ml]) bottle red wine

¾ cup (75 g) frozen cranberries, plus more for garnish

3 cinnamon sticks

15 whole cloves

1 tbsp (15 ml) orange extract

5 tbsp (75 ml) sugar-free honey or sugar-free maple syrup

½ tsp stevia extract or monk fruit extract

1 cup (240 ml) brandy

24 oz (710 ml) sugar-free ginger ale (such as Zevia brand)

⅛ tsp Himalayan salt

Sliced apple, for garnish

In large saucepan or Dutch oven, combine the wine, frozen cranberries, cinnamon sticks and whole cloves and bring to a boil over high heat. As soon as the mixture reaches a boil, immediately decrease the heat to low and simmer for 30 minutes.

Remove from the heat and strain into a large bowl or pitcher. Allow the mixture to cool to room temperature, then add the orange extract, honey, stevia extract, brandy, ginger ale and salt. Mix to combine. Pour into a pitcher and serve. Garnish with sliced green apples and additional frozen cranberries, if desired.

Substitution Note:

To make this **Paleo**, use regular honey or regular maple syrup instead of the sugar-free version and omit the stevia or monk fruit extract.

448 THE ULTIMATE KETO COOKBOOK

Makes 7 to 8 servings

½ cup (120 ml) water

1 cup (250 g) frozen strawberries

3 tbsp (45 ml) sugar-free honey or sugar-free maple syrup (or to taste)

¼ tsp stevia extract or monk fruit extract (or to taste)

¼ tsp Himalayan salt

1 cup (135 g) frozen rhubarb

1 (25.4-oz [750-ml]) bottle rosé

1 tsp pink pitaya (optional, for color)

Strawberry Rhubarb Rosé Slush

Does anyone else miss the slushies from our childhoods? They were bright red or blue and usually found at a gas station or summer festival. This recipe is the adult version! Depending on the brand of rosé you use, the color will vary but is typically a light pink. Feel free to use your favorite natural food coloring to punch up the color. I used Suncore Foods pink pitaya. If you don't have an ice cream machine, you can still make this recipe. Instead, pour the prepared finished mixture into several ice-cube trays. Freeze until solid. Then whenever you want a cocktail, throw as many cubes into the blender as you'd like and purée until it's a slush consistency. For the best results and to avoid freezer burn, I recommend using ice-cube trays that come with a lid.

If you will be using an ice cream maker, chill the bowl in the refrigerator for an hour.

In a small saucepan, add the water, frozen strawberries, honey, stevia, salt and frozen rhubarb. Cook over high heat for 10 to 12 minutes. During this time, the fruit will give off its juices and reduce down to a pulp. Remove the pan from the heat and transfer into a medium bowl or a high-speed blender. Blend with an immersion blender or purée in a high-speed blender for 2 to 3 minutes. Add the wine and stir to combine. Add the pitaya powder if you wish and blend more. Pour the mixture into an ice cream maker and turn on for 30 minutes or as directed by the manufacturer.

Leftover rosé slush can be stored in a sealed container in the freezer. Due to the alcohol it will not freeze solid and can be put back in the blender at any time.

Recipe Note:

Check the sweetness level before adding the mixture to the ice cream maker. If more sweetener is desired, add an additional 3 tablespoons (45 ml) of sugar-free honey and ¼ teaspoon of stevia extract. I provided this range due to the fact that every bottle of rosé is different. Some are sweeter than others, so adjust the sweetness of this recipe to your taste.

Substitution Note:

To make this **Paleo**, use regular honey or regular maple syrup instead of sugar free and omit the stevia or monk fruit extract.

Makes 2 servings

Classic Margarita

This is a simple yet delicious margarita recipe. It comes together quickly; for the best flavor make just before serving.

Combine the tequila, lime juice, orange extract, honey, stevia extract and salt in a medium bowl.

Dip the rims of two glasses into water or lime juice. Choose the desired salt, sweet and salty or sweet option for the rim and spread it on a small plate. Dip the rim of each glass in the plate until the sugar/salt sticks. Add ice to the glasses. Pour in the margarita and garnish with lime wedges.

Substitution Note:

To make this **Paleo**, use regular honey instead of sugar free and omit the stevia or monk fruit extract. Use granulated honey for the rim.

Margarita

½ cup (120 ml) tequila

3 tbsp (45 ml) lime juice, plus more for rims

1 tsp orange extract

3 tbsp (45 ml) sugar-free honey

¼ tsp stevia extract or monk fruit extract

¼ tsp Himalayan salt

For the Rim

Water or lime juice, for dipping

Salty: 4 tbsp (72 g) Himalayan salt

Sweet and salty: 2 tbsp (36 g) Himalayan salt + 2 tbsp (25 g) keto granulated sugar

Sweet: 4 tbsp (50 g) keto granulated sugar

Lime wedges, for garnish

EGG FREE · NUT FREE · DAIRY FREE · VEGETARIAN

Makes 3 to 4 servings

Frozen Strawberry Mango Margarita

Do you ever really need a specific reason to enjoy a darn good margarita? I don't think so. These strawberry mango margaritas will make your friends and family think you are the best bartender around and they'll never believe they are sugar free. They mix together really quickly and I recommend making them just before you are ready to serve. You can use your favorite tequila for these margaritas but I recommend choosing a tequila that is 100% blue agave.

Margarita

3 cups (650 g) whole ice cubes

2 cups (300 g) whole frozen strawberries

2 tsp (10 ml) mango extract

3 tbsp (45 ml) sugar-free honey

¼ tsp stevia extract

¼ tsp Himalayan salt

½ cup (120 ml) tequila

For the Rim

Water or lime juice, for dipping

Salty: 4 tbsp (72 g) Himalayan salt

Sweet and salty: 2 tbsp (36 g) Himalayan salt + 2 tbsp (25 g) keto granulated sugar

Sweet: 4 tbsp (50 g) keto granulated sugar

Lime slices and strawberries, for garnish

Add the ice cubes, strawberries, mango extract, honey, stevia extract, salt and tequila to a high-speed blender. Blend on high for 2 to 3 minutes. If the mixture becomes too thick, add 1 to 2 tablespoons (15 to 30 ml) of water and blend until desired consistency is reached.

Dip the rims of the glasses into water or lime juice. Choose the desired salt, sweet and salty or sweet option for the rim and spread it on a small plate. Dip the rim of each glass in the plate until the sugar/salt sticks. Add the margarita mixture to the glasses and garnish with lime slices and strawberries.

Substitution Note:

To make this ***Paleo***, swap 2 tablespoons (30 ml) of regular honey or agave for the sugar-free version and omit the stevia extract. Use granulated honey for the rim.

EGG FREE · **NUT FREE** · **DAIRY FREE** · **VEGETARIAN**

Makes 3 to 4 servings

Frozen Pineapple Lime Margarita

This margarita is great if you are in the mood for something a little sweet and a little tangy. The sweetness of the pineapple really enhances the sourness of the lime but without the drink tasting too sour. The matcha powder gives this drink its color without altering the flavor but you could also use food coloring to get the desired color. These margaritas mix together really quickly and I recommend making them just before you are ready to serve. You can use your favorite tequila for these margaritas, but I recommend choosing a tequila that is 100% blue agave.

Margarita

6 cups (1.3 kg) whole ice cubes

1 tbsp (15 ml) pineapple extract

4 tsp (20 ml) lime juice

¼ cup (60 ml) sugar-free honey

¼ tsp stevia extract or monk fruit extract

½ tsp sea salt

1½ tsp (2 g) matcha powder (for color) or a few drops of green food coloring

½ cup (120 ml) tequila

For the Rim

Water or lime juice, for the rim

Salty: 4 tbsp (72 g) Himalayan salt

Sweet and salty: 2 tbsp (36 g) Himalayan salt + 2 tbsp (25 g) keto granulated sugar

Sweet: 4 tbsp (50 g) keto granulated sugar

Add the ice cubes, pineapple extract, lime juice, honey, stevia extract, salt, matcha powder or food coloring and tequila to a high-speed blender. Blend on high for 2 to 3 minutes. If the mixture becomes too thick, add 1 to 2 tablespoons (15 to 30 ml) of water and blend until desired consistency is reached.

Dip the rims of the glasses into water or lime juice. Choose the desired salt, sweet and salty or sweet option for the rim and spread it on a small plate. Dip the rim of each glass in the plate until the sugar/salt sticks. Add the margarita mixture to the glasses and serve.

Substitution Note:

To make this **Paleo**, swap ¼ cup (60 ml) of regular honey or agave for the sugar-free version and omit the stevia extract. Use granulated honey for the rim.

EGG FREE · **NUT FREE** · **DAIRY FREE** · **VEGETARIAN**

Makes 4 servings

Peach Hibiscus Margarita

The hibiscus adds a pop of color and a hint of earthiness to this peach margarita. It is refreshing and sweet and great for any occasion.

Margarita

1 cup (240 ml) water

3 tsp (3 g) dried hibiscus flowers

4 cups (870 g) ice cubes

½ cup (120 ml) tequila

1 tbsp (15 ml) peach extract

¼ cup (60 ml) sugar-free honey

1 tbsp (15 ml) lime juice, plus more for rims

¼ tsp stevia extract or monk fruit extract

¼ to ½ tsp Himalayan salt

For the Rim

Water or lime juice, for dipping

Salty: 4 tbsp (72 g) Himalayan salt

Sweet and salty: 2 tbsp (36 g) Himalayan salt + 2 tbsp (25 g) keto granulated sugar

Sweet: 4 tbsp (50 g) keto granulated sugar

Bring the water to a boil in a kettle or in the microwave. Place the dried hibiscus flowers in a small heatproof bowl. Pour the boiling water over the dried hibiscus flowers and steep for 5 to 7 minutes. Strain out the hibiscus flowers and pour the liquid into a large glass or mug. Place the liquid in the refrigerator for 30 to 45 minutes or until cold.

In a high-speed blender, add the ice cubes, tequila, peach extract, honey, lime juice, stevia extract and salt. Take the hibiscus tea out of the refrigerator and add to the blender.

Blend on high for 2 to 3 minutes or until combined.

Dip rims of glasses into water or lime juice. Choose the desired option for the rim and place on a small plate. Turn the glass top in the plate until the sugar/salt sticks. Add the margarita mixture to the glasses and serve.

Recipe Note:

I recommend preparing this drink just before serving. If the margarita is too thick, add water 1 tablespoon (15 ml) at a time until you reach your desired consistency.

Substitution Note:

To make this **Paleo**, use regular honey or maple syrup instead of the sugar-free version and omit the stevia or monk fruit extract. Use granulated honey for the rim.

EGG FREE   NUT FREE   DAIRY FREE

Makes 4 servings

2½ cups (375 g) strawberries (fresh or frozen)

3 tbsp (27 g) keto powdered sugar

½ cup (120 ml) water

2 tbsp (18 g) gelatin

½ tsp pitaya coloring or pink food coloring

1 tsp lime juice

4 tbsp (60 ml) sugar-free honey

½ tsp stevia extract or monk fruit extract

¼ tsp Himalayan salt

1 tsp peach extract

¾ cup (180 ml) white rum

Peach Strawberry Daiquiri Jello Shots

Instead of drinking a cold daiquiri, enjoy these mess-free jello shots. These jello shots are perfect for parties and you don't have to worry about the shots getting watered down as drinks do when they melt.

Cook the strawberries and powdered sugar in a saucepan over medium heat until the strawberries have broken down into a smooth mixture. If using fresh strawberries, add 2 teaspoons (10 ml) of water. Purée the fruit using a regular or immersion blender until smooth. Strain the seeds out and place the liquids back into the saucepan. Heat the purée to a low simmer.

In a small bowl, combine the water and gelatin. When the gelatin absorbs the water without any dry spots, add it to the fruit purée, then remove the pan from the heat. Stir until the gelatin melts into the purée. While the fruit purée is cooling, add the pitaya coloring, lime juice, honey, stevia extract, salt and peach extract. When the purée is cool, mix in the rum and pour into the mold(s) of your choosing. Allow the jello to set in the refrigerator for at least 1 hour before serving.

Substitution Note:

To make this **Paleo**, use 7 tablespoons (105 ml) honey and omit the stevia or monk fruit extracts.

Makes 4 servings

Dairy-Free Piña Colada

If you like piña coladas, you will love this keto version. I used pineapple extract instead of actual pineapple but you won't be able to tell the difference. Because there is no fruit, the color does not match the real thing, so to give it a slightly yellow color, add some turmeric. I recommend making this right before serving. You may be able to make it an hour or two ahead and keep it in the freezer. Most important, enjoy every last drop!

4 cups (870 g) ice

½ cup (120 ml) white rum or coconut rum

½ cup (120 ml) unsweetened full-fat coconut milk from a can, shaken

2 tbsp (30 ml) pineapple extract

4 tbsp (60 ml) sugar-free honey

¼ tsp stevia extract or monk fruit extract

¼ tsp Himalayan salt

¼ tsp turmeric (optional, for color)

Add the ice, rum, coconut milk, pineapple extract, honey, stevia extract, salt and turmeric (if using) to a high-speed blender. Blend on high for 2 to 3 minutes or until combined. If the mixture is too thick, add water, 1 tablespoon (15 ml) at a time until your desired consistency is reached. Pour into glasses and serve immediately.

Substitution Note:

To make this **Paleo**, use regular honey instead of sugar free and omit the stevia extract or monk fruit extract.

Makes 2 servings

¼ cup (60 ml) vodka

¼ cup (60 ml) Homemade Kahlua (page 432)

3 tbsp (45 ml) sugar-free honey or sugar-free maple syrup

¼ tsp stevia extract or monk fruit extract

Ice cubes

½ cup (120 ml) unsweetened full-fat coconut milk or heavy cream

Brandied Cocktail Cherries (page 472), for garnish

Dairy-Free White Russian

This cocktail is unbelievably delicious. It tastes exactly like classic White Russians. Once you make and age the Homemade Kahlua (page 432) you can quickly make this drink whenever you wish.

Combine the vodka, kahlua, honey and stevia or monk fruit extract in a small container and stir. Place a few ice cubes into two glasses. Divide the vodka mixture evenly between the glasses. Divide the coconut milk evenly between both glasses. Garnish with cherries.

Recipe Note:

To have the vodka mixture and coconut milk separate and achieve the same look as seen in the photo, place the vodka mixture and coconut milk in separate containers and chill in the freezer for 10 minutes before adding them to the serving glasses.

Substitution Note:

To make this ***Paleo***, use regular honey or maple syrup instead of sugar free and omit the stevia extract.

Makes 2 servings

The Blue Hawaiian

If you are already a fan of the Blue Hawaiian cocktail, then you won't believe your taste buds when you try my keto version. Instead of using real fruit, I use fruit extract. Blue spirulina and matcha work together to give this drink the prettiest blue–green color without changing the taste. If you don't have matcha on hand, use a little green food coloring instead.

---

3 cups (650 g) ice

¼ cup (60 ml) Homemade Blue Curaçao (page 435)

¼ cup (60 ml) coconut rum

1 tbsp (15 ml) pineapple extract

¼ cup (60 ml) coconut cream

3 tbsp (45 ml) sugar-free honey

¼ tsp stevia extract or monk fruit extract

¾ to 1 tsp blue spirulina powder

¾ to 1 tsp matcha powder

Brandied Cocktail Cherries (page 472), for garnish

Whipped cream or coconut cream, for garnish (optional)

Combine the ice, blue Curaçao, coconut rum, pineapple extract, coconut cream, honey, stevia extract, blue spirulina powder and matcha powder in a high-speed blender. Blend on high for 2 to 3 minutes. Pour the liquid into glasses and garnish each with a brandied cherry and whipped cream or coconut cream, if desired.

Substitution Note:

To make this **Paleo**, use regular honey instead of sugar free and omit the stevia extract.

EGG FREE   NUT FREE

DAIRY FREE   VEGETARIAN

Makes 2 servings

3 to 4 fresh strawberries, chopped

8 to 10 fresh mint leaves, roughly chopped

3 tbsp (45 ml) sugar-free honey

¼ tsp stevia extract

2 tbsp (30 ml) lime juice

¾ cup (180 ml) white rum

¼ to ½ cup (60 to 120 ml) sugar-free ginger ale (such as Zevia)

Strawberry Mint Mojito

This mojito is fresh and delicious. The mojito was one of the first cocktails I fell in love with and I haven't gotten sick of it yet! I highly recommend this version—it is perfectly sweetened but without all the sugar.

In a pitcher, muddle the strawberries and mint leaves. Add the honey, stevia extract, lime juice and rum. Stir to combine. Strain the mixture and divide between two highball glasses. Top each glass with ginger ale to taste.

Substitution Note:

To make this **Paleo**, use regular honey instead of sugar free and omit the stevia extract.

Makes 2 servings

2 mint leaves, plus more for garnish

¼ cup (38 g) frozen blackberries, plus more for garnish

½ cup (120 ml) sugar-free ginger ale (such as Zevia brand)

½ to ¾ cup (120 to 180 ml) vodka (see Recipe Note)

2 tbsp (30 ml) lime juice

1 tbsp (15 ml) sugar-free honey

¼ tsp Himalayan salt

Blackberry Lime Moscow Mule

This Moscow Mule is refreshingly fizzy. If you wish to experiment, feel free to swap out the blackberries for any other berry of choice.

Muddle or crush the mint and blackberries in a pitcher. Add the ginger ale, vodka, lime juice, honey and salt. Stir to combine or use a cocktail shaker. Strain into two Moscow Mule mugs or glasses of choice. Garnish with extra blackberries and mint leaves.

Recipe Note:

You can vary the strength of this drink based on your preference. Start with the lower amount of vodka and add more to taste.

Substitution Note:

To make this **Paleo**, use regular honey instead of sugar free and omit the stevia extract.

EGG FREE   NUT FREE

DAIRY FREE   VEGETARIAN

Makes 5 to 6 servings

4 cups (870 g) ice

½ cup (120 ml) Dairy-Free Irish Crème (page 444)

¼ cup (60 ml) espresso or coffee

¼ cup (60 ml) vodka

6 tbsp (90 ml) sugar-free maple syrup

½ tsp monk fruit extract

¼ tsp Himalayan salt

Brandied Cocktail Cherries

1½ cups (230 g) pitted fresh cherries

½ cup (120 ml) brandy

¼ cup (60 ml) water

3 whole cloves

¼ tsp ground nutmeg

¼ cup (60 ml) sugar-free honey or sugar-free maple syrup

¼ tsp stevia extract or monk fruit extract

¼ tsp Himalayan salt

Dairy-Free Mudslide

The original Mudslide was created by accident. Someone ordered a White Russian but the bartender was out of cream, so they improvised by using Irish cream instead and the Mudslide was born. This delicious cocktail tastes a bit like a milkshake. But don't be deceived, there is most certainly a little kick to it.

Combine the ice, Irish crème, espresso, vodka, maple syrup, monk fruit extract and salt in a high-speed blender. Blend on high for 2 to 3 minutes. Pour into glasses and garnish each with a brandied cherry.

To make the cherries, combine the cherries, brandy, water, cloves, nutmeg, honey, stevia extract and salt in a small Mason jar. Seal the jar and refrigerate for 3 days. Serve the cherries with your favorite beverages. Store in the refrigerator for up to 1 month.

Recipe Note:

For a thicker consistency, add an extra cup (216 g) of ice and blend.

Substitution Note:

To make this **Paleo**, use regular maple syrup or regular honey instead of sugar free and omit the stevia or monk fruit extract.

Makes 2 servings

¼ cup (60 ml) vodka

½ cup (120 ml) Harvest Spice Liqueur (page 440)

3 tbsp (45 ml) sugar-free honey

¼ tsp stevia extract or monk fruit extract

¼ tsp Himalayan salt

½ cup (120 ml) coconut cream

Ice cubes

Brandied Cocktail Cherries (page 472), for garnish

Harvest Spice Cocktail

This cocktail is pretty scrumptious. It's my fall-flavored take on a white Russian. Instead of kahlua, I used the Harvest Spice Liqueur. For the best results, make the base and chill separately from the coconut cream. Then combine in a glass over ice. It should separate and look similar to the photo featured. It's just as good mixed all together, too.

Mix the vodka, liqueur, honey, stevia extract and salt in a small bowl or jar and set aside. Place the coconut cream in a small bowl or jar. Place both jars in the freezer for 10 to 15 minutes to chill.

Fill two glasses halfway with ice cubes. Divide the harvest spice base between the glasses, then divide the coconut cream between the glasses. Garnish with cherries.

Recipe Note:

Coconut cream comes from a chilled can of unsweetened full-fat coconut milk. Skim the cream off the top.

Substitution Note:

To make this **Paleo**, use regular honey instead of sugar free and omit the stevia or monk fruit extract.

EGG FREE · **NUT FREE** · **DAIRY FREE** · **VEGETARIAN**

Makes 2 servings

¼ cup (6 g) packed basil leaves, finely chopped, plus 2 whole leaves for garnish

½ cup (115 g) blueberries, plus more for garnish

1 tbsp (15 ml) sugar-free honey

⅛ tsp Himalayan salt

¾ cup (180 ml) sugar-free ginger ale (such as Zevia brand)

¼ tsp purple food coloring or Suncore Foods wolfberry powder (optional, for color)

Ice cubes

Blueberry Basil Mocktail

This mocktail is perfect for anyone who wants a fun party drink without alcohol. This would also be a great option to share with kiddos.

In a tumbler or large pitcher, muddle the basil and blueberries. Add the honey, salt, ginger ale and food coloring (if using). Stir to combine. Divide between two glasses filled with ice.

Recipe Note:

Measure with whole basil leaves first, then finely chop.

Substitution Note:

To make this **Paleo**, use regular honey instead of sugar free.

Makes 4 servings

Dairy-Free Eggnog

This eggnog evokes a warm and cozy feeling and makes an excellent holiday drink. Enjoy this drink straight, or mix in your favorite rum or brandy for an extra kick.

2 (14.5-oz [430-ml]) cans unsweetened full-fat coconut milk

3 tbsp (45 ml) sugar-free maple syrup

¼ tsp stevia extract or monk fruit extract

1 tsp vanilla extract

2 tsp (5 g) ground cinnamon

2 tsp (5 g) ground nutmeg

¼ tsp ground ginger

4 large egg yolks

¼ tsp Himalayan salt

¼ cup (60 ml) rum or brandy (optional)

Place the coconut milk, maple syrup, stevia extract, vanilla, cinnamon, nutmeg, ginger, egg yolks, salt and rum (if using) in a blender. Mix on high for 1 to 2 minutes, until light and frothy. Pour into a clean 28-ounce (828-ml) or 32-ounce (946-ml) glass jar. Seal the jar and store in the refrigerator. Serve the eggnog over ice, or mix with hot or cold coffee.

Use the eggnog within 2 weeks. If your eggnog thickens in the refrigerator, add ¼ to ½ cup (60 to 120 ml) of water and mix before serving.

Substitution Note:

To make this **Paleo**, use regular maple syrup instead of sugar free and omit the stevia or monk fruit extract.

Keto Basics

In this chapter you will find a hodgepodge of some simple-to-make dairy-free options. Everything from cheese and whipped topping to homemade yogurt.

Makes 2 cups (300 g)

Dairy-Free Chèvre (Goat Cheese)

Truth be told, the flavor of goat cheese is really unique and is hard to duplicate exactly, but I think this cheese is pretty darn close. Try one of my recipes with mix-ins (page 483), which make this goat cheese even more special. I'm not even a big goat cheese lover in general, but I could eat this cheese every single day. I rarely use tofu in recipes but this recipe is worth it.

½ cup (66 g) raw unsalted cashews or raw unsalted macadamia nuts

10 oz (283 g) firm and dry tofu

½ cup (120 g) refined coconut oil

1 tbsp (15 ml) lemon juice

½ tsp Himalayan salt

Place your cashews in enough water to cover them and let them soak for 30 minutes or longer. Drain, place on a kitchen towel and pat dry.

Prep your tofu by getting as much of the water out as possible. Place the tofu, coconut oil, lemon juice, salt and cashews in a blender or food processor (use the tamper on your blender if you have one; see the introduction to the Homemade Dairy-Free Feta recipe on page 488). Process the mixture until it is totally smooth and creamy. Using a spatula, scrape the whipped mixture into a sealable container. Place in the refrigerator for 4 to 6 hours, or longer. After this point it will be ready to shape into a goat cheese log.

Recipe Note:

Using a tofu press is a great way to guarantee that enough water gets pressed out. If your tofu has a lot of liquid, you will end up with a cheese that can't be rolled into a log; instead it will be a softer spread.

(continued)

Cherry Honey Walnut Chèvre Log

Handful of no-sugar-added dried cherries

Handful of walnuts

1 cup (150 g) Dairy-Free Chèvre (Goat Cheese; page 481)

2 tsp (10 ml) sugar-free honey or sugar-free maple syrup

⅛ tsp stevia extract or monk fruit extract

Salt and pepper, to taste

Finely chop the cherries and walnuts and spread them on a plate.

Place the goat cheese in a bowl and mix in the honey, stevia extract and salt and pepper. Place the goat cheese on a piece of parchment paper and carefully roll it into a log. To get the shape perfect, gently roll it on the countertop. This gets a little bit messy, so the parchment paper can help. When it is the shape of a log, roll it in the chopped cherries and walnuts on the plate.

Wrap in plastic wrap and place in the refrigerator for 6 to 8 hours. It will firm up as it chills. Store in the refrigerator for 1 to 2 weeks.

Garlic Black Pepper Chive Chèvre Log

1 cup (150 g) Dairy-Free Chèvre (Goat Cheese; page 481)

2 tbsp (6 g) finely chopped chives, plus more for garnish

½ tsp garlic powder

Salt and pepper, to taste

Place the goat cheese in a bowl and stir in the chives, garlic, salt and pepper. Place the goat cheese on a piece of parchment paper and carefully roll it into a log. To get the shape perfect, gently roll it on the countertop. This gets a little bit messy, so the parchment paper can help. When it is the shape of a log, roll it in a little extra chopped chives.

Wrap in plastic wrap and place in the refrigerator for 6 to 8 hours. It will firm up as it chills. Store in the refrigerator for 1 to 2 weeks.

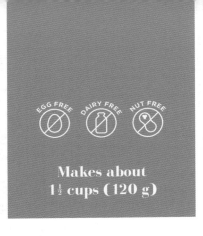

**Makes about
1½ cups (120 g)**

Dairy-Free Whipped Topping

Making whipped cream dairy free is so much fun. It will stay fresh and fluffy in the fridge for up to a month. It does require a few extra steps compared to making regular whipped topping but it is well worth the effort. Gelatin is used to stabilize it, so it behaves just like the real thing!

2 tbsp (30 ml) hot water

1 tsp vanilla extract

½ tsp gelatin

¼ cup (60 ml) sugar-free honey or sugar-free maple syrup

¼ tsp stevia extract or monk fruit extract

2 (13.5-oz [398-ml]) cans unsweetened full-fat coconut milk (chilled in refrigerator overnight)

In a microwave-safe bowl, whisk together the hot water, vanilla and gelatin until there are no clumps remaining. Microwave for 20 seconds.

Scrape the gelatin mixture into the bowl of a stand mixer and add the honey and stevia extract. Using the whisk attachment, whip on high speed for 6 to 7 minutes, until the mixture thickens. (You can also use a hand mixer.)

Open the chilled cans of coconut milk, and scoop out only the creamy, solid portion on top. Leave the watery liquid in the can. (Use the water for other recipes or for smoothies.) Add the coconut cream to the bowl and whip until the mixture is frothy and thickened, 1 to 2 minutes. Use immediately or store in the refrigerator for up to 1 month.

Makes 3 servings

10 oz (283 g) bag fresh or frozen riced cauliflower

1 tbsp (15 ml) oil, butter or butter-flavored coconut oil

Himalayan salt, pepper and any other seasonings, to taste

Simple Cauli Rice Three Ways

If you are eating keto, then you will eventually try cauliflower rice. I'm calling for a 10-ounce (283-g) bag of pre-riced cauliflower as that's what I'm finding most brands are selling. However, do not fret if your bag isn't that exact amount; a bit more or less will still work. While all three variations of this flexible recipe are easy, I recommend making a big batch ahead of time and storing it in the fridge (for up to 5 days), as it's a convenient thing to have on hand to serve with all kinds of meals.

In a Skillet

Add the riced cauliflower to a 10-inch (25-cm) skillet. Cook over medium heat with the oil and seasonings of choice until the cauliflower is cooked to preferred doneness. I cook between 5 to 10 minutes.

Tip:
If I am using frozen cauliflower and want my rice a little bit more dry and crisp, I cook it in a dry pan for a few minutes, allowing all the water to evaporate off the cauliflower rice before adding the oil.

Oven Roasted

Preheat the oven to 425°F (220°C). Line a rimmed baking sheet with parchment paper. Spread the cauliflower rice on the pan, drizzle with the oil and sprinkle on spices of choice. Roast 15 to 20 minutes until the cauliflower reaches preferred doneness.

Grilled

Preheat a grill to 375–425°F (190–220°C). Anywhere in that range is fine; the cauliflower is flexible and can be cooked along with most other foods that are grilled. Place the cauliflower rice on a piece of aluminum foil. Mix in the oil and spices of choice and wrap up. Once the grill is hot, place the packet of foil in and cook for 15 to 20 minutes, or until the cauliflower rice is tender and lightly golden brown.

Homemade Dairy-Free Feta

This faux cheese mimics feta exactly. It will blow your mind. To make this cheese, I had the best results using my high-speed (Vitamix) blender using the tamper. (A twister jar on a Blendtec would work well too.) If you don't have these options, the next best thing would be a food processor.

10 oz (283 g) super-firm, dry tofu (see Recipe Notes)

¾ cup (180 ml) melted refined coconut oil (see Recipe Notes)

1 tbsp (15 ml) lemon juice

2 to 3 tsp (10 to 15 ml) apple cider vinegar (to taste)

2 tsp (5 g) onion powder

1¼ tsp (7.5 g) Himalayan salt

A few hours before making the feta, take the tofu out of the refrigerator and press out as much water as you can. Use a tofu press for the best results. Let it come to room temperature.

Place the tofu, coconut oil, lemon juice and 2 teaspoons (10 ml) of the apple cider vinegar into your blender or food processor. Process until the mixture is completely smooth and creamy. Then, add the onion powder, salt and remaining 1 teaspoon of apple cider vinegar if you want a little more tang. Taste as you go to make sure the seasoning is exactly how you like it. Real feta is very salty and on the sour side, so if you want a stronger-tasting feta go for the full amount of apple cider vinegar.

Using a spatula, scrape the whipped feta into a sealable container. Place the container in the refrigerator. In 4 to 6 hours you can use a fork to break apart the cheese into traditional feta chunks. This feta will have the best taste 1 to 2 days later. If your feta remains creamy and smooth, this means there was too much water in the tofu. You can use this creamier version as cream cheese or mock goat cheese instead and the next time get more water out of the tofu or try a different brand. Store in the refrigerator for up to 2 weeks.

Recipe Notes:

- It's important to use the driest/firmest square of tofu available. The drier and firmer it is, the more like feta your end result will be. If the tofu is watery and soft, you will end up with a cheese more like cream cheese or goat cheese texture rather than feta. Online you can order a tofu press that squeezes out the excess liquid.

- Be sure to use refined coconut oil in this recipe. It has a milder flavor and is better for this cheese. Also make sure you use the type of coconut oil that gets hard when it's cold. (Not the oil that stays liquid no matter the temperature.) The oil firming in the refrigerator is what makes this recipe work.

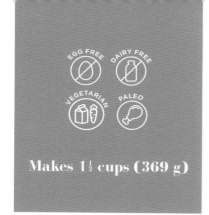

EGG FREE · DAIRY FREE · VEGETARIAN · PALEO

Makes 1¼ cups (369 g)

1½ cups (174 g) blanched almond flour

3 cups (720 ml) water

⅓ cup (80 ml) lemon juice

Dairy-Free Ricotta Cheese or Sour Cream

I had been using homemade almond milk for my dairy-free cheese recipes and I got the crazy idea to try using the milk to make ricotta, the same way that I make real ricotta—and it worked! I was shocked, amazed and beyond excited. This recipe can either be turned into ricotta (by letting the majority of the liquid drip out) or if you let only a little of the liquid drip out, you end up with the creamy sour cream. Be sure to use blanched almond flour in this recipe.

Place the almond flour and water in a blender and process until smooth and creamy. Pour the milk into a saucepan and bring it to *just barely* a boil over medium heat. This is extremely important: if it is not hot enough it won't work, and the same is true if it is too hot. So, as soon as you see the mixture start to bubble, turn off the heat and pour in the lemon juice. Give it a little stir just to mix in the lemon juice and then leave it in the pan, without stirring, for 30 minutes.

While the cheese is separating (the cream and water will separate and curdle), place a piece of cheesecloth over a strainer and place the strainer over a bowl or in a clean sink. When the mixture has separated, gently pour the contents of the pot into the cheesecloth. Let the water drip slowly (if you wish to help speed up the process, you can lift the cheesecloth and squeeze it very gently). Allow it to drip to the thickness of your preference. Thick is ricotta; thin is sour cream. The water that drips should be a clear yellowish color for the most part; if the cheese is going straight through the cheesecloth, this means the cheese did not separate correctly and your water was either too hot or too cold.

Store the cheese in a sealed container in the refrigerator for up to 2 weeks.

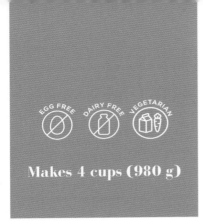

Homemade Cashew Yogurt

These days you can find tons of dairy-free yogurt options at most grocery stores. When I'm in the mood to make it at home, this is one of my go-to recipes. Macadamia nuts are lower in carbs than cashews, so if you are looking to keep carbs as low as possible opt for macadamias. You will need a yogurt maker for this recipe.

3 cups (400 g) raw unsalted cashews or macadamia nuts

2 to 3 cups (480 to 720 ml) water (plus more for soaking)

1 tbsp (15 ml) raw honey (or sweetener of choice, but it *must* be a real sugar in order to ferment)

½ tsp yogurt starter

Soak the cashews or macadamia nuts for 8 hours in water to soften them and to make them more easily digestible. Drain the cashews.

To a high-speed blender, add the cashews, water (2 cups [480 ml] for a nice thick yogurt, 3 cups [720 ml] for a traditional yogurt texture) and raw honey. Blend on high for a few minutes until the mixture is completely smooth. Add the starter and blend until incorporated.

Pour the mixture into a yogurt maker and ferment for at least 7 hours. A 7-hour fermentation will produce a mild tang, while 16 hours will produce a more intense tang. Taste and experiment to find your desired tanginess. Refrigerate immediately after fermentation to halt fermentation and to thicken even more.

Suggested Brands

I tested out *many* products and brands while writing this cookbook and compiled a list of my absolute favorites. These ingredients performed the best and should be used whenever possible in my recipes. In some situations if you don't use them, the recipe may not turn out the same.

Almond flour: These days it is so much easier to come by high-quality blanched almond flour. I buy mine from Costco or Honeyville. The key is to always look for the word "blanched," otherwise your baked goods will not turn out.

Baking powder: For the best results, I have come to depend heavily on Bob's Red Mill double-acting baking powder! It is not always the easiest to find in stores, but is usually available online.

Bouillon: My favorite brand is Better than Bouillon, available in most grocery stores. Just be sure to purchase organic as it is substantially cleaner—their non-organic products often use dairy.

Butter: I always use salted butter in my recipes! Salt makes everything taste better.

Butter substitutes: Earth Balance brand buttery sticks work great anytime that a recipe requires a stick of butter. Anytime that melted butter is called for I really like to use Nutiva Organic Coconut Oil with Non-Dairy Butter Flavor. The ingredients are pretty clean, and the flavor is great! You may find that adding a little more salt when using these subs benefits your finished recipe. I typically use salted butter so using one of these swaps will usually mean you are using a tiny bit less salt than I have.

Cassava flour: Cassava is not considered a low-carb or keto ingredient. However, I chose to include it in a few recipes in a small quantity to get the very best final result possible. I highly and always recommend Otto's brand cassava flour—they have the best flour period.

Coconut milk: There are many brands of coconut milk available, most of which will work just fine in these recipes. But, I would like to give a special shout-out to the Native Forest brand as their cans are BPA free! We use their Coconut Cream Premium and Coconut Milk Classic.

Curry paste: Throughout the book I call for Thai curry paste (red and green). I buy both from the brand Thai Kitchen. They are not spicy and add excellent flavor. Other brands may bring more heat.

Extracts: To create a lot of fun flavors that are not typically keto, I used quite a few unique flavored extracts from OliveNation. I was genuinely impressed with the quality and taste of each one. Their entire collection is available online.

Garbanzo bean flour: Bob's Red Mill garbanzo bean flour is the easiest to find in stores and it will work great in any of my recipes.

Lupin flour: My current preferred brands are Lupina and Small Town Specialties. Be sure to read reviews before purchasing lupin flour online as some brands often arrive rancid. Lupin flour is made from a bean (not a nut), but is a distant relative to the peanut. Be sure to give this warning to anyone with a nut allergy before serving a dish made with this ingredient and allow them to make an educated decision before taste testing, so that they can do so with caution.

Meat: Sourcing good meat is of utmost importance. I really, truly love US Wellness Meats! Their meats are shipped frozen and arrive in pristine condition (unlike other popular subscription box meat services whose meat often arrives in broken packaging). The company has wonderful ethics, and the prices are reasonable. I feel good putting in my order with a company that supports sustainable farming practices, never uses growth hormones or feeds their animals antibiotics and most important treats the animals humanely.

Oat fiber: Not all oat fibers are created the same. Some brands are heavy and coarse. I used Lifesource Foods Oat Fiber throughout the book and I highly recommend this product. I order it online, and it is quite affordable. If you don't use this brand, your results may vary.

Psyllium husk powder: There is a *big* difference between psyllium husk and psyllium husk powder. They do not work the same in recipes. For all of my recipes I use psyllium husk *powder* and my preferred brand is NOW Foods.

Salt: Throughout this book I used pink Himalayan salt as it has nutritional benefits and is easy to come by in stores these days at an affordable price. All types of salt are not the same when it comes to how salty they are, so if you do not use Himalayan, know that you may need to adjust and use more or less to taste.

Shortening: Regular shortening is made from processed oils that not only have no nutritional value, but are quite bad for us. Instead I recommend Spectrum brand Organic All-Vegetable Shortening. It is available in many grocery stores or online. If you cannot find shortening, another great option for recipes is lard.

Superfruit powders: One of my favorite things to work with has become the Suncore Foods superfruit powders. They add gorgeous natural color to recipes, while also adding a boost of nutrition. They can be used in so many different applications and offer up a vibrant color solution to food coloring. These powders can be purchased online.

Keto Sugar Options

There are many brands and many options, and many of them are the same exact type of product. I have heard people say things like, "This brand does not have an aftertaste." But the truth is that all sugar alcohols typically have an aftertaste and produce a cooling sensation in your mouth. What makes the biggest difference is how much of these sugar replacements you use. I was able to get around the aftertaste in the majority of my recipes by limiting the amounts I used and combining different sweeteners to reach a really balanced taste. The following suggestions are based on best performance, accessibility and price. Please note that xylitol is incredibly toxic to animals—be sure to keep all sugar-free sweeteners from your beloved pets.

Allulose: This is another liquid sweetener. I like the brand Wholesome. This sweetener can be used in place of sugar-free maple syrup and sugar-free honey whenever they are called for in this book in equal quantity. Allulose has a neutral flavor that will work in all recipes.

Chocolate chips: Many assume that stevia-sweetened chocolate is the only option. Turns out that most brands of dark chocolate have the same net carb count as Lily's, and truth be told they taste better. I'm not a big fan of stevia in chocolate so I opt for a few more carbs. But if you are trying to keep carbs as low as possible opt for Lily's. If you are dairy free, the lowest carb option I have found is Enjoy Life's dark chocolate morsels.

Keto brown sugar: For brown sugar substitutes I have two favorites: Brown Sugar Swerve and Sukrin Gold Brown Sugar Alternative. The Sukrin Gold in particular has a great flavor and is a must when making caramel. Outside the United States Sukrin Gold is labeled as gluten free, in the United States it is not due to the fact it contains malt extract. The company has made statements that Sukrin Gold is significantly below the United States' threshold for gluten-free products (close to 1ppm). For most this won't cause a reaction—however, I wanted to make this info clear for celiacs.

Keto granulated sugar: For erythritol, I recommend HaleFresh brand. You can't beat the price and it does what it needs to do in recipes. I order it online. For granulated sugar, I recommend Swerve; it is ground a bit finer, which is always a plus with baking. Swerve can be found in most major grocery stores these days. Both options can be used every time I call for keto granulated sugar.

Keto honey: Finding a sugar-free honey substitute made from xylitol was a game changer for my recipe-developing process. I love Nature's Hollow Honey Substitute! It can cause some digestive upset for some people; if you find this is the case for you, swap it out for Lakanto brand sugar-free maple syrup in recipes.

Keto powdered sugar: Powdered erythritol has gotten much easier to find online and in stores. I use two brands: Lakanto and Swerve. Just keep in mind that they do have an aftertaste and so quantity used makes a big difference.

Liquid monk fruit: I discovered that monk fruit extract is really versatile and can be swapped for stevia in the same ratio when using the liquid version. I really like both Lakanto Liquid Monk Fruit Extract and NOW Foods Liquid Monk Fruit Sweetener. Both are available online.

Maple syrup: There are many brands of sugar-free maple syrup available in stores. Most, however, have sugar-free sweeteners that can cause digestive upset or just really are not good for you. My favorite brand by far is Lakanto Maple Flavored Sugar-Free Syrup. It's the easiest to digest and will work beautifully in all of my recipes. Order online, or you may be able to find it in some stores.

Stevia: When I hear that someone doesn't like stevia, I tend to assume it is because they tried one of the many not-great brands. Stevia can have an awful aftertaste. I have come to love liquid stevia from two brands: NuNaturals and Trader Joe's. The key is to not use too much, which is why you will often see stevia combined with another sugar-free sweetener in this book.

Acknowledgments

Marissa Spinks—Marissa, thank you for always being a joy to be around. I enjoy your love of music, and that I can always count on seeing you dancing on the other side of the kitchen, no matter what song is playing. You are a creative, hardworking powerhouse. I truly appreciate you!

Rich Angell—To the most encouraging husband out there and my unpaid publicist, sharing about me and what I do with anyone who will listen. Rich is also the first to offer to help with the dishes! Rich, you are the light of my life, my greatest happiness and because of you I get to chase my dreams.

Chloe, Cliff, Corbyn and Camille—Our little furry "angells." The four cutest kitchen helpers I could ever ask for. I am blessed beyond measure to be surrounded by their love each and every day.

Special thanks to Page Street Publishing for the opportunity to publish this giant book.

About the Author

Brittany Angell is the author of *The Essential Gluten Free Baking Guides Part 1 & 2*, the bestselling cookbook *Every Last Crumb* and is founder of the fast growing allergen-free food blog BrittanyAngell.com. She strives to serve the entire allergy-free community by developing creative, unique and hard-to-find recipes that are gluten free, low carb, dairy free, egg free, nut free, Paleo, grain free and keto. As a worldwide leader in food allergy awareness, Brittany is a sought-after author, speaker and consultant to corporations and restaurants seeking to capitalize on the expanding gluten- and allergy-free market.

Brittany's foray into the food allergy world began in January 2010 after many months of unsuccessfully solving her health issues through traditional means. Once she took her health into her own hands through education and research, she was led to several specialists and was diagnosed with Hashimoto's disease and lead poisoning accompanied by various food allergies and intolerances. Through food and holistic care she has turned her health around and become a positive advocate to help others do the same thing.

Brittany resides in Cleveland, Ohio, with her husband and four rat terriers.

Nutritional Information
(per serving unless otherwise noted)

Serving sizes are generous and can be adjusted to meet dietary needs. The type of sugars selected will affect total carb counts. Choose your keto sweeteners accordingly.

Acai Blueberry Lavender Smoothie Bowl
Calories 277.4; Total Carbs 18.2g; Net Carbs 14.1g; Protein 3.8g; Fat 21.7g

Air Fryer Chicken Cordon Bleu
Calories 492.9; Total Carbs 4.4g; Net Carbs 4.2g; Protein 64.6g; Fat 23.2g

Al Pastor–Inspired Chicken and "Rice"-Stuffed Poblano Peppers
Calories 189.6; Total Carbs 24.4g; Net Carbs 12.6g; Protein 24.5g; Fat 7.8g

Almond Flour Cake Base
Calories 203.3; Total Carbs 13.4g; Net Carbs 19g; Protein 6.1g; Fat 18.4g

Almond Joy Pudding (Nutrition for Total Recipe)
Calories 629.6; Total Carbs 57.8g; Net Carbs 38.3g; Protein 11.2g; Fat 42.6g

Almond Milk (Nutrition for Total Recipe)
Calories 1028.6; Total Carbs 38.6g; Net Carbs 19.3g; Protein 38.6g; Fat 90.0g

Apple Cinnamon Bars
Calories 424.4; Total Carbs 35.3g; Net Carbs 10.1g; Protein 14.2g; Fat 13.1g

Asian Chicken Salad with Tangerine Ginger Dressing
Calories 705.4; Total Carbs 20.4g; Net Carbs 9.0g; Protein 37.0g; Fat 53.3g

Asian Pork Belly Tacos
Calories 525.9; Total Carbs 25.0g; Net Carbs 9.5g; Protein 7.9g; Fat 46.3g

Asian Sesame-Crusted Chicken Wings (Nutrition for Total Recipe)
Calories 2350.7; Total Carbs 15.7g; Net Carbs 6.1g; Protein 165.2g; Fat 177.9g

Avocado Basil And Lime Soup
Calories 179.3; Total Carbs 8.4g; Net Carbs 2.7g; Protein 4.4g; Fat 15.5g

Banana Chai Chocolate Bars
Calories 237.7; Total Carbs 16.8g; Net Carbs 4.3g; Protein 6.9g; Fat 21.0g

Banana Cream Pie Glazed Donuts
Calories 237.9; Total Carbs 39.6g; Net Carbs 3.6g; Protein 8.2g; Fat 17.7g

Beet Ginger Lime Yogurt Dressing (Nutrition for Total Recipe)
Calories 796.2; Total Carbs 59.9g; Net Carbs 35.3g; Protein 12.9g; Fat 62.9g

Berry Brie Burgers
Calories 353.3; Total Carbs 10.7g; Net Carbs 5.2g; Protein 30.7g; Fat 20.8g

Black Goji Berry Protein Balls
Calories 58.3; Total Carbs 1.1g; Net Carbs .6g; Protein .6g; Fat 6.4g

Blackberry Almond Caramel Scones
Calories 230.9; Total Carbs 28.9g; Net Carbs 2.4g; Protein 12.5g; Fat 18.3g

Blackberry Lime Moscow Mule
Calories 158.9; Total Carbs 10.4g; Net Carbs 3.7g; Protein 0.3g; Fat 0.1g

Blackberry Lime Muffins
Calories 147.8; Total Carbs 22.5g; Net Carbs 3.9g; Protein 5.0g; Fat 1.5g

Blackberry Lime Yogurt (Nutrition for Total Recipe)
Calories 204.2; Total Carbs 25.1g; Net Carbs 21.1g; Protein 9.4g; Fat 8.3g

Blackberry Swirl Cheesecake Brownies
Calories 266.9; Total Carbs 21.9g; Net Carbs 8.3g; Protein 4.8g; Fat 22.1g

Blueberry Basil Mocktail
Calories 45.5; Total Carbs 14.8g; Net Carbs 7.5g; Protein 0.4g; Fat 0.2g

Blueberry Lavender Yogurt (Nutrition for Total Recipe)
Calories 71.8; Total Carbs 40.7g; Net Carbs 34.5g; Protein 9.5g; Fat 9.4g

Blueberry Lemon Crumb Muffins
Calories 233.8; Total Carbs 28.0g; Net Carbs 5.8g; Protein 6.8g; Fat 19.3g

Blueberry Lemon Glazed Donuts
Calories 154.2; Total Carbs 33.7g; Net Carbs 2.5g; Protein 7.0g; Fat 10.2g

Blueberry Lemon Poppy Seed Chicken Salad
Calories 246.7; Total Carbs 11.0g; Net Carbs 7.4g; Protein 20.8g; Fat 14.0g

Boiled Low-Carb Bagels
Calories 194.7; Total Carbs 13.2g; Net Carbs 10.5g; Protein 11.4g; Fat 11.3g

Boiled Low-Carb Soft Pretzels
Calories 194.7; Total Carbs 13.2g; Net Carbs; 10.5g; Protein 11.4g; Fat 11.3g

Braised Bourbon Maple-Glazed Pork Roast
Calories 571.5; Total Carbs 14.0g; Net Carbs 4.6g; Protein 50.0g; Fat 20.9g

Brandied Cocktail Cherries (Nutrition for Total Recipe)
Calories 504.7; Total Carbs 81.9g; Net Carbs 32.0g; Protein 2.5g; Fat 0.7g

Breaded Eggplant Fries
Calories 328.9; Total Carbs 39.8g; Net Carbs 22.2g; Protein 13.6g; Fat 16.2g

Buffalo Chicken Burgers
Calories 170.4; Total Carbs 2.5g; Net Carbs 1.8g; Protein 19.1g; Fat 9.7g

Butterfly Pea Flower Smoothie Bowl
Calories 133.9; Total Carbs 9.1g; Net Carbs 7.4g; Protein 2.5g; Fat 9.4g

Caramel Candied Pecan Ice Cream (Nutrition for Total Recipe)
Calories 3666.7; Total Carbs 219.2g; Net Carbs 122.8g; Protein 27.9g; Fat 333.9g

Candied Pecans (Nutrition for Total Recipe)
Calories 941.2; Total Carbs 69.2g; Net Carbs 56.8g; Protein 11.3g; Fat 95.1g

Caramel Pumpkin Cheesecake with Chocolate Crust
Calories 402.3; Total Carbs 26.6g; Net Carbs 8.5g; Protein 7.7g; Fat 36.9g

Carnitas Taco Salad with Crispy Cassava Flour Tortilla Strips
Calories 737.0; Total Carbs 25.5g; Net Carbs 13.1g; Protein 16.5g; Fat 65.3g

Carrot and Zucchini Muffins with Toasted Hemp Seeds
Calories 184.6; Total Carbs; 19.9g; Net Carbs 3.4g; Protein 7.4g; Fat 15.0g

Carrot Cake Protein Balls
Calories 17.5; Total Carbs 1.4g; Net Carbs 0.5g; Protein 0.4g; Fat 1.2g

Celery Root Samosas with Cumin
Calories 73.1; Total Carbs 8.7g; Net Carbs 6.8g; Protein 1.9g; Fat 3.9g

Chai Latte
Calories 430.1; Total Carbs 28.5g; Net Carbs 10.7g; Protein 3.5g; Fat 36.8 g

Cheesy Parsnip Latkes
Calories 123.1; Total Carbs 11.0g; Net Carbs 8.3g; Protein 2.9g; Fat 7.8g

Cherry Honey Walnut Chèvre Log (Nutrition for Total Recipe)
Calories 1050.5; Total Carbs 47.7g; Net Carbs 37.0g; Protein 20.4g; Fat 90.7g

Cherry Mocha Coffee Creamer (Nutrition for Total Recipe)
Calories 858.4; Total Carbs 24.2g; Net Carbs 12.3g; Protein 5.7g; Fat 81.0g

Chicken Eggplant Basil Burgers
Calories 158.4; Total Carbs 3.5g; Net Carbs 2.2g; Protein 18.3g; Fat 8.4g

Chicken Paprikash with Spätzle
Calories 706.0; Total Carbs 23.1g; Net Carbs 16.5g; Protein 47.6g; Fat 48.2g

Chili Lime Parmesan Carrot Fries
Calories 263.0; Total Carbs 20.5g; Net Carbs 13.2g; Protein 7.4g; Fat 18.3g

Chili-Mint Turkey Meatballs (Nutrition for Total Recipe)
Calories 1437.0; Total Carbs 12.3g; Net Carbs 7.9g; Protein 127.2g; Fat 98.8g

Chilled Persian Yogurt Soup
Calories 162.4; Total Carbs 7.5g; Net Carbs 5.9g; Protein 5.5g; Fat 13.2g

Chocolate Chai Protein Balls
Calories 38.0; Total Carbs 3.3g; Net Carbs 0.6g; Protein 1.1g; Fat 2.5g

Chocolate Hazelnut Crepes
Calories 110.5; Total Carbs 10.3g; Net Carbs 1.4g; Protein 5.2g; Fat 8.6g

Chocolate Hazelnut Yogurt (Nutrition for Total Recipe)
Calories 228.2; Total Carbs 34.2g; Net Carbs 14.2g; Protein 10.6g; Fat 9.4g

Chocolate Mousse Pudding (Nutrition for Total Recipe)
Calories 356.5; Total Carbs 47.3g; Net Carbs 15.3g; Protein 10.3g; Fat 19.0g

Chocolate Nut-Free Keto Cake
Calories 113.6; Total Carbs 11.1g; Net Carbs 2.2g; Protein 4.3g; Fat 8.4g

Chocolate Peanut Butter Cups
Calories 137.4; Total Carbs 8.9g; Net Carbs 6.0g; Protein 2.8g; Fat 10.8g

Chorizo And Beef Tex-Mex Chili
Calories 283.6; Total Carbs 16.9g; Net Carbs 11.7g; Protein 19.7g; Fat 16.0g

Chorizo with Chimichurri Sheet-Pan Meal (Nutrition for Total Recipe)
Calories 206.9; Total Carbs 4.9g; Net Carbs 4.6g; Protein 12.3g; Fat 14.9g

Cilantro Lime Marinade (Nutrition for Total Recipe)
Calories 672.5; Total Carbs 25.9g; Net Carbs 5.0g; Protein 0.8g; Fat 68.8g

Cilantro Slaw
Calories 86.8; Total Carbs 19.8g; Net Carbs 14.3g; Protein 3.7g; Fat 0.4g

Cilantro-Lime Avocado Pasta
Calories 142.4; Total Carbs 9.0g; Net Carbs 4.1g; Protein 2.7g; Fat 12.0g

Cincinnati Chili
Calories 318.9; Total Carbs 20.6g; Net Carbs 10.2g; Protein 28.0g; Fat 16.1g

Citrus Pork with Thai Slaw
Calories 695.4; Total Carbs 38.9g; Net Carbs 23.4g; Protein 33.3g; Fat 48.7g

Citrus Rose Angel Food Cake
Calories 154.7; Total Carbs 22.3g; Net Carbs 21.0g; Protein 5.1g; Fat 4.9g

Classic Margarita
Calories 215.3; Total Carbs 28.1g; Net Carbs 2.5g; Protein 0.1g; Fat 0.0g

Classic Scoop-and-Bake Chocolate Chip Cookies
Calories 174.2; Total Carbs 12.6g; Net Carbs 3.5g; Protein 3.6g; Fat 15.7g

Coconut Cream Pie Pudding
Calories 390.6; Total Carbs 42.4g; Net Carbs 7.6g; Protein 8.4g; Fat 23.5g

Coconut Lime Macadamia Protein Balls
Calories 66.5; Total Carbs 2.1g; Net Carbs 0.6g; Protein 1.0g; Fat 6.4g

Coconut Matcha Macadamia Bars with White Chocolate Glaze
Calories 357.1; Total Carbs 18.7g; Net Carbs 4.8g; Protein 7.6g; Fat 34.3g

Coconut, Rum and Pineapple Cream Pie
Calories 266.0; Total Carbs 9.0g; Net Carbs 6.0g; Protein 4.2g; Fat 21.6g

Corned Beef Hash Frittata Cups
Calories 101.0; Total Carbs 1.5g; Net Carbs 1.4g; Protein 8.7g; Fat 6.5g

Cranberry Orange Yogurt (Nutrition for Total Recipe)
Calories 198.4; Total Carbs 23.0g; Net Carbs 19.6g; Protein 8.9g; Fat 8.0g

Cream Cheese Frosting
Calories 51.0; Total Carbs 0.4g; Net Carbs 0.4g; Protein 0.5g; Fat 5.3g

Cream Cheese Swirl Brownies
Calories 207.1; Total Carbs 20.0g; Net Carbs 6.9g; Protein 4.5g; Fat 16.4g

Creamy Pumpkin Chicken Noodle Soup
Calories 243.4; Total Carbs 8.4g; Net Carbs 4.8g; Protein 16.7g; Fat 16.0g

Creamy Tomatillo and Jalapeño Chicken Chili
Calories 320.5; Total Carbs 11.1g; Net Carbs 9.1g; Protein 24.4g; Fat 20.8g

Crispy Asian Pork Belly (Nutrition for Total Recipe)
Calories 2931.1; Total Carbs 38.9g; Net Carbs 8.2g; Protein 43.3g; Fat 295.0g

Crispy Green Curry Drumsticks
Calories 130.0; Total Carbs 1.5g; Net Carbs 1.3g; Protein 16.4g; Fat 6.1g

Crispy Tandoori Drumsticks
Calories 176.1; Total Carbs 2.5g; Net Carbs 2.3g; Protein 16.5g; Fat 10.9g

Crispy Vegetarian Falafel
Calories 375.9; Total Carbs 23.5g; Net Carbs 13.9g; Protein 15.6g; Fat 27.8g

Czech "Bread" Dumplings
Calories 73.8; Total Carbs 5.0g; Net Carbs 4.0g; Protein 4.3g; Fat 4.3g

Dairy- And Egg-Free Chocolate Chunk Cookies
Calories 214.6; Total Carbs 16.7g; Net Carbs 7.0g; Protein 5.6g; Fat 17.6g

Dairy-Free Chèvre (Goat Cheese) (Nutrition for Total Recipe)
Calories 1508.1; Total Carbs 27.3g; Net Carbs 24.6g; Protein 31.4g; Fat 144.0g

Dairy-Free Chili con Queso (Nutrition for Total Recipe)
Calories 2640.7; Total Carbs 49.0g; Net Carbs 29.8g; Protein 33.1g; Fat 269.6g

Dairy-Free Cotton Candy Ice Cream (Nutrition for Total Recipe)
Calories 1531.5; Total Carbs 49.4g; Net Carbs 23.9g; Protein 16.6g; Fat 135.7g

Dairy-Free Eggnog
Calories 164.3; Total Carbs 11.7g; Net Carbs 8.3g; Protein 3.2g; Fat 8.8g

Dairy-Free Fettuccine Alfredo with Broccoli
Calories 194.7; Total Carbs 6.8g; Net Carbs 4.4g; Protein 2.8g; Fat 18.5g

Dairy-Free Irish Crème (Nutrition for Total Recipe)
Calories 850.5; Total Carbs 20.4g; Net Carbs 10.1g; Protein 4.5g; Fat 64.4g

Dairy-Free Marshmallow Ube Ice Cream (Nutrition for Total Recipe)
Calories 1423.4; Total Carbs 48.2g; Net Carbs 15.2g; Protein 11.5g; Fat 135.5g

Dairy-Free Matcha Frappuccino
Calories 331.2; Total Carbs 11.2g; Net Carbs 9.0g; Protein 3.2g; Fat 31.2g

Dairy-Free Mudslide
Calories 47.8; Total Carbs 3.6g; Net Carbs 0.4g; Protein 0.1g; Fat 1.4g

Dairy-Free Piña Colada
Calories 166.5; Total Carbs 13.8g; Net Carbs 3.5g; Protein 0.5g; Fat 6.3g

Dairy-Free Pistachio Chip Ice Cream (Nutrition for Total Recipe)
Calories 1916.5; Total Carbs 72.4g; Net Carbs 39.7g; Protein 21.9g; Fat 171.0g

Dairy-Free Ricotta Cheese or Sour Cream (Nutrition for Total Recipe)
Calories 1012.4; Total Carbs 43.0g; Net Carbs 24.1g; Protein 37.6g; Fat 87.2g

Dairy-Free Tangerine Creamsicle Ice Cream (Nutrition for Total Recipe)
Calories 1487.3; Total Carbs 52.9g; Net Carbs 16.5g; Protein 11.0g; Fat 139.7g

Dairy-Free Whipped Topping (Nutrition for Total Recipe)
Calories 1833.2, Total Carbs 65.9g; Net Carbs 25.9g; Protein 10.2g; Fat 171.9g

Dairy-Free White Queso
Calories 217.8; Total Carbs 13.6g; Net Carbs 7.1g; Protein 9.1g; Fat 15.1g

Dairy-Free White Russian
Calories 355.2; Total Carbs 29.8g; Net Carbs 5.8g; Protein 0.5g; Fat 8.5g

Dublin Coddle Stew
Calories 712.4; Total Carbs 16.4g; Net Carbs 11.5g;Protein 41.4g; Fat 54.8g

Espresso Yogurt (Nutrition for Total Recipe)
Calories 169.0; Total Carbs 12.2g; Net Carbs 12.0g; Protein 8.6g; Fat 8.0g

Fluffy Cinnamon Rolls with Caramel Filling and Cream Cheese Frosting
Calories 265.4; Total Carbs 18.2g; Net Carbs 13.0g; Protein 9.6g; Fat 20.5g

French Onion Quiche
Calories 495.6; Total Carbs 12.6g; Net Carbs 9.1g; Protein 15.0g; Fat 44.2g

French Vanilla Coffee Creamer (Nutrition for Total Recipe)
Calories 184.9; Total Carbs 26.8g; Net Carbs 16.3g; Protein 0.8g; Fat 8.0g

Frozen Coconut Milk
Calories 401.6; Total Carbs 4.7g; Net Carbs 4.7g; Protein 2.4g; Fat 40.2g

Frozen Pineapple Lime Margarita (Nutrition for Total Recipe)
Calories 506.9; Total Carbs 73.6g; Net Carbs 4.8g; Protein 0.8g; Fat 0.0g

Frozen Strawberry Mango Margarita
Calories 128.0; Total Carbs 19.8g; Net Carbs 5.3g; Protein 0.3g; Fat 0.1g

Frozen Yogurt
Calories 54.0; Total Carbs 2.2g; Net Carbs 0.5g; Protein 1.6g; Fat 4.9g

Garlic Black Pepper Chive Chèvre Log (Nutrition for Total Recipe)
Calories 61.2; Total Carbs 15.1g; Net Carbs 13.4g; Protein 16.1g; Fat 72.0g

General Tso's Meatloaf
Calories 209.6; Total Carbs 5.8g; Net Carbs 2.3g; Protein 19.0g; Fat 13.0g

Greek-Style Frittata Cups
Calories 118.1; Total Carbs 2.4g; Net Carbs 1.9g; Protein 6.3g; Fat 9.3g

Green Curry and Lemongrass Soup
Calories 108.0; Total Carbs 9.1g; Net Carbs 6.8g; Protein 2.9g; Fat 7.2g

Green Goddess Deviled Eggs
Calories 43.8; Total Carbs 1.2g; Net Carbs 0.4g; Protein 0.3g; Fat 4.3g

Grilled Keto Cauliflower Couscous
Calories 88.0; Total Carbs 7.3g; Net Carbs 4.3g; Protein 2.9g; Fat 6.2g

Grilled Tilapia
Calories 335.8; Total Carbs 1.0g; Net Carbs 0.6g; Protein 59.5g; Fat 10.8g

Grilled Vietnamese Lemongrass Chicken
Calories 250.2; Total Carbs 15.6g; Net Carbs 9.8g; Protein 36.3g; Fat 5.3g

Grilled Vietnamese Lemongrass Chicken – Sauce
Calories 89.3; Total Carbs 11.7g; Net Carbs 1.7g; Protein 0.7g; Fat 6.9g

Harvest Spice Cocktail
Calories 186.7; Total Carbs 17.9g; Net Carbs 2.9g; Protein 0.5g; Fat 8.5g

Harvest Spice Liqueur (Nutrition for Total Recipe)
Calories 1270.3; Total Carbs 41.8g; Net Carbs 6.2g; Protein 0.3g; Fat 0.7g

Harvest Turkey Meatballs with Cranberry Sauce Sheet-Pan Meal
Calories 635.9; Total Carbs 39.3g; Net Carbs 22.7g; Protein 37.5g; Fat 39.8g

Healthier Grenadine (Nutrition for Total Recipe)
Calories 261.6; Total Carbs 69.7g; Net Carbs 28.6g; Protein 1.7g; Fat 0.9g

Hearty Beef Empanadas
Calories 197.6; Total Carbs 4.3g; Net Carbs 2.4g; Protein 8.8g; Fat 17.0g

Hollandaise Drizzle
Calories 257.0; Total Carbs 0.9g; Net Carbs 0.8g; Protein 2.9g; Fat 27.3g

Homemade Blue Curaçao (Nutrition for Total Recipe)
Calories 1281.4; Total Carbs 105.5g; Net Carbs 13.5g; Protein 2.1g; Fat 0.1g

Homemade Bouquet Garni
Calories 2.5; Total Carbs 0.5g; Net Carbs 0.3g; Protein 0.1g; Fat 0.1g

Homemade Cashew Yogurt (Nutrition for Total Recipe)
Calories 2287.8; Total Carbs 140.5g; Net Carbs 126.8g; Protein 72.9g; Fat 175.4g

Homemade Dairy- and Sugar-Free White Chocolate (Nutrition for Total Recipe)
Calories 6728.0; Total Carbs 63.9g; Net Carbs 12.8g; Protein 20.6g; Fat 745.8g

Homemade Dairy-Free Feta (Nutrition for Total Recipe)
Calories 1655.4; Total Carbs 11.6g; Net Carbs 10.3g; Protein 20.1g; Fat 169.7g

Homemade Frangelico (Nutrition for Total Recipe)
Calories 2887.2; Total Carbs 165.6g; Net Carbs 4.6g; Protein 45.1g; Fat 162.0g

Homemade Kahlua (Nutrition for Total Recipe)
Calories 1684.5; Total Carbs 119.5g; Net Carbs 29.5g; Protein 0.1g; Fat 0.1g

Homemade Limoncello (Nutrition for Total Recipe)
Calories 1240.0; Total Carbs 93.6g; Net Carbs 11.0g; Protein 0.4g; Fat 0.1g

Homemade Protein Balls (Fat Bombs) Base
Calories 181.7; Total Carbs 9.8g; Net Carbs 1.7g; Protein 4.8g; Fat 14.3g

Homemade Ranch Rub – Single (Nutrition for Total Recipe)
Calories 110.1; Total Carbs 24.4g; Net Carbs 17.6g; Protein 4.9g; Fat 1.2g

Homemade Ranch Rub Chicken and Cheddar Sheet-Pan Meal
Calories 309.8; Total Carbs 12.4g; Net Carbs 7.9g; Protein 28.2g; Fat 16.8g

Honey Mustard Marinade (Nutrition for Total Recipe)
Calories 594.7; Total Carbs 45.4g; Net Carbs 4.8g; Protein 0.7g; Fat 55.1g

Hungarian Beef Goulash with Dumplings
Calories 582.5; Total Carbs 16.4g; Net Carbs 11.9g; Protein 53.6g; Fat 33.4g

Indian Butter Chicken
Calories 623.1; Total Carbs 10.1g; Net Carbs 7.1g; Protein 34.7g; Fat 49.4g

Indian Dosas with Aloo Gobi Filling
Calories 351.3; Total Carbs 17.8g; Net Carbs 13.2g; Protein 11.5g; Fat 28.0g

Indian Paneer Korma
Calories 893.4; Total Carbs 26.1g; Net Carbs 17.0g; Protein 31.5g; Fat 76.5g

Instant Pot Pork Carnitas with Orange Soda
Calories 554.8; Total Carbs 6.1g; Net Carbs 3.9g; Protein 54.3g; Fat 33.8g

Irish Cream Pie
Calories 231.8; Total Carbs 5.9g; Net Carbs 3.1g; Protein 4.1g; Fat 20.6g

Jalapeño Goat Cheese Ground Beef Meatballs
Calories 80.0; Total Carbs 1.4g; Net Carbs 0.8g; Protein 7.4g; Fat 5.1g

Jalapeño Popper Sausage Burgers
Calories 386.1; Total Carbs 5.8; Net Carbs 5.3g; Protein 22.8g; Fat 29.9g

Kale Salad
Calories 47.4; Total Carbs 10.4g; Net Carbs 6.3g; Protein 2.9g; Fat 0.4g

Keto Caramel (Nutrition for Total Recipe)
Calories 1219.5; Total Carbs 106.8g; Net Carbs 46.8g; Protein 5.6g; Fat 110.5g

Keto Cheezits (Nutrition for Total Recipe)
Calories 1311.2; Total Carbs 43.5g; Net Carbs 15.5g; Protein 77.0g; Fat 103.7g

Keto Flaky Biscuits
Calories 179.1; Total Carbs 9.3g; Net Carbs 3.1g; Protein 9.2g; Fat 14.3g

Keto Grits
Calories 119.0; Total Carbs 3.4g; Net Carbs 2.2g; Protein 4.1g; Fat 10.4g

Keto Hamburger Buns & Rolls
Calories 257.9; Total Carbs 15.9g; Net Carbs 5.2g; Protein 10.8g; Fat 18.3g

Keto Samoa Cookies
Calories 207.1; Total Carbs 19.7g; Net Carbs 6.2g; Protein 4.1g; Fat 21.0g

Keto Tortilla Chips (Nutrition for Total Recipe)
Calories 1106.4; Total Carbs 61.3g; Net Carbs 6.2g; Protein 60.1g; Fat 93.0g

Keto Twix Bars
Calories 349.2; Total Carbs 24.1g; Net Carbs 12.0g; Protein 4.6g; Fat 29.7g

Keto Unicorn Bark (Nutrition for Total Recipe)
Calories 6748.0; Total Carbs 67.9g; Net Carbs 15.8g; Protein 21.6g; Fat 745.8g

Key Lime Pie Yogurt (Nutrition for Total Recipe)
Calories 232.0; Total Carbs 14.1g; Net Carbs 11.3g; Protein 5.7g; Fat 17.4g

Kung Pao Wings (Nutrition for Total Recipe)
Calories 3069.1; Total Carbs 106.1g; Net Carbs 24.1g; Protein 217.2g; Fat 207.8g

Lavender Simple Syrup
Calories 56.2; Total Carbs 22.3g; Net Carbs 2.3g; Protein 0.0g; Fat 0.0g

Lavender Vanilla Latte
Calories 109.7; Total Carbs 4.3g; Net Carbs 1.1g; Protein 1.0g; Fat 10.8g

Lemon Herb Butter Scallop Scampi
Calories 380.0; Total Carbs 16.9g; Net Carbs 14.6g; Protein 48.0g; Fat 15.1g

Lemon Pitaya Poppy Seed Pudding (Nutrition for Total Recipe)
Calories 402.7; Total Carbs 45.1g; Net Carbs 25.4g; Protein 12.0g; Fat 21.8g

Lemon Poppy Seed Bars With Dragon Fruit Glaze
Calories 179.1; Total Carbs 15.4g; Net Carbs 3.6g; Protein 6.5g; Fat 15.1g

Lemon Poppy Seed Dressing (Nutrition for Total Recipe)
Calories 2069.0; Total Carbs 42.0g; Net Carbs 9.2g; Protein 2.0g; Fat 221.9g

Lemon Poppy Seed Mayonnaise (Nutrition for Total Recipe)
Calories 807.1; Total Carbs 7.2g; Net Carbs 4.7g; Protein 2.9g; Fat 86.1g

Lemon Poppy Seed Muffins with Toasted Slivered Almonds
Calories 225.2; Total Carbs 25.1g; Net Carbs 3.4g; Protein 8.2g; Fat 19.3g

Lemon Poppy Seed Yogurt (Nutrition for Total Recipe)
Calories 193.8; Total Carbs 16.8g; Net Carbs 15.2g; Protein 9.7g; Fat 10.5g

Lemon Ricotta Pancakes
Calories 83.8; Total Carbs 10.4g; Net Carbs 0.8g; Protein 6.3g; Fat 5.7g

Lime Sherbet (Nutrition for Total Recipe)
Calories 549.3; Total Carbs 103.5g; Net Carbs 22.9g; Protein 2.4g; Fat 32.0g

Low-Carb Chicago Deep-Dish Pizza
Calories 426.4; Total Carbs 15.5g; Net Carbs 11.0g; Protein 25.8g; Fat 29.9g

Low-Carb German Spätzle
Calories 309.3; Total Carbs 17.0g; Net Carbs 12.5g; Protein 20.3g; Fat 18.5g

Low-Carb Marble Bundt Pound Cake
Calories 620.0; Total Carbs 57.9g; Net Carbs 8.1g; Protein 17.9g; Fat 55.2g

Maple Apple Cinnamon Turkey Sausage (Nutrition for Total Recipe)
Calories 1637.1; Total Carbs 26.8g; Net Carbs 12.4g; Protein 114.7g; Fat 120.1g

Maple Balsamic Dressing (Nutrition for Total Recipe)
Calories 1168; Total Carbs 46.2g; Net Carbs 34.1g; Protein 1.0g; Fat 109.2g

Maple Pecan Bacon Pork Sausage
Calories 251.0; Total Carbs 3.2g; Net Carbs 0.7g; Protein 15.7g; Fat 20.0g

Margarita Lime Glazed Donuts
Calories 242.4; Total Carbs 68.8g; Net Carbs 1.9g; Protein 11.1g; Fat 13.8g

"Marry Me" Sauce
Calories 261.5; Total Carbs 27.2g; Net Carbs 18.7g; Protein 19.5g; Fat 9.6g

Masala Grilled Whole Red Snapper
Calories 340.6; Total Carbs 33.1g; Net Carbs 25.0g; Protein 50.0g; Fat 4.8g

Matcha Crepes
Calories 108.0; Total Carbs 3.2g; Net Carbs 1.3g; Protein 5.1g; Fat 8.4g

Mediterranean Lamb Sheet-Pan Meal
Calories 537.3; Total Carbs 11.3g; Net Carbs 6.7g; Protein 40.2g; Fat 36.5g

Mixed Berry Bars with Lemon Glaze
Calories 237.1; Total Carbs 18.4g; Net Carbs 4.4g; Protein 8.7g; Fat 19.4g

Mocha Chip Granola - Dry Mixture (Nutrition for Total Recipe)
Calories 4082.9; Total Carbs 136.6g; Net Carbs 51.5g; Protein 123.4g; Fat 359.1g

Mocha Chip Granola - Wet Mixture (Nutrition for Total Recipe)
Calories 783.7; Total Carbs 131.0g; Net Carbs 5.0g; Protein 3.7g; Fat 48.2g

Mongolian Beef (Nutrition for Total Recipe)
Calories 2260.6; Total Carbs 63.3g; Net Carbs 29.6g; Protein 185.1g; Fat 133.1g

Moroccan Vinaigrette
Calories 230.4; Total Carbs 11.3g; Net Carbs 4.5g; Protein 1.1g; Fat 20.8g

Mulled Wine Cranberry Sangria
Calories 178.7; Total Carbs 13.5g; Net Carbs 6.2g; Protein 0.2g; Fat 0.0g

Nacho Ground Beef Meatballs
Calories 92.4; Total Carbs 1.7g; Net Carbs 1.2g; Protein 8.1g; Fat 5.9g

No-Bake Hazelnut Fudge Brownies
Calories 260.5; Total Carbs 13.0g; Net Carbs 3.0g; Protein 4.1g; Fat 24.6g

No-Bake Key Lime Tarts
Calories 295.6; Total Carbs 11.7g; Net Carbs 3.1g; Protein 3.7g; Fat 27.2g

No-Bake Snickers Bars
Calories 646.4; Total Carbs 37.7g; Net Carbs 19.5g; Protein 7.7g; Fat 56.3g

Nut-Free Thai "Peanut" Chicken Wings (Nutrition for Total Recipe)
Calories 3185.6; Total Carbs 37.6g; Net Carbs 11.8g; Protein 227.1g; Fat 234.6g

One-Pot Honey Mustard Chicken with Celery Root
Calories 484.2; Total Carbs 40.6g; Net Carbs 9.5g; Protein 43.8g; Fat 21.0g

Pancetta and Rosemary Cauliflower Mash
Calories 319.6; Total Carbs 18.4g; Net Carbs 0.0g; Protein 12.4g; Fat 23.8g

Parsnip Poutine
Calories 935.8; Total Carbs 74.2g; Net Carbs 55.7g; Protein 29.5g; Fat 62.3g

Pasta Primavera
Calories 273.9; Total Carbs 23.4g; Net Carbs 15.8g; Protein 5.2g; Fat 20.0g

Pasta with Dairy-Free Vodka Sauce
Calories 298.1; Total Carbs 18.5g; Net Carbs 13.8g; Protein 4.7g; Fat 17.1g

Peach Hibiscus Margarita
Calories 100.5 ; Total Carbs 12.2g; Net Carbs 1.9g; Protein 0.0g; Fat 0.0g

Peach Strawberry Daiquiri Jell-O Shots (Nutrition for Total Recipe)
Calories 623.1; Total Carbs 80.1g; Net Carbs 31.8g; Protein 3.0g; Fat 1.1g

Peanut Butter Butterscotch Marshmallow Bars
Calories 438.6; Total Carbs 23.0g; Net Carbs 5.9g; Protein 7.4g; Fat 40.6g

Peanut Butter Frosting (Nutrition for Total Recipe)
Calories 2471.7; Total Carbs 211.2g; Net Carbs 51.2g; Protein 58.0g; Fat 219.5g

Peanut Dressing
Calories 315.5; Total Carbs 5.1g; Net Carbs 3.5g; Protein 2.5g; Fat 32.8g

Pecorino Prosciutto Deviled Eggs
Calories 35.2; Total Carbs 0.5g;
Net Carbs 0.5g; Protein 0.5g;
Fat 3.3g

Peppermint Mocha Coffee Creamer (Nutrition for Total Recipe)
Calories 172.2; Total Carbs 28.8g;
Net Carbs 16.3g; Protein 1.9g;
Fat 8.7g

Peppers and Pork Breakfast Sheet Pan
Calories 161.1; Total Carbs 6.7g;
Net Carbs 5.4g; Protein 9.1g; Fat 10.8g

Perfect Chewy Gnocchi
Calories 289.7; Total Carbs 16.8g; Net Carbs 12.3g; Protein 18.7g; Fat 17.1g

Perfect Fluffy Blueberry Pancakes
Calories 107.8; Total Carbs 13.1g;
Net Carbs 1.4g; Protein 6.2g; Fat 7.5g

Perfect Keto Flatbread
Calories 122.8; Total Carbs 10.4g;
Net Carbs 3.7g; Protein 3.0g; Fat 7.8g

Perfect Keto Vanilla Ice Cream (Nutrition for Total Recipe)
Calories 1403.6; Total Carbs 39.2g; Net Carbs 15.2g; Protein 11.5g; Fat 135.5g

Perfect Low-Carb Brownies
Calories 186.1; Total Carbs 19.3g;
Net Carbs 6.6g; Protein 3.9g; Fat 14.5g

Perfectly Flaky Piecrust
Calories 220.0; Total Carbs 5.8g;
Net Carbs 3.0g; Protein 5.5g; Fat 20.9g

Pesto and Mozzarella Quick Bread
Calories 238.3; Total Carbs 5.9g;
Net Carbs 4.0g; Protein 10.9g; Fat 19.8g

Pickled Carrots
Calories 9.2; Total Carbs 1.8g;
Net Carbs 1.2g; Protein 0.2g; Fat 0.0g

Pineapple and Lime Coconut Rum White Sangria
Calories 97.2; Total Carbs 9.3g;
Net Carbs 5.4g; Protein 0.2g; Fat 0.0g

Pineapple Lime Coconut Cake
Calories 562.4; Total Carbs 48.1g; Net Carbs 5.8g; Protein 13.2g; Fat 49.7g

Pineapple-Mint Dressing
Calories 31.9; Total Carbs 12.8g;
Net Carbs 2.7g; Protein 0.0g; Fat 0.0g

Pink Dragon Fruit Protein Balls
Calories 1063.6; Total Carbs 39.9g; Net Carbs 17.3g; Protein 18.1g; Fat 98.6g

Pizza Frittata Cups
Calories 115.0; Total Carbs 1.7g;
Net Carbs 1.5g; Protein 7.5g; Fat 8.5g

Pizza-Style Ground Italian Sausage Meatballs
Calories 142.2; Total Carbs 2.5g;
Net Carbs 1.9g; Protein 7.0g; Fat 11.6g

PMS Brownies
Calories 533.3; Total Carbs 52.4g; Net Carbs 19.4g; Protein 8.7g; Fat 43.5g

Pork Banh Mi
Calories 327.5; Total Carbs 0.6g;
Net Carbs 0.5g; Protein 43.7g; Fat 15.3g

Pork Banh Mi Kale Salad
Calories 669.7; Total Carbs 22.1g;
Net Carbs 9.8g; Protein 37.0g; Fat 49.9g

Protein Ball Base
Calories 181.5; Total Carbs 9.8g;
Net Carbs 1.7g; Protein 4.8g; Fat 14.3g

Pumpkin Chocolate Chip Muffins
Calories 189.1; Total Carbs 26.0g;
Net Carbs 4.4g; Protein 5.7g; Fat 14.4g

Pumpkin Spice and Chocolate Glazed Donuts
Calories 281.6; Total Carbs 34.0g; Net Carbs 4.2g; Protein 10.3g; Fat 23.0g

Pumpkin Spice Coffee Creamer (Nutrition for Total Recipe)
Calories 158.2; Total Carbs 26.9g; Net Carbs 15.6g; Protein 1.0g; Fat 8.2g

Pumpkin Spice Latte
Calories 239.9; Total Carbs 14.2g; Net Carbs 3.3g; Protein 1.9g; Fat 21.6g

Pumpkin Spice Rum Granola - Dry Mixture (Nutrition for Total Recipe)
Calories 5127.7; Total Carbs 155.9g; Net Carbs 45.0g; Protein 167.4g; Fat 454.2g

Pumpkin Spice Rum Granola - Wet Mixture (Nutrition for Total Recipe)
Calories 525.5; Total Carbs 128.1g; Net Carbs 4.5g; Protein 1.1g; Fat 46.8g

Pumpkin Spice Yogurt (Nutrition for Total Recipe)
Calories 154.5; Total Carbs 24.5g; Net Carbs 16.7g; Protein 6.4g; Fat 4.6g

Quick Peanut Butter Chocolate Chip Cookies
Calories 190.5; Total Carbs 14.2g; Net Carbs 6.0g; Protein 6.6g; Fat 15.5g

Quick Pickled Red Onions and Radishes (Nutrition for Total Recipe)
Calories 290.2; Total Carbs 84.0g; Net Carbs 18.8g; Protein 2.1g; Fat 0.2g

Ranch Dressing (Nutrition for Total Recipe)
Calories 1751.9; Total Carbs 11.4g; Net Carbs 10.6g; Protein 7.8g; Fat 188.1g

Ranch Zucchini Chips (Nutrition for Total Recipe)
Calories 655.4; Total Carbs 24.8g; Net Carbs 16.7g; Protein 9.1g; Fat 62.4g

Raspberry Pink Pitaya Smoothie Bowl
Calories 229.8; Total Carbs 18.1g;
Net Carbs 12.4g; Protein 4.4g; Fat 16.5g

Real Deal Fettuccine
Calories 289.9; Total Carbs 16.8g; Net Carbs 12.4g; Protein 18.7g; Fat 17.1g

Red Velvet Quick Bread
Calories 250.9; Total Carbs 25.0g; Net Carbs 16.4g; Protein 6.8g; Fat 19.3g

Roasted Asiago and Artichoke Stuffed Chicken
Calories 695.6; Total Carbs 5.3g;
Net Carbs 4.9g; Protein 58.3g; Fat 48.9g

Roasted Eggplant Za'atar Dip (Nutrition for Total Recipe)
Calories 593.9; Total Carbs 53.8g; Net Carbs 29.4g; Protein 26.6g; Fat 35.1g

Roasted Pumpkin and Shallot Bacon Soup
Calories 484.0; Total Carbs 14.5g; Net Carbs 11.0g; Protein 18.9g; Fat 39.2g

Roasted Summer Vegetable Soup
Calories 152.1; Total Carbs 16.3g;
Net Carbs 11.5g; Protein 7.5g; Fat 7.2g

Rogan Josh (Nutrition for Total Recipe)
Calories 2311.2; Total Carbs 68.1g; Net Carbs 48.3g; Protein 200.7g; Fat 137.5g

Roasted Garlic Sausage Sheet Pan
Calories 490.5; Total Carbs 8.5g;
Net Carbs 7.4g; Protein 17.3g; Fat 43.8g

Rosemary Garlic Sous Vide Steak
Calories 1279.4; Total Carbs 6.1g;
Net Carbs 4.5g; Protein 122.2g; Fat 82.3g

Rosemary Parsnip Fries
Calories 605.4; Total Carbs 102.2g; Net Carbs 74.3g; Protein 6.8g; Fat 22.0g

Sage and Cranberry Turkey Sausage
Calories 172.3; Total Carbs 5.5g;
Net Carbs 5.0g; Protein 11.5g; Fat 11.8g

Salad with Sesame Chili Dressing
Calories 966.0; Total Carbs 32.8g; Net Carbs 21.1g; Protein 12.8g; Fat 91.1g

Salt and Vinegar Chicken Wings (Nutrition for Total Recipe)
Calories 1766.7; Total Carbs 7.1g;
Net Carbs 2.9g; Protein 162.5g; Fat 114.9g

Santa Fe Ground Turkey Meatballs
Calories 87.1; Total Carbs 1.8g;
Net Carbs 1.1g; Protein 6.8g; Fat 6.2g

Sausage Bourbon Bacon BBQ Burgers
Calories 344.9; Total Carbs 14.9g; Net Carbs 14.3g; Protein 18.5g; Fat 24.5g

Savory Beet and Thyme Yogurt (Nutrition for Total Recipe)
Calories 230.9; Total Carbs 16.2g; Net Carbs 14.6g; Protein 9.3g; Fat 14.9g

Savory Caprese Biscuits
Calories 202.5; Total Carbs 8.9g;
Net Carbs 2.0g; Protein 13.5g; Fat 15.9g

Savory Herb Butter Dutch Baby with Roasted Tomatoes, Garlic and Ricotta
Calories 243.5; Total Carbs 15.3g; Net Carbs 5.4g; Protein 14.6g; Fat 19.2g

Seedy Spirulina Superfood Granola - Dry Mixture (Nutrition for Total Recipe)
Calories 4154.0; Total Carbs 146.0g; Net Carbs 46.7g; Protein 189.6g; Fat 338.1g

Seedy Spirulina Superfood Granola - Wet Mixture (Nutrition for Total Recipe)
Calories 1038.1; Total Carbs 140.7g; Net Carbs 102.4g; Protein 7.3g; Fat 58.4g

Sesame-Crusted Salmon
Calories 345.0; Total Carbs 3.0g; Net Carbs 1.1g; Protein 26.9g; Fat 24.8g

Shallot, Bacon and Sage Butternut Squash Mash
Calories 558.2; Total Carbs 73.7g; Net Carbs 60.8g; Protein 13.6g; Fat 27.9g

Shortbread Sugar Cookies
Calories 153.9; Total Carbs 11.7g; Net Carbs 2.0g; Protein 3.2g; Fat 13.5g

Simple Cauli Rice Three Ways
Calories 55.4; Total Carbs 3.8g; Net Carbs 1.6g; Protein 1.8g; Fat 4.3g

Simple Garlic Naan
Calories 395.5; Total Carbs 14.2g; Net Carbs 7.6g; Protein 17.1g; Fat 32.5g

Smoked Cracklin' Pork Belly Chili
Calories 367.6; Total Carbs 9.9g; Net Carbs 6.1g; Protein 16.0g; Fat 29.7g

Smoky Cracklin' Pork Belly
Calories 401.2; Total Carbs 3.4g; Net Carbs 0.7g; Protein 7.2g; Fat 40.2g

Smothered Pork Chops
Calories 1101.7; Total Carbs 13.1g; Net Carbs 11.2g; Protein 39.3g; Fat 100.8g

Spicy Thai Basil Beef
Calories 355.4; Total Carbs 7.9g; Net Carbs 6.0g; Protein 20.9g; Fat 26.7g

Spinach and Artichoke Pesto Soup
Calories 197.0; Total Carbs 9.7g; Net Carbs 6.7g; Protein 7.1g; Fat 15.2g

Spinach and Goat Cheese Quick Bread
Calories 176.6; Total Carbs 4.8g; Net Carbs 2.5g; Protein 6.4g; Fat 15.3g

Steak Fingers with Caramelized Onion Gravy
Calories 245.4; Total Carbs 2.1g; Net Carbs 1.8g; Protein 30.7g; Fat 13.3g

Strawberry Cheesecake Glazed Donuts
Calories 271.5; Total Carbs 41.6g; Net Carbs 4.2g; Protein 7.8g; Fat 20.5g

Strawberry Lemonade Cake
Calories 625.6; Total Carbs 32.1g; Net Carbs 6.2g; Protein 13.1g; Fat 58.8g

Strawberry Mint Mojito
Calories 234.5; Total Carbs 20.6g; Net Carbs 4.6g; Protein 0.2g; Fat 0.1g

Strawberry Rhubarb Rosé Slush (Nutrition for Total Recipe)
Calories 820.5; Total Carbs 93.2g; Net Carbs 54.2g; Protein 5.4g; Fat 0.4g

Sugar-Free Marshmallows (Nutrition for Total Recipe)
Calories 776.7; Total Carbs 191.0g; Net Carbs 16.7g; Protein 15.4g; Fat 22.8g

Sugar-Free Teriyaki (Nutrition for Total Recipe)
Calories 258.4; Total Carbs 60.2g; Net Carbs 19.9g; Protein 0.4g; Fat 9.2g

Sugar-Free Buttercream (Nutrition for Total Recipe)
Calories 2148.6; Total Carbs 271.9g; Net Carbs 1.3g; Protein 1.5g; Fat 220.3g

Super Green Breakfast Bowl with Sesame-Crusted Soft-Boiled Eggs
Calories 826.6; Total Carbs 15.5g; Net Carbs 6.0g; Protein 19.3g; Fat 79.7g

Sweet and Salty Peanut Granola Bars
Calories 349.6; Total Carbs 16.1g; Net Carbs 7.5g; Protein 11.4g; Fat 29.8g

Sweet and Sour Ground Pork Meatballs
Calories 117.0; Total Carbs 5.7g; Net Carbs 2.7g; Protein 7.5g; Fat 7.1g

Taco Cups
Calories 271.2; Total Carbs 11.6g; Net Carbs 9.0g; Protein 16.6g; Fat 17.4g

Taco Frittata Cups
Calories 134.6; Total Carbs 1.8g; Net Carbs 1.5g; Protein 11.6g; Fat 8.8g

Taco Spaghetti
Calories 331.7; Total Carbs 15.8g; Net Carbs 10.0g; Protein 24.0g; Fat 20.3g

Tangerine Ginger Dressing
Calories 288.4; Total Carbs 6.8g; Net Carbs 2.6g; Protein 0.8g; Fat 29.2g

Tequila Lime Chicken Salad with Avocado Cilantro Dressing
Calories 1167.6; Total Carbs 23.4g; Net Carbs 10.6g; Protein 52.0g; Fat 91.9g

Tequila Lime Ground Turkey Meatballs
Calories 83.8; Total Carbs 1.1g; Net Carbs 0.7g; Protein 6.4g; Fat 5.4g

Thai Green Curry Deviled Eggs
Calories 31.8; Total Carbs 0.8g; Net Carbs 0.6g; Protein 0.2g; Fat 3.2g

Thai Iced Tea
Calories 38.0; Total Carbs 16.6g; Net Carbs 1.6g; Protein 0g; Fat 0g

Thai Noodle Steak Salad with Sesame Chili Dressing
Calories 671.9; Total Carbs 2.5g; Net Carbs 2.3g; Protein 58.9g; Fat 45.5g

Thai Peanut Marinade (Nutrition for Total Recipe)
Calories 1072.6; Total Carbs 46.2g; Net Carbs 22.0g; Protein 14.2g; Fat 100.2g

Thai Pumpkin Ramen Noodle Soup
Calories 225.8; Total Carbs 13.7g; Net Carbs 6.8g; Protein 4.3g; Fat 18.5g

The Blue Hawaiian
Calories 280.5; Total Carbs 24.7g; Net Carbs 5.0g; Protein 2.3g; Fat 10.5g

Traditional Cut-Out Sugar Cookies
Calories 60.1; Total Carbs 6.6g; Net Carbs 0.8g; Protein 1.5g; Fat 5.4g

Vanilla Angel Food Cake with Lavender Lime Glaze
Calories 64.5; Total Carbs 7.8g; Net Carbs 6.8g; Protein 5.7g; Fat 1.0g

Vanilla Bourbon Strawberry Shortcake with Mascarpone Whipped Cream
Calories 2041.2; Total Carbs 33.0g; Net Carbs 22.3g; Protein 16.9g; Fat 209.6g

Vanilla Crepes
Calories 104.1; Total Carbs 2.7g; Net Carbs 1.1g; Protein 4.9g; Fat 8.4g

Vanilla Nut-Free Cake Base
Calories 121.5; Total Carbs 9.9g; Net Carbs 1.8g; Protein 3.9g; Fat 8.2g

Zesty Ranch Chicken Wings (Nutrition for Total Recipe)
Calories 1754.7; Total Carbs 6.1g; Net Carbs 4.2g; Protein 163.0g; Fat 115.0g

Zucchini Walnut Bars
Calories 350.8; Total Carbs 31.2g; Net Carbs 8.9g; Protein 9.1g; Fat 30.3g

Index